PRAISE FOR
"WARLORD: NO BETTER FRIEND, NO WORSE ENEMY"
By Ilario Pantano and Malcolm McConnell

The vitally important (*New York Post*) and controversial memoir by the devoted Marine Lieutenant and family man who reenlisted in the wake of 9/11, led an infantry platoon in Iraq—and was charged by the U.S. Military with murder.

"(Warlord) is suspenseful and thrilling, sobering and upsetting but wonderful to read."

—**Jon Stewart,** Host of *The Daily Show*

"Pantano's story is a tough, gritty, no-holds-barred saga of war by one who knows what it's like to be caught in a crossfire."

—**Oliver L. North,** Host of *War Stories* on Fox News Channel and former U.S. Marine

"Every tenth page of Warlord should be stamped 'this is not a work of fiction.' Some men run from a fight, some hold their own; Ilario is the rare hero that runs to a fight. He is one tough mother!"

—**James Carville,** *New York Times* bestselling author, political strategist, and former U.S. Marine

"I couldn't put down 2nd Lt. Ilario Pantano's new book, *Warlord*. Put it at the top of your summer reading list . . . The writing is riveting. The timing fortuitous. The message timeless. Pantano has given us more than just a war story. This is an American story."

—**Michelle Malkin,** *New York Times* bestselling author

"Ilario was a dedicated, professional and patriotic field officer. What did the military do with such a prize? They hauled him up on murder charges for killing the enemy. This story is Emblematic of what went wrong with this war."

—**Cyrus Nowrasteh,** Writer/producer, *The Path to 9/11*

"Now and then from the battlefront come tales which, despite the confusion of emotion and the limited field of vision see through the smoke and the pall to provide us insights which count in the strategic view . . . *Warlord* is such a dispatch . . . Unvarnished and personal . . . A human drama, gritty and self-effacing."

—**Greg Copley,** Award-winning Historian

"Suspenseful and involving . . . Good Courtroom Drama, excellent war reporting, and absorbing psychology."

—**Booklist**

"Vivid . . . Compelling . . . *Warlord* is full of arresting scenes . . . and his experience is described with a gripping style that carries the reader back and forth from the Iraqi battlefield to the courtroom."

—***The Weekly Standard***

12/31/15

HAPPY NEW YEAR

HOWARD + RUTH CHAPMAN —

GRAND THEFT
HISTORY

How Liberals Stole Southern Valor
in the American Revolution

*What A JOURNEY WE HAVE BEEN ON
TOGETHER — THIS BOOK WOULD NOT HAVE*

ILARIO PANTANO

BEEN POSSIBLE WITHOUT YOUR SUPPORT —

AND YOUR DAUGHTER JILL!

THANK YOU FOR BEING SUCH WONDERFUL

PARENTS AND GRAND PARENTS

THE BEST IS YET TO COME !

Semper Fi

A POST HILL PRESS BOOK

Ilario

Pantano

GRAND THEFT HISTORY
How Liberals Stole Southern Valor in the American Revolution
© 2015 by Ilario Pantano
All Rights Reserved

ISBN: 978-1-61868-872-9
ISBN (eBook): 978-1-61868-873-6

Cover Design by Ryan Truso
Interior design and typesetting by Neuwirth & Associates

Post Hill Press
275 Madison Avenue, 14th Floor
New York, NY 10016
http://posthillpress.com

CONTENTS

This book is dedicated to
Jack Hawke
and to Truth, Justice
and the American Way.

"So, we've got to teach history based not on what's in fashion but what's important . . . If we forget what we did, we won't know who we are. I'm warning of an eradication of the American memory that could result, ultimately, in an erosion of the American spirit."

—Ronald Reagan, "Farewell Address to the Nation,"
January 11, 1989

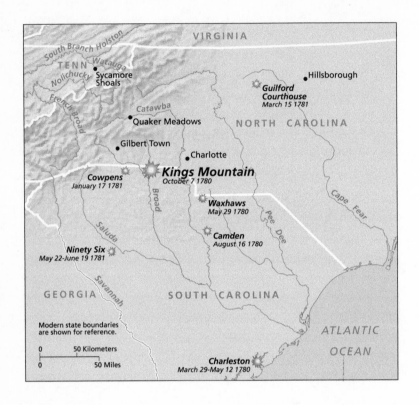

Map of Southern Battles in 1780-1781 Courtesy of the National Park Service.

Battlefield locations and websites are provided in the appendix.

PREFACE

"Most Authors seek fame, but I seek for justice."

—David Crocket,
1834, two years before he was killed while
defending the Alamo[1]

The metal marker put up in 1941 alerted travelers to the nearby site of Buford's Massacre. But even with the sign, I labored to find the spot until the wood line gave way to grassy fields. There stood the flagpole and finally the small brick wall and an iron fence surrounding a mound of sun bleached stones. Every twenty minutes or so, a car would drive by, interrupting my daydream. Screams. Shots. Smoke. Hooves. Iron, wood and hot blood mixed with courage, exhaustion, and terror. I imagined the lines of British cavalry rushing to overtake the fleeing rebels.

235 years ago there had been a pile of American bodies, many of them run through with bayonets. Today there was a mile marker and a pile of rocks.

This wasn't my first battlefield. As a Marine grunt and later a contractor, I had fought in three wars of my own and chronicled some of those experiences in my first book, *Warlord*. But this was different. Now, I was an errant knight on a quest. I had spent the past six years reading piles of manuscripts and traveling endless miles of Southern backroads searching for clues. I was driven by a profound sense of injustice and the suspicion of a crime first uncovered in my mother's backyard.

It was easy to overlook Moores Creek Battlefield. Dozens, maybe hundreds of times, I had driven past the vintage brown sign indicating the turnoff twenty miles north of Wilmington on the way to my mother's house. But the day I took that turn was the day that this quest for justice was set in motion. Down a few side roads past cotton fields, double-wides, and timber trails, I would come to find a supremely important, yet little remembered, piece of hallowed ground. What happened at Moores Creek changed the fate of a colony and ultimately a nation. Unraveling the elements that had conspired to deny me, an author and devotee of military history, the knowledge of this consequential locale was more than a mystery.

It became my mission.

■

"King George and Broadswords!!" shouted wet loyalists, pulling themselves out of the cold river. Moores Creek Bridge had been booby trapped by the rebels who had stripped its planks and greased the remaining beams. The loyalists that escaped drowning pulled themselves from the water right into the teeth of a patriot ambush.

Despite the loyalists' near two-to-one numerical superiority, well-aimed musket fire and cannons with nicknames like "Old Mother Covington" tore them to pieces. It is one of the first skirmishes of the American Revolution, lasting only minutes, but it would have ramifications beyond the blueberry fields of Pender County. On February 27, 1776, that final broadsword charge of recorded history would drive North Carolina towards independence.

Weeks later, on April 12, 1776, North Carolina became the first colony to authorize its delegates to vote for Independence in what became known as the Halifax Resolves. The Resolves in turn led a fellow Southern colony, Virginia, to propose a resolution of independence, from which the Declaration of Independence was born.

The patriot (Whig) victory at Moores Creek gave momentum to the political revolt and had tactical implications as well. The activity and spirit of British loyalists (Tories) in the South was chilled by this first decisive fight. In defeating the column of troops heading towards the coast, the heroic rebels denied the British fleet ground forces that they would need weeks later in their assault on Charleston, South Carolina.

On June 28, 1776, the British attack on Charleston's defensive battery at Sullivan's Island would fail, thanks to the grit and determination of outnumbered Southern patriots. The royal armada was bristling with over 300 cannons. The hastily constructed sand and palmetto log fort had just ten guns, but by the end of the daylong battle nine British warships would limp home, not soon to return.

The soft palmetto palm trunks absorbed the impact of the British shells. Instead of splintering under the onslaught, the fort and its defenders withstood and delivered a punishment of their own. Four years later, when the British finally returned to the Carolinas after pacifying the North, Southern patriots would grind them and their loyalist cronies to a halt. The blue state flag of South Carolina, with its crescent moon and palmetto tree, pays homage to the gallant defenders of Sullivan's Island.

There once was a time when all Americans knew of the Southern colonists' valor, and their critical role in our freedom. Yet today, Moores Creek, Sullivans's Island, and the other Southern battles that I will detail have been virtually eliminated from modern texts.

■

As I stood overlooking Moores Creek and absorbed its consequence, I was stunned by my ignorance and that of my fellow citizens who, like me, had never heard of it. The question that burned was "why not?"

I started to dig. But in the course of many years, volumes, and miles I have come to learn that the reasons most Americans don't know their true history are even more important than the actual history itself.

The deliberate omission and whitewashing of the South's role in America's founding isn't accidental. It is part of an elaborate effort to undermine regional influence by eroding the cultural foundations. In short, Moores Creek, Sullivan's Island, and other military engagements represent more than forgotten histories. The collective valor of the South has been stolen in yet one more attack of the ongoing culture war.

This aspect of the culture war involves the rewriting of the past in order to shape political outcomes in the future. It is more than editorial interpretation, poetic license or simple North vs. South regional bias. It is a thought crime of the highest order with serious consequences for the entire nation. It is Grand Theft History.

OPENING
ARGUMENT

How the Liberal War on Southern Culture
is Rewriting America's Past

"When you put it all together in America, you've got a real stew of fighting here.

It's not just about Guns, it's not just about Obama, it's somewhat about region; this whole cause–lost cause of the Confederacy, there's some of that there. There's some country mouse versus city mouse piece to it. It's really traditional America fifty years ago, one hundred years ago and anything that looks like the future. And they don't like the looks of the future."

—Chris Matthews, *Hardball with Chris Matthews, MSNBC,*
May 6, 2013

The case I am going to present is about two wars. The first was fought 235 years ago by the thirteen colonies but ultimately was won by the Southern four. The second war is being fought today in a carefully orchestrated war on America's founding culture of God, Guns, and Guts and is tearing the national fabric.

Race-baiting, abortion, amnesty, gun control, global warming, and the "Wars on . . . Women, Drugs, Christmas, and Poverty" are only the latest skirmishes in a larger ideological and demographic struggle between progressives and conservatives for money, power, and control of the Republic. While the news media provides real time revisionism to support the Leftist agenda, the truths of our national origin and identity are under Orwellian attack by Marxist historians determined to dismantle the America of our founders. Their efforts in this academic theater of the culture war I have labeled Grand Theft History.

Grand Theft History is the improper and intentional omission or distortion of historical fact to the significant detriment of one or more parties. My thesis is that liberal historians and others have committed criminal acts and I acknowledge that the burden of proof lies with me. Therefore I need to prove, beyond a reasonable doubt, that each element of the crime is met. If I don't succeed, then the defendants must be acquitted.

My argument begins with establishing that Southerners had something of value that was taken away from them: their rightful place in American history. The loss of that and its significance, is one of the elements that needs to be proved. I have more than enough exhibits to enter into evidence to establish this element.

The next element is omission and misstatement of historical fact. You, the reader, are the ultimate judge and jury. I will be providing a number of exhibits that speak to this as well. I hope to make it quite clear that the history books either underemphasize or omit many of the key Southern battles and their significance that people, at the time, recognized.

Next we will prove that these misstatements or omissions did not happen by accident. Rather, we will establish that this was intentional. Accordingly, we will establish a motive and opportunity through the provided exhibits.

Finally, we will establish that all of this was improper. This element is proved not only by the exhibits but also by my arguments. Indeed, it is worth noting that the entire country is damaged by this crime. In other words, by creating and encouraging a false narrative about the South and our nation's origins, liberals have injured and continue to imperil the unity of the United States to our common detriment.

The question of appropriate punishment is what we turn to finally. We might borrow from civil, as opposed to criminal law, and set forth what is often called a prayer for relief where we, as civil plaintiffs, petition the court of public opinion for what we want from the defendants. Typically there are two types of relief: money damages and injunctive relief, where the court orders the defendant to either do something or stop doing something. We are not interested in seeking monetary compensation. Instead, since part of the argument is that what liberal pseudo-historians have done is improper, I point not only to the damage but also to the fact that they have not met their duty to report the historical record accurately. I demand that they start doing so immediately.

This is my prayer.

MAKING THE CASE

"Extremely Unexpected"
"Totally Defeated"

To the war-weary British public, newspapers like *The London Gazette* in 1780 spelled defeat at the hands of Southern Colonists. Yet as we shall see, most of the recent popular history books gloss over the Southern struggle that led to the British Surrender at Yorktown.

The history of America, like all peoples, is messy. The history of the South, no more or less than the rest of the country, but in the over-reactions of the 1960s and 70s, the baby has been thrown out with the bath water. In this case the baby is in many ways the origins of America, its culture of freedom and independence.

Some may be scratching their heads given the well-worn stereotypes of racism and bondage associated with the South. But there is so much more to the story. This is an ex-Yankee's effort to shed light on the truth of America's founding and credit a region and culture that has been demonized in the centuries that have followed and today finds their worldview under a constant and withering attack.

Allow me introduce you to the South that you've never heard of: The South that Saved America. Let the hysterics subside and then we will explore the crime: How pervasive political correctness and cultural revisionism has led to Grand Theft History. Just a quick word on why this matters. In many ways, the South has become the living embodiment of conservative ideologies, practices and principles. While I am not apologizing for them, there is an undeniable reality that fifty years after the civil rights movement and 150 years after the civil war, the South is still in the crosshairs for its past sins.

Why? Not because of what the South had at one time been guilty of, after all we are a forgiving nation. Look around and see how quickly we forgive and then support our former enemies: from millions dead in the Holocaust to the Mercedes dealership in one generation. No, the South remains unforgiven less for what it has done than for what it represents today: a convenient proxy for conservative ideals writ large at a time when statist atheism is sweeping the country.

In *Rise of the Southern Republicans*, Merle and Earl Black describe the crossover of regional to political scorn:

> For many decades rebels and Yankees (and their descendants) would continue to fight the political equivalent of the Civil War through the nation's two major political parties. Battlefield sectionalism funneled most victorious northerners as well as most defeated southerners toward enduring standing decisions regarding their political friends and certainly their political enemies.[2]

Some of the bias is willful, but it is compounded by ignorance. Try mentioning "War" and "the South" and the automatic, almost reflexive reaction of your peers will be an assumption that you meant the War Between the States. There are over 16,000 books written on the Civil War, but this isn't one of them[3]. Instead we will explore the South's role in our first grasp at liberty in the Revolution that shook the world, as ragtag colonists defied an empire. This overlooked dimension to America's history tells us much about who we are as a country and what we are becoming.

RECLAIMING THE SOUTH'S STOLEN VALOR

The Stolen Valor Act of 2013 makes it a crime to lie about an individual's service in war or to wear military medals that you did not earn. Unfortunately, this law makes no provision for the wholesale annihilation of a peoples' contribution to the freedom and independence of a nation. Southern boys die in disproportionately high numbers than troops from the rest of the country, and they have in every war this country has ever fought, from the Revolution to the War on Terror, which leads me to the stolen valor of the South. For veterans, valor and service in wartime are particularly important. Failure to recognize that service and sacrifice is acutely distressing.

The lopsidedness of the South's contribution in blood and toil compared to the recognition it has received is beyond unfair. It is criminal.

Consider this: In 1780, there was more combat action in South Carolina than all of the other twelve colonies combined[4].

Furthermore, the vicious guerilla actions in a backcountry of shifting allegiances pitted brother against brother and neighbor against neighbor. The burden carried by those few patriots against impossible odds, and with little support, was enormous. The fighting was so fierce that the British resorted to paying Indians to murder Southerners. They even imported Yankee loyalists—volunteers from New York, New Jersey, and Connecticut—in order to help them subdue the Southern rebels.[5]

As General George Washington wrote to the President of the Congress on November 7, 1780:

> While our Army is experiencing almost daily want, that of the enemy at New York is deriving ample supplies from a trade with the adjacent states of New York, New Jersey and Connecticut, which has by degrees become so common, that it is hardly thought a crime . . . I believe that most nations make it a capital (offense) for their subjects to furnish their enemies with provisions and Military stores during the War.[6]

In 1780, forces of the Crown were on the cusp of victory. Five years into a stalled rebellion, shortages and mutinies in Northern colonies were leaving George Washington fearful. War-weary fence-sitters watched as the British racked up the Northern cities and set their sights South. If all went according to plan, Royal naval power would land a force at Charleston, South Carolina (1780) that would pacify the wild backcountry and sweep North to consolidate gains and extinguish the rebellion once and for all. Back-to-back British victories at Charleston and Camden led to the capture of America's Southern

Army. Washington struggled with mutinies and turncoat Northern merchants supplying the British. Even his own friend, the "Hero of Saratoga," Benedict Arnold, turned traitor. It just wasn't the kind of thing you did when your side was winning.

But the rising tide of success would cause the British and their newly dominant loyalist sympathizers to overplay their hand. British Dragoons led by the swashbuckling Banastre Tarleton set upon a column of retreating patriots. Tarleton's men slaughtered the American forces led by Col. Buford after many had surrendered. Outrage began to spread at the merciless brutality of "Buford's Slaughter." Neutrality no longer an option, the Southern patriots were driven by accumulated indignations and began to darken the Carolina backcountry with more blood than any other colony.

Burning Presbyterian bibles didn't help the loyalists in their terror war. It backfired and launched the patriots into action on July 12, 1780 with a fledgling victory at "Huck's Defeat." Captain Christian Huck and his New York Dragoons had been busy lighting the countryside aflame, literally. Huck's "atrocities" on the men and women of the South Carolina backcountry were met head-on by this first successful act of resistance since the British arrival at Charleston. Huck, along with thirty loyalists, were killed in an early morning ambush and dozens more loyalists were wounded or captured. The patriots lost only one man.

Word carried and momentum built. The battle of Musgrove's Mill, SC on August 19, 1780 set the stage for what was possible when 200 militia beat a combined force of 500 "regular" provincials and loyalists. Colonel Isaac Shelby and his fellow partisans ambushed and defeated a superior force of loyalists. Shelby's Overmountain Men utilized techniques that had been well-honed fighting Indians—techniques, speed, and violence of action that would help him to win the bigger fights to come.

Musgrove's Mill, SC was the first time that a significant force of uniformed British sympathizers (provincials) were beaten by militia partisans in the South.

It wouldn't be the last.

■

"That all but hopeless year 1780. But the Autumn showed a
sudden turning of the tide."
—Woodrow Wilson, *A History of the American People*[7]

Roused to action, the "*Overmountain* Men" spontaneously converged from Virginia, the Carolinas, and Tennessee in their hunting
shirts and tomahawks. They saved the Revolution on a bloody hilltop
called King's Mountain on October 7, 1780. The epic two-week movement preceding the fight is a marvel of logistics. From several different
directions, bands of partisans traveled hundreds of miles through wil-
derness and converged on their prey in unison. The battle itself was
one of the most lopsided defeats of the entire war.

The forces engaged were numerically matched and the Loyalists had
the high ground, but it was not enough to save them from slaughter.
"Give 'em Indian play boys," the patriots shouted, darting from tree to
tree. Surging forward and falling back, the battle was fluid and quick.
In less than an hour, the defenders of the Crown, many from New York,
New Jersey, and Connecticut, were crushed. Twenty-eight patriots were
killed, compared to two hundred and twenty-five loyalists, a 10-1 ratio.
Another seven hundred loyalists were captured. Violence would beget
violence as the accumulated indignities of the previous year were paid
back with executions. The rebel code word of that day was "Buford," in
homage of their brothers' slaughter at British hands.

The carnage was brutal, as one quarter of the British combat power
in the South was reduced in a matter of hours. Corpses were so plen-
tiful that wolves prowled the grounds for years after, feasting on remains. Adding to the perception of British impotence, the butchery
took place just miles from the main British Army in the South, commanded by the infamous Lord Cornwallis. Bodies were desecrated.
Prisoners were hung and a message was sent. This was the dark side
of war but it was instrumental in winning back the hearts and minds
of the wavering Carolinians.

"The Gen. has the pleasure to congratulate the Army on an
important advantage lately obtained, in North Carolina, over
a corps of fourteen hundred men, British Troops, and new
Levies, commanded by Colonel Ferguson . . .

They came up with the enemy at a place called King's Mountain, advantageously posted, and gave him a Total Defeat . . .

These advantages will in all probability, have a very happy influence on operations in that quarter, and are a proof of the spirit and resources of the country."

—Gen. George Washington, Oct. 27, 1780[8]

A renewed vigor would sweep the colonies as word spread of the patriot victory at King's Mountain. British morale was crushed on both sides of the Atlantic, and the conditions were set for the battles that would follow, from Cowpens, to ultimate victory.

The British came to acknowledge the effect of King's Mountain:

"[British defeat at King's Mountain] was immediately productive of the worst Consequences to the King's affairs in South Carolina, and unhappily proved the first Link of a Chain of Evils that followed each other in regular succession until they at last ended in the total loss of America."

—Sir Henry Clinton, Commander-in-Chief, British forces in North America[9]

Americans in turn, later appreciated that this was the tipping point:

"The victory was of far-reaching importance, and ranks among the decisive battles of the revolution. It was the first great success of the Americans in the South, the turning point in the Southern campaign, and it brought cheer to the patriots throughout the union. The loyalists of the Carolinas were utterly cast down and never recovered the blow; and its immediate effect was to cause Cornwallis to retreat from North Carolina, abandoning his first invasion of that state."

—Theodore Roosevelt, The Winning of the West[10]

For generations, it was celebrated. The anniversary was important to the young nation:

"The battle of King's Mountain stands out in our national memory not only because of the valor of the men of the Carolinas, Georgia, Tennessee, Kentucky, and Virginia, who trod here 150 years ago, and because of the brilliant leadership of Colonel Campbell, but also because the devotion of those men revived the courage of the despondent Colonies and set a nation upon the road of final triumph in American independence."

—President Herbert Hoover, Oct. 7, 1930
Address on the 150th Anniversary of the Battle of
King's Mountain[11]

Just three months after the British defeat at King's Mountain, the patriots landed a series of fatal blows. The new American commander, Daniel Morgan, would pay the British back for his scars at the whipping post. In the opening days of 1781, Morgan delivered a humiliating defeat to Banastre Tarleton, the ruthless British officer that had slaughtered Col. Buford's men the previous year, at the battle of *Cowpens, SC*. Rich with daring military strategy and maneuver, Morgan's victory at Cowpens, a double envelopment, left British historians and generals to bitterly acknowledge their fate in the wake of that upset. Tarleton and his chief, General Cornwallis, were both shaken after the damaging loss of troops in what would be lamented by the British high command as the "Unfortunate day of Jan. 17."

Desperate to salvage the situation and crush the rebels, Cornwallis chased Gen. Greene over 900 miles in the "Race to the Dan." At Guilford Courthouse, NC, the armies collided. Fighting was fierce—some say the worst of the war. Cornwallis was forced to turn British cannons on his own men in order to halt the surging Americans. Patriots left the field to fight another day, but the British Army had been bloodied. Too weakened to give chase, they "cannot stand anymore victories like that one." Cornwallis and his commanders were convinced the Carolinas were futile (read: dangerous). He pinned his hopes on Virginia, but instead of comfort he found only death, despair, and the French.

The French supplied thousands of ground troops and dozens of ships in order to surround the peninsula of Yorktown. The 30-ship

French fleet pounded Cornwallis's positions and kept the British navy at bay. French siege guns and techniques reduced British defenses to rubble in days. Cornwallis surrendered just as his commander, Gen. Clinton, departed New York with long delayed reinforcements. But it was too late. When news reached Britain, Lord North cried, "It is finished."

As a student and practitioner of warfare who fought in the first Gulf War and later led Marines in Falluja, Iraq in 2004, I know how critical it is to assess a military situation through the eyes of your enemy. I also know the importance of checking your sources. My personal history has been manipulated right before my eyes. For example, my Wikipedia page was started and run by a Canadian anti-war protestor who blamed me for "Bush's war." The point being, you have to dig deep. Thanks to the democratization of information that was once the exclusive domain of ivory tower academics, we can now all dig deep via internet archives, Google Books, etc.

The records that we need in this case are well-preserved, thanks to the sophistication of the British war machine with centuries of precedence and practice. Paperwork, reporting, and the flow of information in a global empire is critical, thus the historical record is strongest from the British side. A detailed record of correspondence reveals that the British soldiers and their commanders knew that they had lost the American Revolution in the South in 1780-81. The British Parliament knew it was the end when a battered Cornwallis surrendered at Yorktown. The British press knew and in turn so did the British people. Their history books would become our history books, and they taught generations of American Southern valor.

This argument isn't about the war. I am making the case for what people knew about the war, when they knew it, and when forces conspired for them to stop knowing it.

■

America's victory in the revolution was achieved in the South by Southern hands according to British and American soldiers, politicians and the early historical accounts. As we approach the War Between the States, we start to see divergent histories in the 1850s. But in the years following the war all the way to the 1950's, the South still retained its honor.

As recently as 1957, Winston Churchill lauded the contributions of the South in his *History of the English Speaking Peoples*[12]. But less than two decades later, at the height of the civil rights movement, such a stand would become politically incorrect and subsequent British and American historians would begin the whitewash. By the bicentennial, the South had become a four-letter word and its history was deleted from the national conscience and forgotten. Churchill is not the only modern British historian to celebrate the martial virtue of the South only to have follow-on "historians" selectively edit it out of existence, but for now we will return to the 18th century histories on both sides of the Atlantic.

BODY OF EVIDENCE

Exhibit A is the British ground truth, as reported in detail by their officers and journals (Clinton, Cornwallis, Tarleton, etc.). Rivalries and feuds would play out for years in the English papers with recriminations giving us insight to the critical moments and actions by the men who lived them. In the wake of the defeat there was a battle for public opinion: How had the world's greatest empire lost a prized colonial possession? Who was to blame?

In an effort to protect careers and legacies, the battle for public opinion basically split along two lines: Those who blamed the Senior Commander, General Clinton, or Clinton's deputy, the man charged with the Southern campaign who surrendered at Yorktown, General Cornwallis. Both camps had a number of co-conspirators and surrogates with a variety of reasons for their roles and claims. Some were trying to protect their own reputations and gain glory, others smarted at the shame of defeat they felt had been visited upon them and their fellow soldiers unfairly.

The controversy took many different forms, with letters to officials, and ultimately the newspapers, followed by pamphlets of bundled correspondence to show timelines and try and prove culpability in books with elaborate storytelling and fanciful denials and delusions.

The press in London at that time was in support of the opposition party and against the war effort. The irony of a sympathetic press affecting the fate of a rebellion should not be lost on a generation that has witnessed the blame games of recent unpopular wars from Iraq, to Afghanistan, to Vietnam. The "tit-for-tat" of the Clinton-Cornwallis controversy, as it would come to be called, should ring familiar.

The first shot was fired when upon his surrender, Cornwallis dispatched a detailed three-page letter outlining the actions that he took to defend his men and the possessions of the crown and laying the blame for his surrender squarely at the feet of his superior, who had promised to reinforce him, but never did. The Cornwallis letter, written October 20, 1781, would make its way to the decision makers in London. It was not the first account of the loss that any of them would hear or read, but it firmly established culpability with Cornwallis's boss, General Clinton. The effect on Clinton was real and immediate. He left New York for London to clear his name and thus began a series of exchanges laying blame for the defeat at Yorktown and the loss of America on various actions, inactions, and subordinates.

In the end, parliament would open up an investigation as to the cause of the loss, but the Government would change before the investigation was formally concluded. The summary judgment cast blame on the Admiralty and the Navy's failure to reinforce Cornwallis. It was in fact unthinkable that the empire with the world's greatest navy had been outgunned. But the truth runs deeper and there was plenty of blame to go around. And it did as Clinton was still writing books to clear his name in 1794, thirteen years after the surrender at Yorktown. The point of this work, which Exhibit A: British Correspondence will verify, is that the actions in the South led to the loss of the colonies.

Ultimately the two sides of the Clinton-Cornwallis controversy shaped up as follows: Clinton, Tarleton, and George Hanger on one side versus Cornwallis, Roderick Mackenzie, and Charles Stedman on the other. The commanders and some of their loyal deputies all had a bone to pick. Each of the participants fired off letters and ultimately wrote books attacking or defending their role in the results of the British defeat. For example, Clinton responded with a series of published letters refuting Cornwallis and then in 1783 published a book of his own: *Narrative of Lieutenant Gen. Sir Henry Clinton,*

K.B. Relative to His Conduct During Part of His Command of tl King's Troops in North America, Particularly That Which Respects the Unfortunate Issue of the Campaign of 1781.

But Clinton didn't stop there. Nor did his critics. After a particularly unflattering portrayal in Stedman's *The History of the Origin, Progress, And Termination of the American War*, Clinton responded by publishing *Observations on Stedman's History of the American War* (1794). From these works and others we have a window of detail without parallel into the most important campaign of the war, the one which cost Britain a jewel and won Americans their freedom.

Exhibit B is related through the early American histories. Our founders knew the South's true influence on the war's conclusion. Washington, John Adams, Thomas Jefferson, the Continental Congress, and dozens of nineteenth century historians tell us what was once common knowledge. When did things change? For example, why did a recent tally of Southern battlefields get cut by 60 percent in a 2007 National Park Study when the count of Northern battlefields was left unchanged?[13]

How did we go as a country from the Congress asking for God's blessings on Southern soldiers, to "God Damn the South?" [14]

CROOKS, CRONIES AND THE CONSEQUENCES: STEALING THE VALOR OF THE SOUTH

The marginalization of Southern history hasn't stopped with the Revolutionary War. Beyond the Star Spangled Banner, most Americans are clueless about another dark time for a young America: The War of 1812.

The North was ready to surrender as Washington, DC lay broken and burning. The odds quickly turned against the young republic. But once again, Southern soldiers saved the day in fierce campaigns waged in the South. The British, thirty years after the Revolution, had command of the Northeast, but it was Andrew Jackson, who came of age in that latter-day revolutionary fight in the Carolina backwoods, who would lead Southern boys to vanquish the Indians and then destroy a superior force of redcoats at the Battle of New Orleans.

Meanwhile, Northern states from Rhode Island to Massachusetts were negotiating separate deals with England, and their treachery and cowardice would expose them to ridicule and political marginalization until the Civil War. Humiliation and sectional hatred that had run hot since before the Declaration of Independence would only continue to smolder until the flames engulfed these United States in 1861.

America's North vs. South friction predates the colonies and transcends false notions of post-Civil War "northern virtue." In fact, there is a political and deeply cynical motive for the liberal destruction of Southern history: Since the 1990s, the South has become politically and economically ascendant. Southerners spearheaded the GOP takeover of the U.S. Congress in 1994, hosted the Olympics in 1996, and occupied the White House from 1992 to 2008. Southern states have the fastest growing economies and populations. Today, the powerful Tea Party block of conservative Republicans in Congress is a largely Southern phenomenon.

The Left's resultant hostility towards Southern culture has even been acknowledged by prominent Democrats like former Virginia Senator Jim Webb. Southern culture, with its red state conservative values, is "the greatest inhibitor of the plans of the activist Left and cultural Marxists for a new kind of society altogether . . . [and] the greatest obstacles to what might be called the collectivist taming of America," according to Webb[15]. How has the Left, firmly ensconced in academia and entertainment, responded to the political and economic influence of the South? By attacking the cultural legitimacy of its conservative beliefs (God), institutions (Guns), and its valor (Guts) through the crime of Grand Theft History. On college campuses today, those attacks are concealed under the veneer of being "politically correct."

David Horowitz, conservative luminary and author, who himself was a campus radical in the 1960s, has written extensively on the "radical attempt to turn schools into agencies for social change." In his book, *Indoctrination U*, Horowitz describes the modern-day liberal indoctrination on campuses across the country:[16]

"Political correctness" is a term that describes an orthodoxy or party line, in this case reflecting the agendas of the Left. Ideas that oppose left wing orthodoxy—opposition to racial preferences, belief in innate differences between men and women, or, more recently, support for America's War in Iraq—are regarded as morally unacceptable or simply indecent. The proponents of such ideas are regarded as deviants from the academic norm, to be marginalized and shunned.[17]

Adjacent to Columbia University in New York, Roger Baldwin began the American Civil Liberties Union (ACLU) as a communist organization determined to undermine the United States and its values. First formulated to rescue a crop of communist bombers from jail, the ACLU's next target would be the Holy Bible. The Battlefield? Dayton, Tennessee, in what would become known as the "Scopes Monkey Trial." The play and subsequent film version of the trial, *Inherit the Wind*, would go on to misinform tens of millions of Americans, and it is still used as a teaching tool today.[18] *Inherit the Wind*'s savage tarring of the South, its flagrantly atheist protagonists and its mean-spirited depiction of Christianity have made atheists out of millions of school children. I was one of them.

The trending atheism and counter culture that is being promoted today as new, hip, and trendy has century-old roots in Marxist influences seeking to undermine the United States. And it is working. Broken families, failing school systems and incarceration rates are on the rise in America. So are suicides, the leading cause of death for the first time over car accidents. "Coincidentally" we are experiencing a record decline in faith: One out of five Americans now claim no belief in God and 70 percent of those atheists vote liberally. After watching the Democratic National Convention reject God from their platform on live television in 2012, it would appear that killing God is good politics for the Left and they've enlisted some help along the way.

Hollywood, despite its perceived self-importance, could not change the terms of the debate on American history without the path that has been lit by academics and pseudo historians. Films like *Inherit the Wind*, *Cool Hand Luke*, *Cape Fear*, *Deliverance*, and even *the Water Boy* have skewered Southern culture.

More recent efforts have been less subtle. 2012 Academy Award-winning *Django: Unchained* uses the word "nigger" 120 times.[19] The lead character, a freed black slave played by Jamie Foxx, shoots an unarmed woman and the murder is seemingly justified because the victim is southern and white. Foxx would later brag on live television that, "it is fun to kill white people."[20] The same cabal of Hollywood brand names who produced and starred in the conveniently timed Bush-bash *W.* by Oliver Stone (2008), have funded, filmed, and distributed the Socialist-Anarchist vision of Howard Zinn to our schools.[21]

"We lost the elections but we won the textbooks."
—Todd Gitlin,
the self-described "political activist in the New Left
of the 1960s." Currently chairs the Ph.D program at
Columbia University School of Journalism[22]

The distinctly anti-Southern bias of New York's Columbia University communists, shared by Karl Marx as recorded in his congratulatory correspondence to Abraham Lincoln, is alive and well today.[23] For example Howard Zinn, who once called the South "the worst place in the world," received his MA and PhD at the Columbia University History Department under the mentorship of generations of communist deans. Zinn, a self-described "Socialist Anarchist" with a robust FBI file, is the top selling anti-American "academic" historian. More than two million copies of his leftist screed occupy college and high school campuses—more than any other author.

Today the Columbia History Department is chaired by Eric Foner, who personally and professionally is descended from a long line of Marxists. Foner, considered a "leader" in Southern history has, like Zinn, "revised" views of American history with a distinctly anti-southern bias.

Foner was influenced by a peer of Zinn's and a fellow Leftist professor, Fawn Brodie, whose salacious character assassination *Thomas Jefferson: An Intimate History* (1974) set in motion an industry of attacking America's founding by destroying its fathers.

Since World War Two, only three history books about early America have been #1 *New York Times* bestsellers: *Alistair Cooke's America* by PBS host Alistair Cooke (1973), *John Adams* (2001) and *1776* (2005), both by David McCullough. None of these "history" books discuss, much less credit, the role of the South in the American Revolution.

Other books that completely ignore or misrepresent the role of the South may not have achieved the #1 slot, but their consistent sales year after year have given them command of the history market from the suburban book club to the elementary school library.

You might spot the trend here beyond the South-bashing, since David McCullough who, like Alistair Cooke, hosted a show on PBS for over a decade, joined "yellow-dog Democrat" Ken Burns and Michael Moore in contributing the maximum level allowed by federal law to Barack Obama in 2008.

If you doubt the role of liberal politics in regional bias, consider some of the anti-Southern books written shortly after the Republican surge of the mid 90's. The Gingrich Revolution of 1994 was led by a Georgian and granted control of the House and the Senate to Republicans for the first time in 40 years. *Confederates in the Attic: Dispatches from the Unfinished Civil War*, a 1998 bestseller written by a former (labor) union organizer that identified a clergyman by his "pastor's dog collar." If that language wasn't offensive enough perhaps the "striking consonance between the GOP's Contract with America and the Confederate Constitution" will drive the bias home. The hillbilly-inbred-homicidal-moron narrative is continued en masse with titles like: *Better Off Without 'Em: A Northern Manifesto for Southern Secession, Made in Texas: George W. Bush and the Southern Takeover of American Politics,* and *What's the Matter with Kansas? How Conservatives Won the Heart of America,* to name a few.

A consequence of diminishing the role of the South in our nation's founding, is the marginalization of the values that Southern people hold dear. Faith, family, and love of freedom, the three pillars of American exceptionalism identified by Alexis De Tocqueville, are challenged daily from the courtroom to the classroom. The national character De Tocqueville credits with American success can be simplified to God, Guns, and Guts, or the "3Gs." The 3Gs, as lived by the Louisiana family on "Duck Dynasty," are still revered in the South, but blue state culture warriors from places like New York City have been pressing the attack and are succeeding.

Cultural forces have conspired to turn Christianity into "hate speech" and the South a dirty word. The shame is so deep that even the Southern Baptist Convention was forced to drop the "Southern" from its name. "In regions outside of the South, 'Southern' may con-jure up a regional stereotype that becomes a hindrance to the Gospel," said Roger S. "Sing" Oldham, a spokesman for the Southern Baptist Convention. "Our brothers and sisters in Christ who are of other race and language groups can now identify themselves with something that does not hearken back to a Southern past."[24]

Today, if you defend the South, you are immediately tarred and feathered and presumed to be a simple-minded bigot. Just watch the critics attack my thesis without realizing that is not the case. I was ed-ucated in the finest New York private schools and universities and I do not condone racism. Nor do I condone injustice, especially not at the scale that has been perpetrated on the people of the South and more broadly on the people of the United States to the degree to which they have been made ignorant of their cultural foundations. The reflexive moral superiority of Southern bashers is only possible in a vacuum of knowledge of America's true origins. This is a failure of modern education that conveniently overlooks Northern institutional racism and the countrywide profiteering in all the aspects of the slave trade.

The sin of slavery and its legacy was and is a national one, as de-tailed in the book, *Complicity: How the North Promoted, Prolonged, and Profited from Slavery*, written by a team of three courageous jour-nalists from the *Hartford Courant* in Connecticut of all places. The reporters' investigation boldly revealed that every major Northeastern industry from New York's Tiffany Jewelers and Steinway Pianos, to the Massachusetts mill towns and shipping fleets was complicit in that shameful chapter of our past. In 1861, the Mayor of New York wanted to secede with the slave states because the city's economic ties to the South were so deep.[25]

In her foreword to *Complicity*, Evelyn Brooks Higginbotham, Pro-fessor and Chair of the Department African and African-American Studies at Harvard University, explained:

In this study of how the North promoted, prolonged, and prof-ited from slavery, the authors give a fascinating account of racial inequality in America, revealing that positions do not fall neatly into categories such as North versus South, antebellum versus post bellum, and virtuous versus complicit. . . .

It is worth remembering that the litigants who appealed the Supreme Court in the *Civil Rights Cases of 1883* brought charges of national, not simply southern, discrimination, suing establishments in New York, San Francisco, Kansas and Tennessee.

Decades later, in the 1940s through 1960s, the fight to end Jim Crow and disenfranchisement would be waged not only in Southern cities and Deltas, but also in Northern Cities, where African Americans and their white allies fought for racial justice in regards to education, housing and hiring.[26]

I make no apologies for these shameful chapters of our national past and I am deeply saddened that some have chosen to worsen the cultural divisions instead of heal them, often for political or personal gain. While each individual's motivations for the historical revisionism that I document are beyond the scope of this argument, the fact of the vitriolic institutional anti-southern bias of liberal "intellectuals" is self-evident.

Michael Lind, author of *Made in Texas: George W. Bush and the Southern Takeover of American Politics,* recently contributed to Salon.com: "Today's Tea Party movement is merely the latest of a series of attacks on American democracy by the white Southern minority, which for more than two centuries has not hesitated to paralyze, sabotage or, in the case of the Civil War, destroy American democracy in order to get their way."[27]

What a sad indictment of a people who shed more blood, bore more scars and witnessed more horrors in defense of freedom than any other. Read these accounts, many of which are in first person, for yourself and then ask the question:

Who is actually destroying America?

BODY OF
EVIDENCE

Ballad of Ferguson's Defeat on King's Mountain, 1780

Come all you good people, I pray you draw near,
A tragical story you quickly shall hear,
Of Whigs and of Tories, how they breed great strife,
When they chased old Ferguson out of his life.

Brave Colonel Williams from Hillsboro' came.
The South Carolinians flocked to him amain,
Four hundred and fifty, a jolly brisk crew,
After old Ferguson we then did pursue.

We march'd to the Cowpens- Brave Campbell was there,
And Shelby and Cleveland and Colonel Sevier,
Taking the lead of their bold mountaineers,
Brave Indian fighters, devoid of all fears.

They were men of renown- like lions so bold,
Like Lions undaunted, ne'er to be controll'd,
They were bent on the game they had in their eye,
Determined to take it—to conquer or die.

We march'd from Cowpens that very same night,
Sometimes we were wrong—sometimes we were right,
Our heart's being run in true liberty's mold,
We regarded not hunger, wet, weary nor cold.

Early next morning we came to the ford,
Cherokee was its name—and "Buford"* the word,
We march'd thro' the river, with courage so free,
Expecting the foemen we might quickly see.

---

* "Buford" was the counter sign that day in reference to the Americans that had been butchered without mercy four months prior at the "Battle of the Waxhaws" (Buford's Slaughter) by Lieutenant Colonel Banastre Tarleton. Ballad found among the papers of Robert Long, a revolutionary soldier from Laurens County South Carolina according to King's Mountain historian Bobby Gilmore Moss.

Like eagles a hungry in search of their prey,
We chas'd the old fox the best part of the day.
At length on King's Mountain the old rogue we found,
And we, like bold heroes, his camp did surround.

The drums they did beat, the guns they did rattle,
Our enemies stood us a very smart battle,
Like lightening the flashes, like thunder and noise,
Such was the onset of our bold mountain boys.

The battle did last the best part of an hour,
The guns they did roar—the bullets did shower,
With an oath in our hearts to conquer the field,
We rush'd on the Tories—resolv'd they should yield.

We laid old Ferguson dead on the ground,
Four hundred and fifty dead Tories lay round—
Making a large escort not so wise,
To guide him to his chosen abode in the skies.

Brave Colonel Williams, and twenty five more,
Of our brave heroes lay roll'd in their grave,
With sorrow their bodies we laid in the clay.
In hopes that to heaven their souls took their way.

We shouted the victory that we did obtain,
Our voices were heard seven miles on the plain,
Liberty shall stand—and the Tories shall fall,
Here's an end to my song, so God bless you all

EXHIBIT A

British Ground Truth:
From Private to King in Their Own Words

HISTORY AS HEADLINES:
The London Gazette and *The Annual Register*

"**T**he sword of the state was delivered to the Sovereign," read the cover page of *The London Gazette* on December 15, 1781, which opened with the activity at the Court of St. James, specifically the knighting ceremonies:

> "Earl Ligonier, kneeling, was knighted therewith. Then the Senior knight, presented the Ribbon and Badge to the Sovereign, and His Majesty put them over the new knight's right shoulder, who being thus invested, kissed his Majesty's Hand. . . . "[28]

That Saturday, King George III and his ceremony made the front page of *The London Gazette* along with coverage of regal activities and the proclamations of Loyalty to the Most Gracious Sovereign, pledging support to "defeat the Confederacy of His Majesty's Enemies."

The cover page also bore updates on shipping from Bombay and territorial holdings in the East Indies. And vivid descriptions of "hard fought" battles with Hyder Ali. But it was page two that would change the world. As was customary for the paper of the day, whole correspondences of senior generals recapped battles and actions. These officers were the war correspondents of their day, and they knew it, so their words were carefully chosen for an audience extending beyond their higher headquarters to all of their countrymen and to posterity itself.

The letter was from Lieutenant General Earl Cornwallis, commander of British forces engaged in the Southern Campaign, to Sir

Henry Clinton, the overall commander of British Forces in America. The two men had a fractured relationship before this letter, and it would only become more complicated in the decades after. Some expected that they might duel after the war, but we will consider that later. For now, let us read, as the people of London did, as the parliamentarians did, as the royal staff and diplomats did, and as the Sovereign, King George Himself, read on that cold grey winter day in December of 1781:

Sir,

I have the mortification to inform your Excellency that I have been forced to give up the posts of York[town] and Gloucester, and to surrender the troops under my command, by capitulation on the 19th inst. as prisoners of war to the combined forces of America and France.

I never saw this post in a very favourable light, but when I found I was to be attacked in it in so unprepared a state, by so powerful an army and artillery, *nothing but the hopes of relief would have induced me to attempt its defence;* for I would either have endeavoured to escape to New York, by rapid marches from the Gloucester side, immediately on the arrival of General Washington's troops at Williamsburgh, or I would notwithstanding the disparity of numbers have attacked them in the open field, where it might have been just possible that fortune would have favoured the gallantry of the handful of troops under my command. *But being assured by your Excellency's letters that every possible means would be tried by the navy and army to relieve us,* I could not think myself at liberty to venture upon either of those desperate attempts; therefore, after remaining for two days in a strong position in front of this place, in hopes of being attacked, upon observing that the enemy were taking measures which could not fail of turning my left flank in a short time, *and receiving on the second evening your letter of the 24th of September informing that the relief would sail about the 5th of October,* I withdrew within the works on the night of the 29th of September, hoping by the labour and firmness of the soldiers to protract the defence until you could arrive.[29] [Note: Here and in subsequent extracts, italic font has been added for emphasis by the author.]

By the time the above letter was printed, Britons knew the war had already been lost. In fact news had arrived weeks earlier, prompting the King's speech which you shall read later. This October 20, 1781 letter from General Cornwallis is among the most important documents of the Revolution. Cornwallis's letter is the most publicly read accounting, and blame shifting of the war. Not three days after capitulating, he begins heaping fault at the feet of his commander in New York.

Burke's *Annual Register*, a yearly wrap up of essays and historical accounts around the British Empire, would use the text and inference of this letter in crafting the summary of events, not just of capitulation, but of the entire war in the Americas, that would in turn be copied by historians around the world. The ensuing finger-pointing between Cornwallis and Clinton will begin one of the great historical controversies, but for now let us examine the role of the general as correspondent, and the Gazette as a source for *The Annual Register*.

THE LONDON GAZETTE

The London Gazette proudly proclaims itself "An alternative to scurrilous gossip and rumour." Its history page and searchable online database is a wonderful resource:

> The state already held incomparable sources of information from overseas: during peacetime the various British embassies could be relied upon to relay strategic and political news back home and, in times of war, the dispatches of the British generals served a similar purpose— both sources acting effectively as the foreign correspondents of their day ... From the beginning the Gazette readership was not the general public but the mercantile class, the legal profession and officers of the state serving at home and abroad. Whilst this guaranteed a large circulation—6,000 copies by 1704—over 1,000 of these were provided free to office holders and often sold on for a profit.[30]

Published twice a week averaging about four pages, it grew to eight pages by 1785 in order to publish insolvency (bankruptcy) announcements.

The Cover page of *The London Gazette*, 13 Feb. 1781, records the activity of the King at the Court of St. James as was typical at the time. The pages that follow are then dedicated to the affairs at the empire's edge, which include letters from the field commanders such as Cornwallis. It is through this narrative view that the British public, and more importantly, the political class, got a relatively unfiltered view of success or failure in the colonies. Today you can see these perfectly preserved issues for yourself on the Gazette's website (see end notes) as part of the internet's democratization of information, once reserved for elite scholars with access, time, and money.

The letter printed in this issue provided the first account of the Battle of King's Mountain for the British audience:

Recorded in the Gazette (London Gazette), issue 12162, 13 Feb. 1781, Pg. 2

Dateline: Whitehall, February 17, 1781

Extract of a letter from the Earl of Cornwallis to Sir Henry Clinton, dated Camp at Wynnesborough (SC), December 3, 1780

> . . . a few words about poor Major Ferguson. . . . As he had only militia and the small remains of his own corps, without baggage or artillery, and as he promised to come back if he heard of any superior force, I thought he could do no harm, and might help keep alive the spirits of our friends in North Carolina, which might be damped by the slowness of our motions . . . A numerous and unexpected Enemy came from the Mountains; as they had good horses their movement was rapid . . . [Major Ferguson] was not aware that the enemy was so near him; and in endeavoring to execute my orders . . . joining me at Charlotte Town, he was *attacked by a superior force and totally defeated on King's Mountain.*[31]

This letter would be combined with other reports from the colonies creating a foundation that by yearend would produce the *Annual Register*. Here is how *The Annual Register or a View of the History,*

Politics and Literature for the Year 1781 described the Battle of King's Mountain:

> Ferguson was tempted to stay longer in the mountainous country which partly borders on, and partly forms a part of Tyron County in North Carolina, than was absolutely necessary, under the hope of cutting off a Col. Clarke, who was returning from an expedition into Georgia; and was the more encouraged in his delay from his not having an idea that there was a force in the country at all able to look him in the face. A numerous fierce and unexpected enemy, however, suddenly sprung up in the depths of the deserts. The scattered inhabitants of the mountains assembled without noise or warning under the conduct of six or seven of their militia colonels, to the number of 1600 daring, well mounted and excellent horsemen.
>
> Col. Ferguson had already received orders from Lord Cornwallis for his return, and was on his way to pass the Catawba for that purpose. But discovering, as he crossed the King's Mountain, that he was eagerly pursued by a thick cloud of cavalry, he took the best position for receiving them which time and the place would admit of, and which happened to be by no means a bad one. But his men being neither covered by horse nor artillery, and being likewise dismayed and admonished, *at finding themselves so unexpectedly surrounded and attacked on every side by this cavalry, were not at all capable of withstanding the impetuosity of their charge. A total rout ensued.* The colonel with 150 of his men were killed upon the spot. About the same number were wounded; and the prisoners including the latter exceeded 800. The Americans say they took 1500 stand of arms and state Ferguson's force at 1400 men.
>
> The fall of this officer, who possessed very distinguished talents as a partisan, and in the conduct of irregular warfare, was, independently even of his detachment, no small loss to the service . . . *This was the first reverse of fortune which Earl Cornwallis had experienced in his military career, but she seemed now to take vengeance for the delay: for the state of his force, and the nature of the war considered, few things could have been more peculiarly unlucky in the present juncture . . .* "[32]

The story of the massacre at King's Mountain riveted generations. And it would soon populate the history books of the nineteenth century. Of those volumes, it wasn't an American or even a Briton who captured this story or the other dramas of our revolution best, according to Library of Congress historian Daniel Boorstin. It was an Italian, Charles Botta, whose history book "became the first standard account for Americans of All parties. John Adams called Botta the 'best,' and Jefferson predicted it would become 'the common manual of our revolutionary History.'"[33]

Here is a sampling of Charles Botta's writing on King's Mountain as it was first written in Italian in 1809 and then translated to English in 1820:

> At every step they swore to exterminate him. At length they found him. But Ferguson was not a man that any danger whatever could intimidate. He was posted on a woody eminence which commands all the adjacent plain and has a circular base. It is called King's Mountain . . . The carnage had been dreadful; the Royalists had to regret above eleven hundred men in Killed wounded and prisoners, a loss extremely serious in the present circumstances . . . The Mountaineers, after this victory, returned to their homes. The check of King's Mountain was a heavy blow to the British interests in the Carolinas. The position of Cornwallis became critical. The Loyalists no longer manifested the same zeal to join him; and he found himself with a feeble army in the midst of a hostile and sterile country.[34]

Botta's descriptions written more than twenty years after the war are colorful, fluid, and assured, but what were his sources? By whom was he inspired?

The British ground truth that was delivered through the pages of *The London Gazette* is a prime source, as are subsequent biographies of the participants (note parallels with Stedman in Exhibit A.7). But the most important single source for Charles Botta and dozens of writers who would join him in recounting the American Revolution is the *Annual Register*.

A quick note on the literary and political figure Edmund Burke, who many consider the father of modern conservatism. For centuries, biographers had reported that Edmund Burke edited *The Annual Register* and actually wrote the "Historical Article," the segment of the *Register* that gave a yearly recap of British activities around the globe, during the timeframe of the American Revolution.

This theory of Burke's role in recording America's history had not been seriously challenged (especially given the pro-American tone appropriately delivered by a leading Whig intellectual) until the 1950s, when professor and investigator of literary history Bertram D. Sarason determined "Burke's editorial connection with the Register ended in 1765 . . . No evidence—receipts from (publisher) or confirmation by Burke or his friends—exists to support his editorship after 1765. Concrete evidence does show that Thomas English succeeded Burke in that year."[35]

230 years later, the identity of the author is not what we are contesting. Today the British newsweekly, *The Economist*, does not credit its staff, but is still considered authoritative by many. For attribution purposes we will still credit Burke as editor, even if he was, as Sarason suggests, a "phantom."[36]

It does add a tinge of irony, given the premise of this case, that over time Leftists have worked to erase much of *The Annual Register*'s version of events from American history. Could Burke's role as an early contributor to conservative thought have anything to do with his subsequent diminution? For example, Dr. Edward Feulner, Chairman of the conservative Heritage Foundation, wrote this of Burke:

> If we had to pick the thinkers more responsible than any other for planting the intellectual roots of modern conservative thought, I believe we would select Edmund Burke and Russell Kirk. They were separated by almost two hundred years but united in their adherence to the priceless principle of ordered liberty.[37]

We will save for later an exploration of the motives and mechanisms of this historical rewrite. For now let us satisfy ourselves that whoever wrote the words on *The Annual Register*, the impact is undeniable. Passages or pages would surface as the foundations of dozens of history books on both sides of the Atlantic.

In 1953 Bertram Sarason described the frequency of plagiarism in early American histories and noted, "The Annual Register emerges as a source of first importance . . . devoted to describing the events of the war between England and her colonies. These convenient accounts served as the main source of the histories mentioned."[38]

■

Given *The Annual Register*'s role as a historical "benchmark," we will reference its accounts of three other major battles of the 1781 Southern campaign: Cowpens, Guilford Courthouse and Yorktown. Then using these narratives of the action, we can see the influence of the letters populating *The London Gazette,* which originally described the events as well as the subsequent books derived from them.

While controversy may arise over the importance of one battle over another, or the accuracy of a source, what will become clear is that there is no disputing where the British lost the war, or to whom.

COWPENS

Towards the close of the year (1780), Whilst Lord Cornwallis was making every preparation for a vigorous eruption into North Carolina, General Greene was sent from the northern army by Washington to take command of the southern . . . Greene stands so high with the Americans as an officer, that he holds the next place to Washington in their military estimation . . . the great favorite of that commander.

He brought no troops from the northern army, depending on the resources of the southern colonies for their own defence; but was accompanied by Col. Daniel Morgan, a brave and distinguished partisan who had commanded those riflemen in the northern war, that besides being fatal to many brave officers became so terrible to the Indians under Gen. Burgoyne, and were so far superior to them in their own way, that to use his own expressive words, "they could not be brought within the sound of a rifle shot."

Early in the new year of 1781 . . . Morgan advanced with about 500 regular troops (mostly belonging to Virginia), and some hundreds of militia, with a detachment of one hundred cavalry, Under Col. [William] Washington, upon the Pacelot river.

Tarleton was already on that side, with the legion consisting of 300 cavalry and as many infantry, with the first battalion of the 71st, which was now annexed to it, and one three pounder; and being joined by the 7th regiment, which was marching with another three pounder, he received instructions from the commander in chief (Cornwallis) to strike a blow, if possible, at Gen. Morgan; but at all events, to oblige him to pass the Broad River and thereby prevent any future embarrassment on that side.

Morgan retreated and Tarleton pursued; a state of things that naturally increases confidence and ardour on one side, and generally depresses them on the other. Morgan at length found his enemy so close upon him that he could not pass the Broad River especially as the waters were exceedingly out, without exposing his troops to greater danger, than he thought he should hazard by an encounter. He accordingly, without hesitation, determined at once upon the part which he should take; and choosing his ground boldly prepared for battle.

Tarleton came up with his enemy at eight in the morning (Jan. 17, 1781), and nothing could appear more inviting than the prospect before him. They were drawn up on the edge of an open wood without defenses; and though their number might have been somewhat superior to his own, the quality of the troops was so different as not to admit a doubt of success; which was still farther confirmed by his great superiority in cavalry; so that everything seemed to indicate a complete victory. His line of attack was composed of the 7th regiment, with the foot of the legion, and the corps of light infantry annexed to it. A troop of cavalry covered each flank. The first battalion of the 71st, and the remainder of the cavalry, formed a second line.

Morgan showed uncommon ability and judgment in the disposition of his force. Seven hundred militia, on whom he placed no great confidence, were exposed to open view, as we have seen, in the first line, on the edge of the wood: but the second, composed of the Continental and Virginia troops was out of sight in the wood, where they were drawn up in excellent order, and prepared for all events.

The militia were little capable of sustaining the impetuosity of their assailants, and were soon broken, routed, and scattered on all sides. It is not to be wondered at that those troops who had been so long used to carry everything before them, now meeting with the usual facility, should at once conclude the day to be their own, and pursue the fugitives with the utmost rapidity. In the meantime, the second line having opened on the right and left in the wood, as well to lead the victors on, as to afford a clear passage for the fugitives as soon as the former were far enough advanced, poured in a close and deadly fire on both sides, which took the most fatal effect.

The ground was in an instant, covered with killed and wounded, and those brave troops who had been so long inured to conquer, were by this severe and unthought-of check, thrown into irremediable disorder and confusion.

A total defeat was the immediate consequence. The 7th Regiment lost their colors, and the brave men of the royal artillery, who attended the two pieces of cannon with characteristic intrepidity and magnanimity of their corps, scorning either to abandon or surrender their guns, were cut to pieces by them. The loss every way, in killed, wounded prisoners, exceeded 400 men . . .

This blow, coming so closely upon that at the King's Mountain, produced effects worse than could have been feared from such partial disasters. Indeed they seemed seriously to have influenced all the subsequent operations of the war, and deeply affected its general fortune. The loss of the light troops, especially of the cavalry, could scarcely be repaired; and the nature of war rendered this sort of force one of its more effectual arms.

It was the more grievous to Lord Cornwallis, from being one of those unexpected events which as it could neither be foreseen nor apprehended, no wisdom could possibly provide against. Most of the troops that were now defeated had been much distinguished and constantly successful. It was not even clear that there was any disparity in point of number; and if there had, from long confirmed experience, it could not have been a matter of much consideration. Nor was it even to be supposed, that Morgan would in any possible circumstance have ventured an engagement . . . [39]

GUILFORD COURTHOUSE

Thus ended the very sharp, hard fought, and exceedingly diversified action at Guilford. . . . The loss on the British side, in any comparative estimate, drawn from the length, circumstances, and severity of the action, would appear very moderate; but if considered, either with respect to the number of the army, its ability to bear the loss, or the intrinsic value of the brave men who fell or were disabled, it was great indeed. In the whole it exceeded 500 men; if whom though scarcely a fifth were killed on the spot, many died afterwards of their wounds; and undoubtedly, a much greater number were disabled from all future service.

At any rate the army was deprived of about one-fourth in number of its present force. . . . The Americans gave no state of their loss, which would alone have been sufficient reason for concluding it to be very considerable. They only published an account of killed and wounded of the Continental troops, who formed but a small part of their army. It was said that all the houses for many miles were filled with their wounded. The action was spread through so wide an extent of the country, and that so thickly wooded, that the victors could form no estimate of the slain . . . [40]

It is sufficient to observe, that however the Americans were routed, the royal forces were in no condition to maintain a pursuit . . . and though this victory was gained at the entrance to the country in which the loyalists were supposed to be numerous, it does not appear that it was capable of inducing anybody of that people deserving of a name or consideration to join the royal army . . .

Such was the strange and untoward nature of this unhappy war, that *victory now, as we have already seen in more than one other instance, was productive of all the consequences of defeat.*[41]

The news of this victory in England, for a while, produced the usual effects upon the minds of the people in general. Very little time and reflection gave rise to other thoughts; and a series of victories caused, for the first time, the beginning of a general despair. The fact was that while the British army astonished both the old and the new world by the greatness of its exertions and the rapidity of its marches, it had never advanced any nearer even to the conquest of North Carolina. And such was the hard fate of the victors, who had gained much glory at Guilford, as in the first place to abandon part of their wounded, and in the second, to make a circuitous retreat of 200 miles before they could find shelter or rest.[42]

YORKTOWN

Thus was the brave but ill-fated army under Lord Cornwallis by degrees enclosed and surrounded, being shut up by a prodigious naval force on the one side and an army of above 8,000 French, of about as many Continental troops and 5,000 militia, on the others, and with no other cover than the recent earthen works, hastily thrown up, to oppose so great a force, aided by a powerful train of heavy artillery . . . [43]

The desire of extricating Lord Cornwallis and his army, however, prevailed over all considerations of danger and loss, and the British Naval commanders used all the possible expedition in refitting and equipping the fleet in New York. This, however though unavoidably necessary, took up more time than could have been afforded at this juncture . . . It was, however, the 19th of October before the fleet could get clear the bar; Sir Henry Clinton, with above 7,000 of his best forces, having embarked on board ships of war . . . [44]

In this final passage, *The Annual Register* gives Gen. Cornwallis's account, via his October 20, 1781 letter to Clinton, nearly verbatim. The material is drawn from *The London Gazette* on December 15, 1781.

Nothing less than certain hope and expectation of relief, could have induced Lord Cornwallis to attempt a defense of a post, which he deemed too incapable of refitting the force opposed to it, as that which he now occupied. He would otherwise have attempted to retreat, however difficult, or he would have hazarded an encounter in the open field, and trusting the gallantry of these troops, leave the rest to the decision of fortune.* This hope was farther confirmed, by a letter from the commander in chief at New York, dated on the 24th

---

* All drawn directly from Gen. Cornwallis's Oct 20, 1781 Letter.

of September, which informed him that relief would sail from thence about the 5th of October. Thus circumstanced, Lord Cornwallis could not think himself justified in abandoning his position, and in risking the consequences of those desperate measures, which must then of necessity be adopted. On the other hand, it happened most unfortunately, that the delay that occurred in refitting and equipping the fleet, rendered it impossible for Sir Henry Clinton to fulfill his intention.[45]

Clearly the words of Gen. Cornwallis, the most senior British officer actually on the ground in the Carolinas and later Virginia, carried much weight in the reporting that would follow. In the following exhibits we look at his words directly as well as others who were eyewitnesses to the carnage of the Carolinas.

COMMANDER AS CORRESPONDENT:
General Cornwallis

F lush from seizing Charleston and smashing the rebel General Gates at Camden, the tone of Cornwallis's letters in 1780 was triumphant. For those initial moments in the summer of 1780, victory was seemingly assured. But overplaying their hand would hurt the British and the loyalists, whose support they were counting on. Cornwallis was determined to *"punish severely"* any resistance, but that only fueled the patriot fire.

Cornwallis to Lt. Col. Cruger
Camden, Aug 18, 1780

On the morning of the 16th, I attacked and totally defeated General Gate's army; above 1000 were killed and wounded, and about 800 taken prisoners . . . I have given orders that all the inhabitants of this province, who have submitted, and who have taken part in this revolt, should be punished with the greatest rigour, that they should be imprisoned, and their whole property taken or destroyed . . . I have ordered in the most positive manner, that every militia man who had borne arms with us and had afterwards joined the enemy should be immediately hanged.[46]

Cornwallis to Sir Henry Clinton
Camden, Aug 29, 1780

We receive the strongest professions of friendship from North Carolina. Our friends, however, do not seem inclined to rise until

they see our army in motion. The severity of the Rebel government has so terrified and totally subdued the minds of the people,
that it is very difficult to rouse them to any exertions . . . [47]

. . . Major Wemyss is going . . . to disarm in the most rigid
manner, the country between the Santee and Pedee (rivers) and
to punish severely all those who submitted or pretended to live
peaceably . . . I have myself ordered several militia men to be
executed who had voluntarily enrolled and borne arms with us,
and afterwards revolted to the enemy.[48]

. . . Ferguson is to move in to Tryon County with some militia,
whom he says he is sure he can depend upon for doing their duty
and fighting well; but I am sorry to say that his own experience,
as well as that of every other officer, is totally against him.[49]

The Battle of King's Mountain occurred on October 7, 1780. Cornwallis was encamped at nearby Charlotte and was fully aware of the
cost and consequences within days. Evidence of the psychological
impact was manifest when Cornwallis sent out the call for loyalists.
He tells Clinton (below) no one showed up. Just two months prior,
the British had been on top of the world when Cornwallis achieved a
decisive victory against General Gates at Camden on August 16. The
rebel general fled and his army was "entirely dispersed."

In a matter of weeks however, perceptions of British inevitability
began a downward trend that would not recover. The next year, 1781
started badly with a shocking defeat at Cowpens, and then only
seemed to worsen. Ever aware of an audience, Cornwallis's letters still
betray his concerns as they were shared almost daily in the pages of
The London Gazette.

Cornwallis to Sir Henry Clinton (via Lord Rawdon)
Near Catawba River, October 29, 1780

Not a single man, however, attempted to improve the favourable
moment, or obeyed that summons . . . whilst we were waiting
at [Charlotte], they did not even furnish us with the least information respecting the force collecting against us. . . . Whilst this
Army lay at Charlotte, Georgetown was taken from our militia

by the rebels, and the whole country east of the Santee gave such proof of the general defection that even the militia of the high hills could not be prevailed upon to join . . . *the defeat of Maj. Ferguson had so dispirited this part of the country,* and indeed the loyal subjects were so wearied by the long continuance of the campaign, that Lt. Col. Cruger sent information to Lord Cornwallis that the whole district had determined to submit as soon as the Rebels should enter it.[50]

Cornwallis to Lt. Col. Tarleton
Wynnesborough, NC, October 29, 1780

. . . We should want you, always endeavoring to strike a blow if an opening should offer, and taking up all that have been violent against us, to change for our friends who have been everywhere seized and most cruelly treated.[51]

Cornwallis to Maj. Gen. Smallwood
Camp, Nov. 10, 1780

I must now observe that the cruelty exercised on the prisoners taken under Major Ferguson is shocking to Humanity; and the hanging of poor Colonel Mills . . . was an act of savage barbarity . . . I cannot suppose that you can approve of these most cruel murders; but I hope you will see the necessity of interposing your authority to stop this bloody scene, which must oblige me, in justice to the suffering loyalists, to retaliate on the unfortunate persons now in my power.[52]

Cornwallis to Lt. Col. Cruger
Camp, Nov. 11, 1780

The accounts I receive from Col. Kirkland of the supineness and pusillanimity of our militia, takes off all of my compassion for their sufferings. If they will allow themselves to be plundered and their families ruined by a banditti not one-third of their numbers, there is no possibility of our protecting them.[53]

Cornwallis to Lt. Col. Kirkland
Camp, Nov. 13, 1780

... but if those who say they are our friends will not stir, I cannot defend everyman's house from being plundered; and I must say that when I see a whole settlement running away from twenty or thirty robbers, I think they deserve to be robbed.[54]

Cornwallis's editor and biographer Charles Ross observes that in the winter of 1780, "None of these engagements were of importance or had much influence over the subsequent operations, beyond increasing the terror of the Loyalists, who were persecuted by the rebels in the most cruel manner, and not infrequently murdered under circumstances of savage barbarity." Savagery, "plunder" and "retaliation" in the backcountry were taking their toll on the sympathizers. Cornwallis's security, communications, and logistics eroded.[55]

Cornwallis to American Major Gen. Gates
Camp, Dec. 1, 1780

Sir, I think it is proper to present to you that the officers and men taken at King's Mountain were treated with an inhumanity scarcely credible. I feel myself under the disagreeable necessity of making severe retaliation for those unhappy men who were so cruelly and unjustly put to death at Gilbertstown, Sincerely ... Cornwallis[56]

Cornwallis to Sir Henry Clinton
Camp, Dec. 3, 1780

... the (loyalist) militia ... on which alone we could place the smallest dependence, are so totally disheartened by the defeat of Ferguson that of the whole district we could with difficulty assemble 100, and even those, I am convinced, would not have made the smallest resistance if we had been attacked."[57]

Complaints of cruelty and savagery in the backcountry of the Carolinas went both ways. When the war was over, Congress demanded that Cornwallis be returned to America to stand trial. Instead he was appointed Governor of India, but that twist of fate was still years over the horizon. For now let us return the personal imploring of a commander attempting to resuscitate "disheartened" loyalists who have become too terrorized to fight as the South descends deeper into a bloody civil war.

Cornwallis to Sir Henry Clinton
Camp, Dec. 4, 1780

I received from your Excellency the copies of two letters which were sent to you from General Washington, of the 6th and 16th of October, complaining of the cruelty and injustice of the measures pursued by the officers serving under your command in the Southern Colonies . . .

I will not hurt your Excellency's feelings by attempting to describe the shocking tortures and inhuman murders which are everyday committed by the enemy, not only on those who have taken part with us, but on many who refuse to join them.

I cannot flatter myself that your representations will have any effect, but I am very sure that unless some steps are taken to check it, the war in this quarter will become truly savage.[58]

TRULY SAVAGE: UNLEASHING INDIANS

Grabbing an infant in one hand by the ankles and "braining" it against a tree was not uncommon for Indians raiding Anglo settlements. Often ignored, the barbarity of and constant fighting with the Indians was a through-line of America's founding. The use of Indians as proxy soldiers to raid, attack, murder, or kidnap women and children is well documented, yet still somehow ignored, or worse, retold as a uniquely Anglo phenomenon of Indian victimization, when in reality there was no shortage of savagery on all sides.

Cornwallis to Sir Henry Clinton
Camp, Dec. 29, 1780

Sir, when the numerous and formidable body of Back Mountain men came down to attack Major Ferguson, and showed themselves to be our most inveterate enemies, *I directed Lt. Col. Brown to encourage the Indians to attack the settlements* of Watauga, Holstein, and Nolachuckie, all of which are new encroachments on the Indian territories. *The good effects of this measure have already appeared.* A large body of the mountaineers marched lately to join the Rebels near King's Mountain, but were soon *obliged to return to oppose the incursions of the Indians* . . . [59]

COWPENS

Cornwallis was crushed by the defeat of his aggressive deputy Lt. Col. Banastre Tarleton at the battle of Cowpens on January 17, 1781. Rebel General Daniel Morgan did more than disembowel some of Cornwallis's finest troops, he derailed the entire war effort in the South, and in so doing set America on a course for victory. Months later, Cornwallis would lament, "The affair of the 17th of January must be classed among the extraordinary events of the war."[60]

After studying all of Cornwallis's correspondence and producing a book on the General in 1859, Charles Ross, wrote:

The defeat at Cowpens was the most serious calamity which had occurred since Saratoga, and crippled Lord Cornwallis's movements during the remainder of the war. No blame could be attached to him as he had furnished Tarleton with 700 infantry and 350 cavalry—the best troops of the army. Morgan had hardly an equal force, of which only 540 were continentals. The loss of the English was about 600—that of the Americans, according to their own account, was less than 100.

Note the comment about blame, as recrimination of the senior commanders would continue for decades around this ignominious defeat.[61]

Cornwallis to Lord (General) Rawdon,
Camp, Feb. 4, 1781

... Our Friends must be so disheartened by the misfortune of the 17th that you will get but little good from them ... [62]

NORTH VS. SOUTH

In an almost offhand way Lord Rawdon, Cornwallis's deputy who had been present with Clinton and Cornwallis from the start of the Revolution and the first attempt on Charleston, acknowledged another controversial element of America's first civil war. Not only was the backcountry conflict in the Carolinas an American on American phenomena, sometimes pitting families against each other, but it had another familiar strain: North versus South.

Lord Rawdon to Cornwallis
Camp, Mar. 7, 1781

... I know how anxious your lordship must be to hear from us, but the savage cruelty of the enemy, who commit the most wanton murders in cold blood upon the friends of Government that fall into their hands, makes it very difficult to procure a messenger at any price ... In the meantime, (Sumter) summoned by proclamation all the inhabitants to join him, offering to all such as would take part with him a full pardon for their former attachment to us (Britain) and denouncing penalty of death to all who did not range themselves under his standard by the 23rd of February.

To give weight to these threats several persons known to be friendly towards us were inhumanly murdered, tho' unarmed and remaining peaceably at their own houses. Either thro' fear or inclination many joined the enemy ... *The New York Dragoons have distinguished themselves in many successful skirmishes.*[63]

Which contemporary texts teach that the northern colonies were so sufficiently pacified by the British that they could spare volunteers to go south?

Show me a modern American history book that admits New York Dragoons were pillaging and killing Southerners on behalf of the crown. Where does that live in the pantheon of Northern post-civil war self-righteousness?

The following chapter is dedicated to one such Connecticut Yankee, Stephen Jarvis. His story is far from unique, as fellow loyalists from the other Northern colonies were a regular occurrence fighting alongside the royal forces. The strategy of Clinton and Cornwallis had always depended on such loyalists who comprised units like Major Ferguson's "All American Volunteers." Sometimes called provincials, the Americans fighting on behalf of the crown supplemented the professional British soldiers.

Recruited as a young man in 1776, Jarvis's campaigns across the frozen rivers of New York to the impenetrable bayous of the Low Country offer a succinct and engaging snapshot of the entire war. Special attention should be paid to the difference in tone and terror, when he is recounting his fights up north as compared to those in Southern swamps.

STEPHEN JARVIS AND THE CONNECTICUT YANKEES INVADE DIXIE

"*My father was one of those persons called Tories. He lived in the Colony of Connecticut . . . I was the age of Eighteen years when the hostilities commenced between Great Britain and her colonies . . .*"[64]

So begins the gripping firsthand narrative of a Connecticut boy, Stephen Jarvis, who becomes a man while fighting against the Declaration of Independence and those rebels who wanted to break from his beloved crown. After seven years of service in the King's Army, going from private to Colonel, Jarvis leaves the colonies for Canada. He expired at the ripe age of 84, but not before he left us this most interesting firsthand account.

A witness to many of the battles of the revolution from start to finish, including his own internal struggle as he switched from loyalist to patriot and back again, his insight is unparalleled. It is unlikely you have heard Jarvis's story because it doesn't fit the conventional "mainstream" narrative. In 1907, after being discovered by the Jarvis family, the *Connecticut Magazine* published Stephen Jarvis's story in serial, titled: "An American's Experience in the British Army: Manuscript of Colonel Stephen Jarvis, Born in 1756 in Danbury, Connecticut, Revealing the Life of the Loyalists Who Refused to Renounce Allegiance to the King and Fought to Save the Western Continent to the British Empire."

My father was one of those persons called Tories. He lived in the Colony of Connecticut . . . I was the age of Eighteen years when the hostilities commenced between Great Britain and her colonies . . .

Soon after the battle of Bunker Hill, and about the time the British Army evacuated Boston, there was a draft of the [Patriot] Militia of Connecticut to Garrison New York, and I was drafted as one; my father would readily have got a substitute for me, but as he had so strenuously opposed my suit, I was obstinate and declared my intentions of going as a soldier—for this declaration he took me by the arm and thrust me out the door; during the evening, however, I went to my room and went to bed.

The next day was Sunday and I kept out of sight; the next morning we were to march, a brother of my mother was the officer commanding. On leaving the house, I passed my father and wished him "goodbye;" he made no reply, and I passed on to the house of my uncle, the place of rendezvous, but before the troops marched my father so far relented as to come to me and after giving me a severe reproof, ordered me a horse to ride, gave me some money, and I set off.[65]

Jarvis quickly realizes he made a mistake in choosing the rebels against his father's wishes . . .

I repented to my father that I was very sinnable, that I had done wrong in espousing a cause so repugnant to his feelings, and contrary to my own opinion . . . After the British had taken New York, the militia was again called out but I refused to serve.[66]

Jarvis flees, hides, lies, and evades until he is able to join the British cause, which he does with gusto after being told that Americans had killed his father.

This melancholy news determined for me a military life . . . I was a perfect stranger to every individual around me, not a friend to advise, or ask council of, no money in my pocket, the most inexperienced, either of men or of manners, of any almost in existence. Think what my feelings were at this time . . . I however made up my mind that if I ever had the opportunity to meet the enemy—that I would merit a commission, and I applied myself strictly to my duty, and soon merited the notice of my officers . . . [which he did as a member of the Regiment of Queens Rangers.][67]

Jarvis is involved in some minor skirmishes, then deploys to the Chesapeake, and is in combat at Brandywine.

. . . My pantaloons received a wound, and I don't hesitate to say that I should been very well pleased to have seen a little blood also. The enemy stood until we came near bayonet points, then gave us a volley and retired across the Brandywine . . . General Howe commenced his attack late in the afternoon, and this was the signal for our division to advance . . . the battery playing upon us with grapeshot, which did much execution. The water took us up to our breasts, and was much stained with blood.[68]

After taking a hill, Jarvis observed:

. . . We had a most extensive view of the American Army, and we saw our brave comrades cutting them up in great style. The battle lasted until dark, when the enemy retreated and left us master of the field . . . we took up our night's lodgings on the field of battle, which was strewed with dead bodies of the enemy. In this day's hard fought action, the Queens Rangers' loss in killed and wounded were seventy five out of two hundred and fifty . . .

We remained encamped the whole next day, and gave the enemy an opportunity to rally his forces and get reinforcements and take up a position to attack us, which they did, at Germantown, where our army had encamped sending our sick and wounded to Philadelphia. At this battle the enemy were again defeated, and left us in possession of the field . . . It would be endless to enumerate the different actions which took place, but there were too many, in which the Regiment gained great applause at White Marsh, and afterwards at Parkers Bridge, at both places we took and killed a good many.

In short we were continually engaged with the enemy more or less, and had General Howe during the winter, instead of Gambling with the officers every night, to the utter ruin of many of them, attacked General Washington at the Valley Forge, where he might have done, the event of the War would have been very different, but I am only relating those actions in which I am personally concerned . . . [69]

The news of general Burgoyne's capture gave great energy to the enemy. The French also forming an alliance with the Americans, sending troops to America put a different face on things. General Howe, after making a great display in Philadelphia, resigned the command and went home and Sir Henry Clinton took the Command in Chief . . . Nothing of moment took place on our route until we came to Monmouth, where on the morning of the 28th of June, the Queens Ranger met at daylight the advance army of the Americans under command of General Lee. We had a smart brush and Col. Simcoe was wounded. We took some prisoners and returned and joined the Army at Monmouth Courthouse.

Sir Henry Clinton with five thousand of his army attacked Lee and drove him the whole day—took and killed a great many of his men until we fell in with general Washington's whole Army; when we retreated, leaving our wounded in the enemies hands . . . I bore the fatigue of the day very well with only having again a shot through my pantaloons, leaving the mark of the ball on the skin, or rather the powder without drawing blood. The Queens Rangers embarked in flat boats and rowed up to New York . . . where we remained for some time. Our duty during the winter (1778-79) was not severe, the harbor afforded plenty of oysters . . . Our food was for some time very course, our bread oatmeal biscuit full of maggots.[70]

Jarvis and the Rangers continue operations in the North East— New York, New Jersey and Connecticut throughout 1779. He serves beside Gen. Cornwallis and Maj. Ferguson and even has occasion to patrol near his childhood home.

Sir Henry Clinton with a part of the Army embarked for Charlestown [Charleston], and the infantry of the Rangers were also in orders, and the baggage was on board and they were ordered to be re-landed, and the fleet sailed without them, and the Regiment remained in Richmond (New York) all winter. The winter of 1780 was a most severe one; the harbor of New York was even so frozen that cannon were brought from New York to Staten Island upon ice, and during the winter a body of enemy crossed from the Jerseys to Staten Island and invested our post.

At the Narrows the cold was so intense, and after remaining two nights and losing about forty men frozen to death, they returned to the Jerseys . . . in the latter month of March (1780) I was informed that the Regiment were going to embark; the cavalry were to remain behind. He (Commander) asked me "if I had any inclination to go with the regiment." I expressed a desire to go. He said, "Well, my boy, you shall go, and you shall have command . . . ."

We soon embarked, me with my men, saddles and appointments, and after a passage of fourteen or fifteen days, we arrived at Charlestown . . . we never came in contact with any of the enemy during the siege . . . after the town surrendered, the Rangers marched in . . . there was little to excite attention of the reader during our stay. . . . The people from the backcountry coming in daily and taking the oath of allegiance, and before we left Charlestown it was again to appearance a British Colony. We soon left Charlestown and sailed for New York (with Clinton) . . .

We remained in this situation until the fate of Major Andre (Benedict Arnold's Spy Handler), where we were waiting to take possession of the Fort at West Point, when we were removed to Long Island.[71]

Then with a full complement of Northern loyalist troops they mounted for Norfolk Virginia and then shortly thereafter farther south to the Carolinas.

We embarked for Charlestown, myself, men, stores and horses in one vessel and the officers in another. On our leaving Norfolk Captain Saunders had plundered more horses than he was allowed to put on board. He, therefore, distributed them to his officers and among the rest, gave me a very fine horse. At sea we had very boisterous weather, our vessel sprang a leak—never so crazy a vessel went to sea. To save our lives, I threw thirty fine horses overboard, but saved every officer a horse. With great difficulty we got safe into port (at Charlestown).[72]

Jarvis is quickly made a lieutenant.

Earnestly [I] set about recruiting, and in a short time we mustered twenty-six dragoons with which number we were ordered to take the field, after procuring horses and appointments. This was at the time that Lord Rawdon fought the Americans and defeated them at Camden . . . in the meantime, a reinforcement of three Regiments arrived from England . . . At this time we were reinforced with the South Carolina Regiment (local loyalists.)[73]

Jarvis is then sent upon some reconnaissance missions.

I set off a little before sunset in a heavy shower of rain, and before I had proceeded far found that my militia men had left me, and I was reduced to my four dragoons, but as my object was intelligence more than fighting, I proceeded on. I soon discovered six or eight men advancing towards me, and when they came to a certain distance, challenged me.

I said, a friend.

"What friend?"

To the King.

At this declaration one of them dismounted and placed his rifle across his horse. I charged his rifle, [and he] missed fire. He mounted and with his comrades dashed into the woods. I soon came up with him, and by a well-directed stroke laid him in the dust. I ordered my man to secure him and pushed forward after the rest . . . We soon came into the sight of the enemy and charged . . . I rode a very fleet horse and soon gained the advance, and pressed hard on the enemy, who left the roads and took to the woods; I soon came up with one, and my corporal on the other side, and we both made a blow at the same time and gave the fellow his quarters . . . [74]

Skirmishes continue until partisan leader Francis Marion mauls the loyalist forces.

We had got intelligence that General Marion was collecting a body of troops to give us annoyance on our route . . . we marched in this order until we came to a long swamp, a mile or so from Parker's

Ferry, when we heard some few shots in front, and Major Fraser ordered the Cavalry to advance, and seeing some troops a long distance off, and supposing them to be the enemy, charged over this long causeway and fell into an ambuscade, laid by the enemy, and we received the most galling fire ever troops experienced.

We only saw the flash of the pieces, the enemy was so complete hid from our view, and we had only to push forward men and horses falling before and behind. We lost one hundred twenty-five killed and a great many wounded before they could bring their guns to bear upon the enemy . . . [75]

Combat ensues, almost daily.

. . . We had another brush with the Americans at Monks' Corner, where we got completely defeated. It was an attempt to surprise a party at this post, but they got intelligence on our approach, and gave us a complete drubbing. We lost one Captain killed, one captain two subalterns and several men wounded, without injuring a single man of the enemy. They had so completely fortified themselves that having no infantry with us we could not approach them and had to receive their fire without being able to return it, and we returned to our encampment not very well satisfied with our defeat . . . [76]

Jarvis's experience offers a glimpse into the larger phenomenon of early British success in the Northern colonies, followed by the quick victories in the South at Charleston and Camden, summarily overturned by the grinding hostility of the backwoods partisans.

UZAL JOHNSON

Another Yankee who came to know firsthand the efficacy of Carolina backwoodsmen was Uzal Johnson. A fifth-generation American born in Newark, New Jersey April 17, 1757, Johnson was commissioned surgeon of the North Battalion, Second Regiment of the Essex County Militia. Like Stephen Jarvis and many of their peers, Uzal Johnson's loyalties oscillated back and forth until he finally sided with the King.

According to the adjutant General of New Jersey who wrote about Johnson in 1887:

> [W]hen the colonies declared themselves independent, [Johnson] retained his allegiance to the British Crown, and soon after is found in commission as surgeon of the Fifth Battalion of New Jersey Volunteers [Loyalists], afterward transferred to the First Battalion. He went with the New Jersey contingent to South Carolina, and was of great service to the wounded at King's Mountain. He lived in Newark after the war, and died there May 22nd, 1827.[77]

While Johnson's story and diaries are not as vibrant as Jarvis's, he was an eyewitness to British joy in victory, sorrow in defeat, and the fury of the southern partisans.

August 19, 1780:

> Still at Winn's. An express arrived from Camden with the agreeable news of Lord Cornwallis attacking and totally defeating Gen. Gates on the morning of the 16th. Twelve hundred were killed and wounded left in the field. One thousand taken prisoners, eight brass field pieces, being all they had in the field, were taken several stand of colors, all the ammunition wagons, a hundred and fifty wagons of baggage, provisions and stores of different kinds. Gen. De Kalb is among the killed. Among the wounded and prisoners are Gen. Rutherford and Gen. Gregory. All of this with the trifling loss on our side of not more than ten officers killed and wounded, and not more than two hundred and fifty non-commissioned Officers and Privates.
>
> After this, we received orders to pursue Gen. Sumter, he being the only remains of what the rebels can call a corps in these parts at present. At six in the evening, we ordered our wagons forward that we might pursue Sumter with vigour. At seven we got in motion, that very moment, an express arrived from Col. Innes informing us that he had been attacked that morning by a body of rebels at Musgroves Mill, Enoree River, that himself and Major Fraser of his corps were wounded . . .

He must immediately have assistance as many of the militia had left him. This to our great mortification altered the course of our march, and at eleven at night we got in motion. Marched all night . . . A.W. Smith was executed (at Winn's, Saturday the 19th Inst.) for joining the Rebels after he had taken protection and embodied himself with our militia.[78]

Johnson's account of his time on King's Mountain is brief, but he gives us two important windows, one is the actions of fellow Yankee loyalist Andre DePeyster, and the other the bravery of his comrades as they were executed in the aftermath of King's Mountain, recording for posterity, that "they died like Romans."

October 7, 1780:

They advanced up the hill rapidly. As soon as they got to the brow of the hill, the American Volunteers charged them with success and drove them down the hill, but were not able to pursue, our number being too small. We then retreated in order to gain the height and prevent their getting possession of it . . . (after multiple charges and counters, Col. Ferguson) then rushed in amongst the rebels with about half a dozen men. He was soon shot from his horse.

Capt. DePeyster then gave the word to form and charge. The cry throughout the militia line was, "we are out of Ammunition," this being our unhappy condition . . . it was thought most expedient to send out a flag to save a few brave men that had survived the heat of action. The engagement lasted an hour and five minutes . . .

Ten o'clock in the [following] morning, their guard paraded and formed a circle. Capt. DePeyster and the rest of us Officers were ordered within the ring. They then proceeded to trying the [Loyalists] for treason. Thirty of them were condemned and bound under the gallows. We were spectators of this disagreeable day's work. At Seven o'clock in the evening they began to execute them . . . They died like Romans, saying they died for their king and their laws. [79]

Bobby Gilmer Moss, the preeminent modern historian of the battle of King's Mountain, preserved, edited and reproduced Uzal Johnson's diary for posterity, as well as other noteworthy individual histories. Moss offers a "fact is stranger than fiction" episode, noting that Capt. DePeyster was "the Son of a French Huguenot, born into a wealthy New York Family. Fought in Siege of Charlestown, Musgrove's Mills, and King's Mountain where his life was saved by a doubloon in his waist coat which stopped a rifle ball."[80]

COMMANDER AS CORRESPONDENT:
Cornwallis at Guilford

After the defeat at Cowpens, Cornwallis moved quickly to attempt to reverse his fortunes. He chased General Greene 900 miles in an epic pursuit known as the "the race to the Dan (river)." On March 15, 1781 the armies clashed at Guilford Court House in modern day Greensboro, North Carolina. Almost 150 years later, legislation creating the Guilford Courthouse National Military Park was enacted in 1917 making it the first battlefield of the American Revolution preserved by the Federal Government. There was a time, as we shall see, when Southern battlefields were appreciated, but first there was a battle to be won![81]

Charles Ross wrote this of Gen. Cornwallis's experience at Guilford:

This battle, however glorious to the British Arms, was productive of little real advantage, as Lord Cornwallis anticipated . . . The severe loss he had sustained and the want of provisions, arising partly from the disaffection of the country, rendered it impossible for Lord Cornwallis to follow up the blow by pursuing General Greene . . . Nor did his troubles end there for he was followed by General Greene, whose forces effectually prevented supplies being drawn from the open country.[82]

Cornwallis to Lord Germain
Camp, Mar. 17, 1781

... I hoped in my way to be able to destroy or drive out of South Carolina the corps of the enemy commanded by General Morgan ... and I like wise hoped by rapid marches to get between General Greene and Virginia and by that means force him to fight without receiving any reinforcement from that province or, failing of that, to oblige him to quit North Carolina with precipitation and thereby encourage our friends to make good on their promises of a general rising to assist me in re-establishing His Majesty's Government.

The unfortunate affair of the 17th of January was very unexpected and severe blow, for besides reputation, our loss did not fall short of 600 men. However, being thoroughly sensible that defensive measures would be certain ruin to the affairs of Britain in the southern colonies ...

I proceeded by easy marches to Hillsborough, where I erected the King's Standard and invited by proclamation all loyal subjects to repair to it and to stand forth and take an active part in assisting me restore order and constitutional government ... Unluckily, a detachment of rebel light troops had crossed the same day and by accident fell in with about 200 of our friends under Col. Pyle on their way to Hillsborough, who mistaking the rebels for Lt Colonel Tarleton's corps, allowed themselves to be surrounded, and a number of them were most inhumanly butchered, when begging for quarter, without making the least resistance ...

I was determined to fight the rebel army if it approached me, being convinced that it would be impossible to succeed in that great object of our arduous campaign, the calling forth of numerous loyalists of North Carolina, whilst a doubt remained on their minds of the superiority of our arms.[83]

Cornwallis to Lord Rawdon
Camp, Mar 17, 1781

General Greene having been very considerably reinforced ... advanced with an army of about 5,000 or 6,000 men and four

6-pounders to this place. I attacked him on the 15th, and after a very sharp action routed his army and took his cannon. The great fatigue of troops, the number of wounded, and the want of provision, prevented our pursuing the enemy. . . .[84]

Cornwallis to Major General Phillips
Camp, April 10, 1781

I have had a most difficult and dangerous campaign, and was obliged to fight a battle 200 miles from any communication, against an enemy seven times my number. The fate of it was long and doubtful. We had not a regiment or corps that did not at some time give way; it ended however happily, in our completely routing the enemy and taking their cannon. The idea of our friends rising in any number and to any purpose totally failed, as I expected, and here I am getting rid of my wounded and re-fitting my troops at Wilmington, NC . . . Now my dear friend, what is our plan? Without one we cannot succeed, and I assure you that I am quite tired of marching about the country in quest of adventures.

If we mean offensive war in America, we must abandon New York, and bring our whole force into Virginia; we then have a stake to fight for, and a successful battle may give us America. If our plan is defensive, mixed with desultory expeditions, let us quit the Carolinas (which cannot be held defensively while Virginia can be so easily armed against us) and stick to our salt pork at New York, sending now and then a detachment to steal tobacco.

If no reinforcement comes, and that I am obliged to march with my present force to the upper frontiers of South Carolina, my situation will be truly distressing. [Note: if he goes South, trouble. If he leaves and goes North, more trouble] If I was to embark from Hence, the loss of the upper posts in South Carolina would be inevitable. . . . "[85]

Cornwallis to Clinton,
Wilmington, 10 April, 1781

I have, however, the satisfaction of informing you that our military operations were uniformly successful and the victory at Guildford (sic), altho' one of the bloodiest of this war, was very complete. . . . General Greene retreated the night of the action . . . leaving us . . . all the cannon he had in the field. The fatigue of the troops (British) and the great number of wounded put it out of my power to pursue . . . I therefore issued (a) proclamation (to join the crown) . . . Many of the inhabitants rode into camp, shook me by the hand, said they were glad to see us and to hear that we had beat Greene, and then rode home again, for I could not get 100 men in all the . . . country to stay with us even as militia. [Note: Even though Cornwallis "won," no one on the ground perceived it as a victory, not him, not the locals. The tide had turned.]

I cannot help expressing my wishes that Chesapeake may become the seat of war, even (if necessary) at the expense of abandoning New York. Until Virginia is subdued, our hold on the Carolinas must be difficult if not precarious. The rivers of Virginia are advantageous to an invading army, but North Carolina is of all the provinces in America the most difficult to attack (unless material assistance could be got from the inhabitants, the contrary of which I have sufficiently experienced) on account of its great extent, the numberless rivers and creeks, and the total want of interior navigation."[86]

After his "victory" at Guilford Courthouse, Cornwallis begins pushing Clinton hard to reorient the campaign Northwards. Cornwallis has realized that he does not have the men, the momentum or the popular support. He begins decrying the conditions of the Carolinas and in the following pages he reveals his fear of being just one battle away from a psychological defeat that would yield strategic calamity. Suddenly, the odds of this small army of red coats subduing one hundred thousand square miles of swarming forests, mountains, and swamps seemed impossibly grim.

Cornwallis to Lord Germain
Wilmington, 18 April, 1781

I think it incumbent upon me to be explicit to your Lordship, as His Majesty's Minister, on one or two capital points:

The Principle reasons for undertaking the winter's campaign were the difficulty of a defensive war in South Carolina and the hopes that our friends in North Carolina, who are said to be very numerous, would make good their promises of assembling and taking an active part with us in endeavoring to reestablish His Majesty's Government. Our experience has shown that their numbers are not so great as had been represented [by former governors & war hawks] and that their friendship was only passive, for we have received little assistance from them since our arrival in the province, and although I gave the strongest and most public assurances that after refitting and depositing our sick and wounded I should return to the Upper Country, not above two hundred have been prevailed upon to follow us, either as provincials or militia.

This being the case, the immense extent of this country, cut with numberless rivers and creeks, and the total want of internal navigation (maps/roads), which renders it impossible for our army to remain long in the heart of the country, will make it very difficult to reduce this province to obedience by a direct attack upon it.

If therefore it should appear to be in the interest of Great Britain to maintain what she already possesses and to push the war to the Southern Provinces, I take the liberty of giving it as my opinion that a serious attempt upon Virginia would be the most solid plan, because successful operations might not only be attended with important consequences there but would tend to the security of South Carolina and ultimately the submission of North Carolina.[87]

Cornwallis to Lord Germain
Wilmington, 23 April, 1781

Yesterday, I received an express by small vessel . . . brought me the disagreeable accounts that the upper posts of South Carolina were in the most imminent danger from an alarming spirit of revolt among many of the people . . .

I apprehend a possibility of the utmost hazard to this little corps, without the chance of a benefit, in the attempt, for *if we are so unlucky as to suffer a severe blow in South Carolina, the spirit of revolt in that province would become very general and the numerous rebels in this province be encouraged to be more than ever active and violent...*This might enable General Greene to hem me in among the great rivers and by cutting off our subsistence render our arms useless. And to remain here for transports to carry us off would be a work of time, and would lose our cavalry, and be otherwise ruinous and disgraceful to Britain as most events could be.

I have therefore under so many embarrassing circumstances—resolved to take advantage of General Greene's having left the back part of Virginia open and march immediately into that province . . . my force being very insufficient for offensive operations in this province [NC], may be employed usefully in Virginia . . . [88]

Cornwallis to Sir Henry Clinton
Wilmington, April 23, 1781

My present undertaking sits heavy on my mind. I have experienced the dangers and distresses of marching some hundreds of miles in a country chiefly hostile, without one active or useful friend, without intelligence, and without communication with any part of the country. The situation in which I leave South Carolina adds much to my anxiety . . . [89]

Cornwallis to Sir Henry Clinton
Wilmington, April 24, 1781

"I have reflected very seriously on the subject of my attempt to
march into Virginia . . . "

[Note: Cornwallis was so fearful of the Southern backcountry that he warned
Clinton to only reinforce by sea, because the backcountry will swallow the
British army.]

  . . . there is no other method [than by sea] of conveying his
majesty's troops to South Carolina without exposing them to the
most evident danger of being lost.[90]

Cornwallis to General Phillips
Wilmington, 24 April, 1781

My situation here is very distressing. My expresses to Lord
Rawdon (subordinate commander) . . . have all failed. Mountaineers and militia have poured into the back part of that province and I much fear that Lord Rawdon's posts will be so distant
from each other and his troops so scattered as to put him to the
greatest danger of being beaten in detail, and that the worst of
consequences may happen to most of the troops out of Charlestown . . . I cannot get time enough to relieve Lord Rawdon, and
should he have fallen, my army would be exposed to the utmost
danger from the great rivers I should have to pass, the exhausted
state of the country, the numerous militia, the almost universal
spirit of revolt in South Carolina and the strength of Greene's
Army, whose continentals alone are at least as numerous as I am
. . . I shall therefore immediately march up the country . . . I shall
march to the lowest ford on the Roanoke (Virginia).[91]

Cornwallis here summed up his situation: General Greene was far
from defeated, while Cornwallis's army was exhausted and the terrain
had conspired against him.

Cornwallis to Lord Rawdon
Petersburgh, May 20, 1781

As to the extensive frontier which we have hitherto endeavoured
to occupy, I am not certain whether we had not better relinquish
it . . . The perpetual instances of the weakness and treachery of
our friends in South Carolina, and the impossibility of getting
any military assistance from them, makes possession of any part
of the country of very little use . . . [92]

Cornwallis then bemoans the *"the most horrid accounts of the cru-*
elty of the enemy, and the numberless murders committed by them.
If it should be in your power, I should hope you would endeavour to
put a stop to them, by retaliation, or such means as may appear most
efficacious."[93]

In discussing the pending collapse of two forts in the Carolinas,
Cornwallis confesses:

Cornwallis to Sir Henry Clinton
Petersburgh, VA, May 20, 1781

. . . if however General Greene should persevere in carrying on
offensive operations against it, we must I think abandon (forts at)
Camden, and probably Ninety-Six, and limit our defence . . . this
will only be giving up two bad posts, which it is difficult to supply
with provisions, and quitting that part if the country which *for*
some months past we have not possessed.[94]

Cornwallis to Sir Henry Clinton
James River VA, May 28, 1781

. . . I have too often observed that when a storm threatens, our
friends disappear . . . I shall take the liberty of repeating, that if
offensive war is intended, Virginia appears to me the only province in which it can be carried on, and in which there is a stake.
But to reduce the province and keep possession of the country,

a considerable army would be necessary, for with a small force the business would probably terminate unfavourably, though the beginning might be successful.

By my letter of the 20th, your Excellency will observe that instead of thinking it possible to do anything in North Carolina, I am of the opinion *that it is doubtful whether we can keep the posts in the back parts of South Carolina*; and I believe that I have stated in former letters the infinite difficulty of protecting a frontier of 300 miles against a persevering enemy, in a country where we have no water communication, and where only few of the inhabitants are active or useful friends.[95]

Back in Britain, the Secretary of State, Lord Germain also noticed the tenacity of the Southern soldiers. His observations that Southern rebels were "more" spirited and skillful than the resistance in "any other part of the country," were drawn from his own correspondence with Gen. Cornwallis, as well as letters with Clinton. Both of which were reprinted in *The London Gazette.*

Lord Germain to Cornwallis
England, June 4, 1781

The rapidity of your movement thro a country so thinly inhabited and so little cultivated is justly a matter of astonishment to all Europe as well as the rebels in America, and although they appear to make every possible exertion to oppose your progress and *conduct their enterprises in Carolina with more spirit and skill than they have shown in any other part of the country,* His majesty has such confidence in your lordships military talents . . . [96]

Cornwallis to Sir Henry Clinton
Cobham, VA, July 8, 1781

I must again take the liberty of calling your Excellency's serious attention to the question of the utility of a defensive post in this country which cannot have the smallest influence in the war in the Carolinas, and which only gives us some acres of an unhealthy swamp and is forever liable to become prey to a foreign enemy with a temporary superiority at sea.[97]

Cornwallis to Lord Rawdon
Portsmouth, VA, July 23, 1781

I have not the time to explain to you my situation. Suffice it to say that the C [Sir Henry Clinton] is determined to throw all blame on me, and to disapprove of all I have done, and that nothing but the consciousness that my going home in apparent disgust, would essentially hurt our affairs in this country could possibly induce me to remain.[98]

The Clinton v. Cornwallis Blame Game was shaping up, as this previous example is not something you write when victory is assured.

CLINTON v. CORNWALLIS:
"Who Lost the War?"

The Clinton v. Cornwallis controversy, or the war of the pamphlets (or letters) as it came to be known, is one of the great forgotten dramas of the Revolutionary War. The back and forth correspondence between these two men who grew to hate each other as they sacrificed so much of their lives to crush the rebellion is well preserved. Their letters compose a narrative of increasing desperation as a battered Cornwallis allowed himself to be cornered in Yorktown. As summer turns to the fall of 1781, and the requests for support became more urgent, Clinton gave Cornwallis lip service, but the support never arrived.

Even as Cornwallis' tone became a shriek, Clinton's naval captains dallied. General Washington, and his French allies saw the opportunity, and staged a number of deceptions in order to fix Clinton's forces and attention in the North. Washington then snuck his forces out of New York for a quick attack on Cornwallis in Virginia. These gambles, perhaps the biggest of the war, all play out in the pages of Clinton's and Cornwallis's letters. But despite the credit that Washington, Rochambeau, Lafayette and the French fleet deserve, the fact remains: Cornwallis would never have fled to the Carolinas to suckle with his back to the water in Virginia if he had had not been so badly mauled for the past year.

The South set the conditions for a rebel victory and it would unfold with a tick-tock Hollywood would be hard pressed to replicate. Reinforcements were promised. They didn't come. The noose tightened. Reinforcements were promised again, and again they failed to arrive.

Ultimately, Clinton and his armada departed New York on the very day that Cornwallis was surrendering in Virginia!

In 1888, *The New York Times* published a book review on the two-volume collection of letters on the Clinton-Cornwallis Controversy. "*The Campaign in Virginia, 1781: An Exact Reprint of Six Rare Pamphlets On the Clinton-Cornwallis Controversy, With Very Numerous Unpublished Manuscript Notes By Sir Henry Clinton, and the Omitted and Hitherto Unpublished Portions of the Letters in Their Appendixes and from the Original Manuscripts,*" was edited by Benjamin Franklin Stevens and originally published in London in 1887.[99]

In the 2,000 word book review for America's "paper of record" there is scant mention of the actual battles of the Southern campaign, despite those episodes defining the military character and reputation of both Clinton and Cornwallis. The review focuses exclusively on Yorktown and the personal bickering of the two generals, leaving an uninformed reader unaware that King's Mountain, Cowpens, or Guilford Courthouse had in fact ever happened, despite their importance to the big picture.[100]

This is not the first time these battles will be overlooked by Northerners, nor will it be the last, but it is instructive that twenty years after the culmination of the Civil War, *The New York Times* chose to distill the nine years that followed from the first shots at Concord to the evacuation of the British as a single episode at Yorktown. Many more liberal historians will make the same choice, which we will explore later.

By now, I hope to have firmly established the facts of the ground truth. The political drama that will ensue for decades after the end of the war very much revolves around whose fault the loss of America truly was. The correspondence of Clinton and Cornwallis, in the final months before Yorktown is an interesting chess game of pre-staging blame for something that is starting to feel more and more inevitable. Whoever you chose to blame, what is beyond doubt, is that the conditions had been set in the South.

Cornwallis's chronicler and editor of his personal papers, *Correspondence of Charles, First Marquis Cornwallis*, Charles Ross, notes in 1859:

Lord Cornwallis arrived at New York November 19, 1781 and a controversy immediately arose between him and Sir Henry Clinton. Three questions came under discussion: 1st: the policy of the march into Virginia; 2nd: Whether Sir Henry had not ordered Lord Cornwallis to fortify some post on the Chesapeake, leaving him little or no discretion except as to the selection of the place; 3rd : Whether the promises of relief held out [by Clinton] justified Lord Cornwallis in standing a siege . . . [101]

With reference to the relief at Yorktown, there can be no doubt that Sir Henry fully intended to perform what he had promised, and to whom the blame of the delay should be attributed, it is not easy to say. On the 25th of September Lord Cornwallis was assured that the fleet would sail on the 5th of October, or possibly a day or two later . . . but the fleet did not in fact quit New York till the 19th, [the very day of capitulation], nor arrive off the mouth of Chesapeake until the 24th.[102]

The surrender of Cornwallis practically put an end to the war: for though both parties continued in arms for nearly a year and a half longer, no serious encounter took place between them. Indeed, after the resignation of Lord North, March 20, 1782, the speedy termination of hostilities was considered so certain, that a special kind of armistice took place . . . [103]

Congress (by letter dated July 30, from General Washington) ordered Lord Cornwallis to return to America according to his parole. Such a proceeding was too unjustifiable to be persevered in, and the demand was not enforced. The negotiations, however, dragged on in the most unsatisfactory manner to the end of the year, and probably were only brought to a close by the signing of preliminaries of Peace January 20, 1783, when all prisoners were released on both sides . . . Whether the Americans were actuated by petty spite, or a desire to revenge themselves upon the most active general who had been opposed to them, or whether they were swayed by some unknown political reasons, it is of course impossible to say.[104]

Having established the consequences of defeat, notice the tones of the letters and the imbedded recriminations as the date ticked closer to that fateful October day of surrender at Yorktown.

Cornwallis to Lord Clinton
Virginia, June 30, 1781

It is natural for every officer to turn his thoughts particularly to the part of the war in which he has been most employed and as the security at least of South Carolina if not the reduction of North Carolina, seemed to be generally expected from me, both in this country and in England, I thought myself called upon, after the experiment I had made failed, to point out the only mode in my opinion effecting it and to declare that until Virginia was to a degree subjected, we could not reduce North Carolina, or have any certain hold of back country of South Carolina . . . *I will not say much in praise of the militia of the Southern colonies but the list of British Officers and Soldiers killed and wounded by them since last June proves but too fatally, that they are not wholly contemptible . . . "*[105]

Clinton to Lord Germain
New York, July 18, 1781

I can say little to your lordship's sanguine hopes of a speedy reduction of the Southern provinces than to lament that the state of the war there does not altogether promise so flattering an event. Many untoward incidents, of which your lordship was not appraised, have thrown us too far back to be able to recover very soon what we have lately lost there; for if, (as I have often before suggested) the good will of the inhabitants is absolutely requisite to retain a country after we have conquered it, I fear it will be some time before we can recover the confidence of those in Carolina as their past sufferings will make them cautious . . .

I shall therefore most cordially join with your lordship in condemning bad policy of taking possession of places at one time and abandoning them at another, and in the opinion that the war should be conducted, upon permanent and settled plan of conquest, by securing and preserving what has been recovered. But if these maxims have on any occasion been deviated from in the past progress of the war, *I must in justice to myself declare that it has never been warranted by my orders* . . .

And if Lord Cornwallis made a desultory move into North Carolina, and without a force sufficient to protect, or provisions to support them, invited by proclamation the loyalists to join him, and afterwards found it necessary to quit friendly districts of that province before he could have time to give them a fair trial; *I am persuaded your Lordship will acknowledge he did not act under my instructions,* nor were his lordships retreat to Wilmington [Note: Aftermath of Guilford Courthouse], and subsequent move from thence to Virginia in consequence of my orders. For as I for saw the unhappy consequences of them I should surely have endeavoured to have stopt[sic] him . . . *Victory cannot be effected unless there should be an addition to this army.*[106]

Cornwallis to Clinton,
Camp at Virginia, July 24, 1781

I find from your Excellency's letter . . . that neither my march from Cross Creek to Wilmington (NC) or from thence to Petersburg (VA) meet with your approbation. The move was absolutely necessary, such was the situation and distress of the troops; and so great the sufferings of the sick and wounded, that I had no option left.

. . . I knew the whole country East of Santee and Peedee (rivers) would be in arms against us. I therefore did not think I could, with thirteen hundred infantry and two hundred cavalry, undertake such a march . . . without exposing the corps under my command to the utmost hazard of disgrace and ruin.[107]

Now, farther up the chain, Clinton was sensing a loss and was recriminating it back to his higher headquarters . . . "If only we had more troops."

Lord Clinton to Lord Germain
New York, July 25, 1781

Many of the losses we sustained in Carolina may be imputed in part to the lateness of its (troop convoy's) arrival . . . had the Reinforcements sailed as early as was promised, and the three battalions not been detained . . . I should have by this time have made such movements as would have obliged the enemy to be apprehensive . . . instead of meditating the attacks which they now threaten . . . [108]

Lord Clinton to Lord Germain
New York, August 9, 1781

With respect to Lord Cornwallis' having done as much in North Carolina as could have been effected with his force. But I have to lament the causes (King's Mountain, Cowpens, Guilford) which reduced it so low in number (troops) . . . after it became obvious that he was unable to establish himself there, and support and arm loyalists, which were his object[ives].[109]

Then, seven days before surrender at Yorktown . . .

Lord Germain to Lord Clinton,
England, 12 October 1781

. . . unless one of these [Clinton's plans] happens to convince the people of this country that We have friends in America, I cannot answer for the turn things may take here . . . [110]

After the Surrender, Cornwallis was quick out of the gate with the letter of October 20, foisting blame for the loss of the Americas upon Clinton. Clinton didn't fully realize the damage until he returned home to England, when he quickly penned his rebuttal, *Narrative of Lieutenant General Sir Henry Clinton, K.B. Relative to His Conduct During Part of His Command of the King's Troops in North America,*

Particularly That Which Respects the Unfortunate Issue of the Campaign of 1781, in 1783.

In the first ten pages, Clinton blamed Cornwallis (shouldn't have gone to Virginia), Germain (didn't send reinforcements) and Cowpens (Jan. 17). The supreme commander of North America complained about not being understood so he offered a fifty-page apologia with sixty-five pages of appended letters. The opening page and subsequent salvos are offered below:

> Being conscious that during my command in North America, my whole conduct was actuated by the most ardent zeal for the King's service, and the interests of the public, *I was exceedingly mortified, when I returned to England, after a service of seven years in that country, to find that erroneous opinions had gone forth respecting it;* and that many persons had in consequence, admitted impressions to my prejudice. Anxious, therefore to explain what had been misinterpreted or misrepresented, (as indeed might well be expected, from the publication of Lord. C.'s letter of the 20th of October, without being accompanied by my answer to it) . . . *none of the misfortunes of the very unfortunate campaign of 1781 can, with the smallest degree of justice, be imputed to me.*[111]

Clinton went on to single out Cowpens in a footnoted letter:

> I am exceedingly concerned, my Lord, at the very unfortunate affair of the 17th of January [Cowpens]. I confess I dread the consequences.[112]
>
> If, therefore, Lord Cornwallis's letter of the 20th of October, giving an account of the unfortunate conclusion of the campaign, by surrender of Yorktown could ever have been understood to imply the posts were not his Lordship's own choice . . . or that I had ever received information that the ground at either was unfavorable- till the day before he had offered to capitulate, or that I had ever given him any assurances of the exertions of the navy . . . I am persuaded it will appear that those implications are not founded on any orders I gave his Lordship, and cannot be supported by any part of our correspondence . . . [113]

Upon the whole, I am persuaded, that had I been left to my own plans, and a proper confidence had been earlier reposed in me, the campaign of 1781 would probably not have ended unfortunately . . .[114]

While Clinton's rebuttal would appear to be the final and definitive effort to besmirch Cornwallis and save himself, it is far from the last word. Officers up and down the chain began to weigh in. Clinton was again prompted to respond with another book, in response to Stedman, one of Cornwallis's defenders, some fifteen years later. Meanwhile, the most cavalier of Cornwallis's officers also proved himself to be the most disloyal.

"BLOODY" BANASTRE TARLETON AND HIS "UNFORTUNATE" DAY

BANASTRE TARLETON

One of few soldiers of the Revolutionary War to illicit active fan clubs 230 years later, and likenesses in 21st century films, is Banastre Tarleton. A fictionalized composite of Tarleton played opposite Mel Gibson in the 2001 film *The Patriot*.

A gambler, womanizer, and opportunist by all accounts, Tarleton came home from defeat at Yorktown and married the biggest stage actress of the day, Mary "Perdita" Robinson. Ironically, the butcher of "Buford's Slaughter" went on to flaunt his war wounds (missing fingers) and became the only solider of the British occupation to become a parliamentarian, post war.

When Cornwallis snubbed Tarleton by declining to give him a post in India, Tarleton turned on Cornwallis and joined the Clinton attack team. A close read of Tarleton's work shows subtle and blatant biases against Cornwallis, and in favor of Clinton in the coloring of actions as "judicious and necessary." As an Iraq war veteran, I am reminded of apologists for Paul Bremer and his short-sighted decision-making in 2003/4 Iraq that vexed that country, perhaps permanently. For example, the only defenders of Bremer's decision to demobilize the Iraqi army, are the former U.S. officials who did it.[115]

Tarleton's account, *A History of the Campaigns of 1780 and 1781 in the Southern Provinces of North America*, is instructive precisely because he was so controversial, and he knew it. Remember, like me, Tarleton isn't merely telling a story; he was a making a case that he knew would be challenged. Every chapter is followed by the original letters that appeared in that era's *London Gazette*. For example, Chapter One contains thirty-five pages of narrative of the beginning of the Southern Campaign up through the Surrender of Charleston, the defeat of Buford, and the articles of capitulation the colonists were required to abide by. All of that is supported by fifty-two pages of reprinted letters, many of which had appeared previously in *The London Gazette*, giving broad strokes, and also minute detail such as the names of individual soldiers killed and wounded. Chapter Two has thirty-three pages of narrative and thirty-eight pages of supporting letters, etc.

Despite Tarleton's strong desire to whitewash his career, his *History of the Campaigns of 1780 and 1781* is full of great, eyewitness detail, particularly of the events which have come into question over time, from his role in Buford's Slaughter, to his failure to support Ferguson at King's Mountain, leading to Ferguson's demise, to his subsequent drubbing at the hands of Daniel Morgan at Cowpens. Tarleton has a story to tell that, despite being told in the third person, is essential to fully comprehending the ground truth of the Revolutionary War.

Lt Col. Tarleton on Buford's Slaughter

At 2 o'clock in the morning, the British troops being tolerably refreshed continued their pursuit . . . they learned that the Continentals were retreating above 20 miles in their front towards the Catawba settlement to meet their reinforcement. At this period Tarleton might have contented himself with following them at his leisure to the boundary line of South Carolina, and from thence have returned upon his footsteps to join the main army satisfied with pursuing the troops of Congress out of the province; but animated by the alacrity which he discovered both in the officers and men, to undergo all hardships, he put his detachment in motion after adopting a stratagem to delay the march of the enemy: Captain Kinlock, of the Legion, was employed to carry a summons to the American commander, which by magnifying the number of the British, might intimidate him into submission, or at least delay him whilst he deliberated on an answer.

Col. Buford, after detaining the flag for some time without halting his march returned a defiance. By this time many of the British cavalry and mounted infantry were totally worn out, and dropped successively into the rear; the horses of the three pounder were likewise unable to proceed.

In this dilemma, Lt. Col. Tarleton found himself not far distant from the enemy, and, though not in a suitable condition for action, he determined as soon as possible to attack, there being no other ex-pedient to stop their progress and prevent they're being reinforced the next morning . . .

Col. Buford's force consisted of 380 Continental infantry of the Virginia line, a detachment of Washington's cavalry, and two 6-pounders. He chose his post in an open wood, to the right of the road; he formed his infantry in one line, with a small reserve; he placed his colors in the center; and he ordered his cannon, baggage, and wagons to continue their March.

Lt. Col. Tarleton made his arrangement for the attack with all possible expedition: He confided his right wing, which composed of 60 dragoons, and nearly as many mounted infantry, to Major Cochran desiring him to dismount, to gall the enemy's flank, before he moved against their front with his cavalry. Captains Corbet and Kinlock were directed, with the 17th dragoons and part of the legion, to charge the center of the Americans, whilst Lt. Col. Tar-leton, with 30 chosen horse and some infantry, assaulted the right flank and reserve: This particular situation the commanding officer selected for himself, that he might discover the effect of the other attacks. The dragoons, the mounted infantry, and three-pounder in the rear, as they could come up with their tired horses, were ordered to form something like a reserve, opposite to the enemy's center, upon a small eminence that commanded the road, which disposition afforded the British light troops an object to rally to, in case of a repulse, and made no inconsiderable impression on the minds of their opponents.

The disposition being completed without any fire from the enemy, though within 300 yards of their front, the cavalry advanced to the charge. On their arrival within 50 paces, the Continental infantry presented [aimed their rifles], when Tarleton was surprised to hear their officers command them to retain their fire till the British cavalry were nearer. This forbearance in not firing before the dragoons within 10 yards of the object of their attack, prevented their falling in to confusion on the charge and likewise deprived the Americans of the farther use of their ammunition.

Some officers, men, and horses, suffered by this fire; but [Buford's] *battalion was totally broken and slaughter was commenced* before Lt. Col. Tarleton could remount another horse, the one with which he led his dragoons being overturned by the volley. Thus in a few minutes ended an affair which might have had a very different termination.

The British troops had two officers killed, one wounded, three privates killed, 13 wounded; and 31 horses killed and wounded. The loss of officers and men was great on the part of the Americans, owing to the dragoons so effectually breaking the infantry, and to a *report amongst the cavalry, that they had lost their commanding officer [Tarleton], which stimulated the soldiers to a vindictive asperity not easily restrained.*

Upwards of 100 officers and men were killed on the spot.

Three colors, two six-pounders and above 200 prisoners, with a number of wagons containing: two Royals, quantities of new clothing, other military stores; in camp equipage, fell into the possession of the victors. The complete success of this attack, may, in great measure be ascribed the mistakes committed by the American commander.[116]

Lt. Col. Tarleton on Maj. Ferguson

The proclamation issued by the General [Clinton] produced great effect in South Carolina: In most of the districts adjoining to Charlestown, great numbers offered to stand forth in defense of the British government and many did voluntarily take up arms, and place themselves under the direction of Major Ferguson who was appointed to receive and command them. A general revolution of sentiment seemed to take place, and the cause of Great Britain appeared to triumph over that of the American Congress.[117]

Near the end of September, Major Ferguson had intelligence of Clarke's having joined Sumter, and that a swarm of backwoodsmen, by an unexpected and rapid approach to Gilbertown, now threatened his destruction.

[Ferguson] dispatched information to Earl Cornwallis of the superior numbers to which he was opposed, and directly commenced his march to the Catawba. Notwithstanding the prudent plan verging towards the Royal army, and advertising to the British general of his situation, *owing going to some communication, or the distance of his friends, a detachment did not March in time from Charlottetown to yield him assistance.*[118]

[Note: *Cornwallis tasked Tarleton, who claimed "sickness." Tarleton's inaction (later called "yellow" fever by his detractors) contributed to Ferguson's defeat, but he shifts the blame. Cornwallis disputes Tarleton, and in a letter to Bishop Lichtefield, from Calcutta in 1787, Cornwallis says, "Tarleton's is the most malicious and false attack; he knew and approved the reasons for several of the measures which he now blames. My not sending relief to Col. Ferguson, although he was positively ordered to retire, was entirely owning to Tarleton himself: he pleaded weakness from remains of a fever, and refused to make the attempt, although I used the most earnest entreaties."*] [119]

Major Ferguson heard of the enemy's approach at King's Mountain: He occupied the most favorable position he could find, and waited the attack.

The action commenced at 4 o'clock in the afternoon on the 7th of October, and was disputed with great bravery near an hour, when *the death of the gallant Ferguson threw his whole corps into total confusion.*

No effort was made after this event to resist the enemy's barbarity, or revenge the fall of their leader. By American accounts 150 officers and men of the provincials and loyal militia were killed, [many from NY, NJ, and CT] 150 were wounded and 800 were made prisoners.

The mountaineers, it is reported, used every insult and indignity, after the action, towards the dead body of Major Ferguson, and exercised horrid cruelties on the prisoners that fell into their possession . . .

On the 10th, [Tarleton] . . . received certain information of the melancholy fate of Major Ferguson . . . This mortifying intelligence was forwarded to Charlotte town, and the light troops crossed the river, to give protection to the fugitives and to attend the operations of the enemy.

The destruction of Ferguson and his corps marked the period and the extent of the first expedition into North Carolina. Added to the depression and fear it communicated to the loyalists up on the borders, and to the southward, the effect of such an important event was sensibly felt by Gen. Cornwallis at Charlotte town. The weakness of his army, the extent and poverty of North Carolina, the want of knowledge of his enemies designs, and the total ruin of his militia, presented a gloomy prospect at the commencement of the campaign.[120]

Alfred Chesney, South Carolina Loyalist and member of Maj. Ferguson's American Volunteers

Alexander Chesney is another example, of an American conflicted by competing calls for rebellion, or preservation of the status quo. Chesney's story is illustrative of the ping-ponging of loyalties, the power of coercion, and the long painful slog that was the revolution in the South. His experiences shed light on the common struggle for survival and twisted loyalties, and consequences. Alfred Jones edited an edition of Chesney's journal and provides the following insights:

> As a young man Chesney worked with Loyalist refugees, which landed him in prison and had consequences for his family's holdings which he was able to avert by switching sides. Now working for the patriots, he fought off Creek and Cherokee Indians from 1776 until 1779. Chesney switched sides again, when Charleston was captured for the Crown as General Clinton demanded loyalty, Chesney was happy to comply as this was true sentiment. A natural leader with some success at rallying others to the cause of King George, Chesney was appointed a Lieutenant of militia and ultimately came under the fold of Major Patrick Ferguson, a promising British officer who had come down from New York with the British invasion force and had taken part in the seizure of Charleston.
>
> Ferguson in turn had taken command of militia and loyalist volunteers and, as such Chesney, now a captain, was an officer under

Ferguson's command at the calamitous King's Mountain where he was wounded. After being captured in the route, Chesney managed to escape King's Mountain. Fleeing home, hiding in caves and woods, and hop-scotching the homes of different family members, Chesney rejoined the fight and soon found himself under the command of Col. Banastre Tarleton, to which he was a witness of the subsequent mauling of loyalists by General Morgan at the Battle of the Cowpens 17 January, 1781. After this second vanquishing he quit the fight, returning home to find his home looted. He retired to the security of the Charleston area, where he continued to play a part in the British war effort up until he fled to England on a 45-day voyage in 1782.[121]

Chesney mentions being present in a number of fights "the particulars of which, as well as numerous other skirmishes having escaped my memory, scarcely a day passed without some fighting." Shifting loyalty as well as the surging fortunes of the loyalists through the summer of 1780, impressed upon Chesney: " . . . At this period the North Carolina men joined us fast."[122]

Chesney's account of King's Mountain:

We marched to King's Mountain and there encamped with a view of approaching Lord Cornwallis' Army, and receiving support; by Col. Ferguson's orders I sent expresses to the Militia Officers to join us here; but we were attacked before any support arrived by 1500 picked men from Gilbert's-town under the command of Cols. Cleveland, Shelby, and Campbell, all of whom were armed with rifles, well mounted and of course could move with the utmost celerity; so rapid was their attack that I was in the act of dismounting to report that all was quiet and the pickets on the alert when we heard their firing about half a mile off; I immediately paraded the men and posted the officers, during this short interval I received a wound which however did not stop my doing duty; and on going towards my horse I found he been killed by the first discharge.

King's Mountain from its height would have enabled us to oppose a superior force with advantage, had it not been with wood which sheltered the Americans and enabled them to fight in the favorite manner; in fact after driving in our piquets they were able to advance in three divisions under separate leaders to the crest of the hill in perfect safety until they took post and opened an irregular but destructive fire from behind trees and other cover: Col. Cleveland's was first perceived and repulsed by a charge made by Col. Ferguson: Col. Shelby's next and met a similar fate being driven down the hill; last the detachment under Col. Campbell and by desire of Col. Ferguson I presented a new front which opposed it with success; by this time the Americans who had been repulsed had regained their former stations and sheltered.[123]

After escaping the carnage of King's Mountain, Chesney recounts:

The first night I slept in the woods. The next day I was supported by haws grapes as I could find them in the woods. The second or third day in pushing through the woods to get to a ford I heard a noise of some people (whom I knew to be Americans by white paper in their hats) on which I lay down and was so close to them that I could have touched one of their horses in passing; fortunately I was not observed, and soon after crossed the Creek after them. I then made for the Mountains in order to be guided by the Appalachian range and get over the rivers with greater facility.

After crossing Broad-river I met one [John] Heron who had been with me in King's Mountain and who had with some others taken flight early in the action, putting white papers in their hats, by which disgraceful stratagem they got through the American lines.

I passed a night at Heron's house and one before at another man's on whom I could depend, from both I took some provisions all the other nights I slept out; I do not remember the number exactly, must have been nearly a fortnight. I reached home on the 31st of October. I found the Americans had left me little. My wife had a son on the 20th whom I named William which was all the christening he had.

As I did not know where to find any British troops, I continued about home some time [November, 1780] and as the Americans were in possession of the country I was obliged to conceal myself in a cave dug in the branch of a creek under a hollow poplar with my cousins Hugh Cook and Charles Brandon in which we were forced for want of room to lie flat. Cooke's wife brought us food and news every night; I sometimes staid at my father-in- laws, until I heard that Col. Tarleton had defeated Sumter at Black-stocks fort.[124]

Lt. Col. Tarleton

Chesney joined Tarleton and we will resume his first person accounting shortly, once the battle is joined at Cowpens. For now, let us return to Banastre Tarleton's narrative, in which he would attempt to impugn Cornwallis for his handling of Ferguson at King's Mountain:

> *It was now evident beyond contradiction, that the British General had not adopted the most eligible plan for the invasion of North Carolina.* The route by Charlotte town, through the most hostile quarter of the province, on many accounts was not advisable.
>
> Its distance likewise from Ferguson allowed the enemy to direct their attention and force against that officer, which ultimately proved his destruction.[125]

Lt. Col. Tarleton on Cowpens

Earl Cornwallis employed various measures, in order to acquire daily intelligence of the enemy, and to obtain a competent knowledge of the nature of the country in his front. No expense was spared to learn the state of roads, the number of the mills, and the quantities of forage and provisions, between Broad river and the Catawba. This information was peculiarly necessary for a general who is about to invade a province not remarkable for its fertility and which has no navigable rivers to convey supplies to the interior parts of the country.[126]

The strength of the Royal army in South Carolina near the end of the year 1780, allowed Earl Cornwallis the experiment of an enterprise, which the loyalists and British troops in America, as well as the administration in England supposed he could with facility accomplish. The superiority of his force when compared with General Greene's, gave every reasonable assurance, that with proper care of the latter might be destroyed, or driven over the Roanoke ...

When it was imagined that the loyalists, who were computed to be the greater portion of the inhabitants, would make indefatigable exertions to render themselves independent of Congress. Such was the opinion of thousands when the King's troops prepared for this expedition: But their expectations were not verified, though the Continental Army was chased out of the province and the loyal subjects were invited to repair to the king standard in Hillsboro; it therefore becomes necessary to investigate whether the scheme itself was visionary, or the plan to complete it injudicious, or whether the force employed was inadequate to the purpose.

If Earl Cornwallis was not equally sanguine in his expectation of final conquest, it must however, be universally acknowledged, that the present was a favorable crisis for exertion. The strength of the king's troops and the weakness of the enemy strongly recommended his second invasion of North Carolina ...[127]

Operations of the Americans to the westward of Broad river laid immediate claim to the attention of the British. General Morgan, with the Continental light infantry, Col. Washington's cavalry, and large detachments of militia, were reported to be advancing to (fort) Ninety Six. Although the fortifications were in tolerable condition at that place, and sufficiently strong to resist an assault, yet the preservation of the country and its neighborhood was considered so great an object for the Garrison and the Loyalists of the district, that Earl Cornwallis dispatched an aid to camp on 11 January to order Lt. Col. Tarleton over Broad river with his corps of cavalry and infantry, of 550 men the first Battalion of the 71st [regiment] consisting of 200, and two three-pounders, to counteract the designs of General Morgan, by protecting the country and compelling him to repass Broad river.

Tarleton received a letter the next day from his Lordship communicating an earnest wish that the American commander, if within his reach, should be "pushed to the utmost."[128]

Chesney, the eyewitness at Cowpens:

I continued until Tarleton came into Ninety-Six district to go in quest of General Morgan [January, 1781] and sent to the garrison for guides acquainted with Morgan's situation which was then convenient to my house on Pacholet; I joined Col. Tarleton and marched to Fair-forest having failed to get intelligence of Morgan's situation he sent me out [January 16] to endeavour to do so and to make the mills grind for the Army . . .

I swam my horse over a private ford not likely to be guarded, leaving the man behind me to go on more quietly & reconnoiter the swamp. I found the fires burning but no one there, on which I rode to my father's who said Morgan was gone to the Old-fields [literally the "Cow pens"] about an hour before; my wife said the same and that they had used or destroyed my crop and took away almost every thing. I immediately returned to Col. Tarleton and found he had marched towards the old fields.[129]

I overtook them before 10 o'clock near the Cowpens on Thickety Creek where *we suffered a total defeat by some dreadful bad management.*

The Americans were posted behind a rivulet with Rifle-men as a front line and Cavalry in the rear so as to make a third line; Col. Tarleton charged at the head of his Regiment of Cavalry called the British Legion which was filled up from the prisoners taken at the battle of Camden; the Cavalry supported by a detachment of the 71st Regt. under Major McArthur broke the Riflemen without difficulty, but the prisoners on seeing their own Regiment opposed to them in the rear would not proceed against it and broke: the remainder charged but were repulsed this gave time to the front line to rally and form in the rear of their Cavalry which immediately charged and broke the 71st (then unsupported) making many prisoners: the rout was almost total.

I was with Tarleton in the charge who behaved bravely but imprudently the consequence was his force dispersed in all directions the guns and many prisoners fell into the hands of the Americans . . . *The Rebels increased much.*[130]

Lt. Col. Tarleton on his defeat at Cowpens

Tarleton was very careful in recounting his version of the battle of Cowpens. Pay special attention to the end, where he basically blames his men for his own failures:

Upon the advance of the 71st, all the infantry again moved on: the Continentals and back woodsmen gave ground, the British rushed forwards, an order was dispatched to cavalry charge.

An unexpected fire at this instant by the Americans who came about as they were retreating, stopped the British, and threw them into confusion. Exertions to make them advance were useless. The part of the Cavalry which had not been engaged fell likewise into disorder, and an unaccountable panic extended itself along the whole line.

The Americans, who before thought they had lost the action, taking advantage of the present situation, advanced upon the British troops and augmented their astonishment.

A general flight ensued.[131]

Tarleton sent directions to his cavalry to form about four hundred yards to the right of the enemy, in order to check them, whilst he endeavoured to rally the infantry to protect the guns.

The cavalry did not comply with his order and the effort to collect the infantry was ineffectual.

Neither promises nor threats could gain their attention, they surrendered or dispersed and abandoned the guns to the artillery men, who defended them for some time with exemplary resolution.

In this last stage of defeat Lt. Col. Tarleton made another struggle to bring his cavalry to the charge. The weight of such an attack might yet retrieve the day, the enemy being much broken [dispersed] by their own rapid advance, but all attempts to restore order, recollection or courage proved fruitless.

Above two hundred dragoons forsook their leader [Tarleton] and left the field of battle.

The number of killed and wounded in the action at the Cowpens, amounted to near three hundred on both sides, officers and men inclusive: this loss was almost equally shared, but the Americans took two pieces of cannon, the colors of the 7th Rgt., and near four hundred prisoners.[132]

After minimizing the effects of the battle, Tarleton dissects Cornwallis's choices systematically. He lays blame at his former boss's feet, even when the responsibility was Tarleton's own.

> It would be mortifying to describe the advantages that might have resulted from his lordship's [Cornwallis] arrival at the concerted point, or to expatiate upon the calamities which were produced by this event. If an army is acting where no cooperation can take place, it is necessary for the commander and chief to keep as near as possible to his detachments . . . [Note: Tarleton, who had a long record of headlong charges with no support, was blaming Cornwallis for not being closer.][133]
>
> Earl Cornwallis might have conceived, that, by attending to the country and by covering his light troops, he would in all probability have alternately brought Generals Morgan and Greene into his power by co-operative movements.
>
> He might also have concluded, that all his parties that were beaten in the country, if they had no corps to give them instant support or refuge, must be completely destroyed [Note: Again, blaming Cornwallis for Ferguson]. Many instances of this nature occurred during the war. The fall of Ferguson was a recent and melancholy example: that catastrophe put a period to the end of the first expedition into North Carolina, and the affair of the Cowpens overshadowed the commencement of the second.[134]
>
> The defeat of the British [me, Tarleton] must be ascribed to the bravery or good conduct of the Americans . . . or to some unforeseen event, which may throw terror into the most disciplined soldiers or counteract the best concerted designs . . . *when they experience an unexpected shock, confusion will ensue, and flight without immediate support must be the inevitable consequence.*[135]

With these words Tarleton actually summed up the Southern campaign after the grinding molestation of the British, and the shocks of King's Mountain and Cowpens . . . Cornwallis, and Tarleton decided to run, and die. Tarleton goes on to describe the rest of the campaign, including his actions at Yorktown, and all the things that Cornwallis might have done better. We shall close his narrative with the final analysis, after pages and pages degrading Cornwallis, he ultimately throws blame on the Navy for failing to reinforce.[136]

Lt. Col. Tarleton's Closing Shots

A retrospective view on British Operations plainly discovers that the march from Wilmington, NC to Petersburg, VA was formed and executed without the knowledge or consent of Sir Henry Clinton . . . [NOTE: Later in our discovery we will see that Roderick Mackenzie, another eyewitness, will claim Tarleton specifically asked to vacate the Carolinas in favor of Virginia.][137]

Tarleton goes on to list and detail six more of Cornwallis's failures, before closing with this:

Some instances of oversight may, therefore be attributed to his Lordship, which precipitated perhaps, the fate of his own army; but the genuine cause of the great national calamity which put a period to the Continental war must be principally ascribed to [the navy] . . . The Superiority at Sea [of the French Fleet] proved the strength of the enemies of Great Britain, deranged the plans of her generals disheartened the courage of her friends, and finally confirmed the independency of America.[138]

GLORY SEEKERS, FINGER POINTERS, AND THE CHORUS OF CRITICS

RODERICK MACKENZIE

"Death before dishonor" is more than a common military tattoo among soldiers and Marines. The phrase speaks to the importance of honor in a martial society, in the profession of arms. When that honor is impugned, it triggers instant response. In this case, the men that fought and bled beside Tarleton, felt that their honor was besmirched by their Commander's self-serving revisionism. The response was swift and forceful.

"Lieutenant Colonel Tarleton's *History of the Campaigns of 1780 and 1781, in the Southern Provinces of North America* . . . though elaborately worked up, abounds with misrepresentation and error;" begins Roderick Mackenzie's *Strictures on Lt Col. Tarleton's "History of the Campaigns of 1780 and 1781, in the Southern Provinces of North America."* The return salvo in the battle for post-war reputation continued:

> . . . it does injustice to a number of respectable officers, wantons in reflecting unmerited disgrace on an entire corps of the army, and is replete with palpable inconsistencies. When public opinion is thus misled by consummate artifice, it becomes necessary to detect the sophistry that produced the deception.[139]

Our author [Tarleton] insinuates that Earl Cornwallis might have foreseen and guarded against this misfortune [the fall of Ferguson]. The charge is more than disingenuous, and merits a pointed refutation ... [140]

Mackenzie blames Tarleton's failure at Cowpens for the defeat at Yorktown, and then goes on to specifically detail Tarleton's mistakes:

Of all men, Lieutenant Colonel Tarleton should be last to censure Earl Cornwallis for not destroying Morgan's force ... if the troops lost on that occasion [Cowpens] had escaped the misfortune which befell them [defeat under Tarleton's command], and had been combined with the British force at the battle of Guilford, the victory must have been much more decisive, and General Greene would probably have brought off as few of his army as his predecessor in command, General Gates, did at Camden.[141]

"I was [a member] of the detachment in question," Mackenzie emotionally tells us before enumerating Tarleton's blunders:[142]

The first error in judgment to be imputed to Lt. Col. Tarleton, on the morning of the17th of January, 1781, is not halting his troops before he engaged the enemy. Had he done so ...

The second error was the un-officer like impetuosity of directing the line to advance before it was properly formed and before the reserve had taken its ground ...

The third error in this ruinous business, was the omission of giving discretional powers to that judicious veteran McArthur, to advance with the reserve ...

His fourth error was ordering Captain Ogilvie, with a troop consisting of no more than forty men, to charge ...

The next (fifth) and most destructive ... was in not bringing up a column of cavalry and completing the rout that by his own acknowledgment had commenced through the whole American Infantry ...

After what has been said there may not, perhaps, be a better criterion to judge the conduct of those corps, upon whom Lieutenant Colonel Tarleton has stamped the charge of "Total misbehavior" ... [143]

Duly enraged, Mackenzie, then goes on to detail the seasoned nature of their combat experience, implying Tarleton had a top-notch unit, which he handled like an amateur, to deadly consequences. Mackenzie then changes tack and makes the case for Cornwallis's record as a combat leader, and in turn calls out Tarleton's record as over-hyped.

When Earl Cornwallis fought the memorable battle near Camden, his force, considerably under two thousand men, was opposed by upwards of six thousand. At Guilford, his lordship, with not one-third the number of his enemy, obtained a glorious victory over General Greene, the best commander of the American Service.

I venture to affirm, that the disparity of force at Cowpens was smaller than it had been in any engagement during the Southern campaigns, consequently, Lieutenant Colonel Tarleton had it in his power to engage with greater advantages than occurred either previous to his defeat or since.[144]

I leave to Lieutenant Colonel Tarleton all the satisfaction that he can enjoy, from reflecting that *he led a number of brave men to destruction, and then used every effort in his power to damn their fame with posterity.*[145]

Before the departure of Earl Cornwallis from Wilmington, it is well known that various opinions had been formed of the measures most proper to be adopted by the army; the opinion of many was in favor of the plan of following General Greene to South Carolina; the advice of others, which succeeded, was to march to Virginia; among the latter Lieutenant Colonel Tarleton does not wish to be classed.

The event of the march proving unfortunate, he either means to extricate himself from the blame of advising it, or cannot resist his usual practice of censure. General report, however, says he actually recommended the movement of the army, which took place, and expressed his disapprobation of a return to South Carolina by declaring that his lordship [Cornwallis] might as well order the throats of his horses to be cut, as adopt that measure.

Did he not say to an officer (Colonel John Hamilton) on the route to Virginia, at a time when circumstances appeared particularly favourable, *"That this march [to Yorktown] was a child of his own, and that he gloried in it?"*[146]

Mackenzie concludes that Tarleton is the first link:

Lieutenant Colonel Tarleton had hitherto acquired distinguished reputation, but he was greatly indebted for his military fame to good fortune and accident. In all his previous engagements he either had the advantage of surprising an incautious enemy—of attacking them when panic-struck after recent defeats—or of being opposed to undisciplined militia.

He had gathered no laurels by hard fighting against an equal force; his repulse on this occasion [Cowpens] did more essential injury to the British interest, than was compensated by all his victories. *Tarleton's defeat was the first link, in a grand chain of causes, which finally drew ruin, both in North and South Carolina, on the Royal interest.*[147]

GEORGE HANGER

Could such a bold fusillade on Tarleton's character go unanswered? Of course not. Just as Cornwallis had his camp followers, so too did Clinton and his accomplice, Tarleton. Into this corner stepped George Hanger, who identified himself to the world as "Major to the Cavalry of the British Legion, Commanded by Lieut. Col. Tarleton, and Captain in the Hessian Jaeger Corps."

Hanger's book was titled aptly enough *Address to the Army in Reply to 'Strictures' by Roderick Mackenzie on Tarleton's History of the Campaigns of 1780 and 1781.*

On page 122, Hanger responds directly to Mackenzie's implication:

. . . [quoting Mackenzie] essential injury to the British interest . . . "Out of the mouth of your own witness I will judge both you and him! This unhappy quotation contains the antidote to its own venom, and establishes the military fame which professes to depreciate. If you had consulted Lloyd instead of Ramsay [an American historian we will consider shortly], you would have learned that victory is the result of action. "No army conquers merely by resisting: you may repel an enemy; but victory is the result of action."

You having studied in a different school, may naturally condemn Tarleton for the enterprise and perseverance which enabled him to surprise his enemy; for the celerity of his marches, for his instant decision; for that quickness that rapidity of attack, which prevents an enemy from forming, and insures victory with inferior force . . . [148]

Bear in mind, from all these living witnesses to the calamity of the Southern campaign, no one is stepping forward and bellowing, "What about Boston? Or New York? How about Philadelphia? Or Quebec?" No, there is no question in anyone's mind where this war was lost. The only question is by whom, and at which precise battle in the South was it lost.

This is the focal point upon which this argument hinges and I will continue to hammer it home, until the space for any possible doubt is erased. The need to reemphasize this issue is the very fact that it will be so foreign to so many: the Left and modern academia have worked diligently to erase this chapter for reasons we will soon discuss, and instead of platitudes, I am seeking to arm you with unequivocal facts. This happened, and it matters.

Now, let's go back 230 years to the concluding defense of Mackenzie's attack on Tarleton, as Tarleton's deputy Major Hanger fires a closing volley:

Your favorite author (Ramsay) has harped very much on the defeats of Ferguson and Tarleton at King's Mountain and Cowpens; and attributes greatly the destruction of the British Interest in the Southern Parts of America, to these events. Although the actions of King's Mountain and Cowpens, were severely felt at that instant of time, they were only partial misfortunes. I will be so bold as to assert, that these misfortunes did not in any degree contribute to the loss of America, nor could such misfortunes have produced that calamity.

Our ruin was completed by permitting a superior French Fleet to ride triumphant on the American Seas in the Autumn of 1781. That, and that only, ruined our cause in America, and disgracefully put an end to the war—The nail was clinched![149]

CHARLES STEDMAN

Five years after Hanger, Charles Stedman stepped in, offering what will become a highly regarded history book in common circulation on both sides of the Atlantic. In fact it won't be until the 1950s that Stedman is identified as yet one more borrower from the credibility library of *The Annual Register*. But unlike other plagiarizers (an issue we shall revisit in detail later), Stedman was actually there, on the ground with Tarleton and Cornwallis. The facts that Stedman recounts are what they are at a time when, if anyone disagreed, there were cultural and literary, and even lethal, mechanisms by which the offender could be challenged. From physical duels, to dueling letters, articles, pamphlets and books, this was a time when all the participants on both sides of the Atlantic were paying attention to what was being said or written.

One observer at the time even noted that during the war, a duel was imminent: "Sir. H. Clinton was going on an expedition to try and relieve Lord Cornwallis, but they were so ill together, that Sir Henry had owned to Conway that he was determined to challenge (duel) Lord Cornwallis after the campaign."[150] Victors and vanquished were vigorously packaging their actions for posterity, yet none of these first person accounts challenges my narrative of Southern military significance. Let's take Charles Stedman, for example:

> . . . the unwelcome news arrived of the defeat of Maj. Ferguson; the fall of that officer; and the destruction, captivity or dispersion of his whole corps. The total loss of so considerable a detachment, for the operations of which so much was expected, put a stop for the present to the further progress of the commander in chief, and obliged him to fall back into South Carolina, for the protection of its western borders against the incursions of a horde of mountaineers, whose appearance was as unexpected as their success was fatal to the prosecution of the intended expedition.[151]
>
> Ferguson's vigilance nevertheless prevented a surprise. Whilst they were yet some distance he received intelligence of their approach, by means of his emissaries, and immediately began to retreat

towards the British army, sending forward messengers to acquaint Lord Cornwallis with his danger; but these unfortunately were intercepted. When the different divisions of mountaineers reached Gilbert-town which was nearly about the same time, they amounted to upwards of three thousand men. From these, fifteen hundred of the best were selected who, mounted on fleet horses, were sent in pursuit of Ferguson and overtook him at King's Mountain . . .

Already one hundred and fifty of Maj. Ferguson's corps were slain, and a greater number wounded, still however, the unconquerable spirit of that gallant officer refused to surrender: He persevered, and repulsed a succession of attacks from every quarter, until he received a mortal wound.

By the fall of Ferguson his men were undoubtedly disheartened . . . Much had been expected from the exertions of Maj. Ferguson in collecting a force upon the frontiers: and by his unfortunate fall, and the slaughter and captivity, or dispersion of his whole corps, the plan of the expedition into North Carolina was entirely deranged . . . [152]

The King's troops suffered much, encountering the greatest difficulties; the soldiers had no tents; it rained for several days without intermission; the roads were over their shoes with water and mud. At night when the army took up its ground, it encamped in the woods, in a most unhealthy climate, for many days without rum.

Sometimes the army had beef, and no bread; at other times bread and no beef. For five days it was supported upon Indian corn, which was collected as it stood in the field, five ears of which were the allowance for two soldiers for twenty-four hours. They were to cook it as they could, which was generally done by parching it before the fire.

In riding through the encampment of the militia, the author [Stedman] discovered them grating their corn, which was done by two men of a mess breaking up their tin canteens, and with a bayonet punching holes through the tin; this made a kind of rasp, on which they grated their corn: the idea was communicated to the adjutant-general, and it was afterwards adopted throughout the army. The water that the army drank was frequently as thick as puddle.

Few armies have ever encountered greater difficulties and hardships . . . Yet with all their resolution and patience they could not have proceeded but for the personal exertions of the militia. [Note: Eyewitness extolling the criticality of partisan support—so when that support is removed, the effect is deadly.][153]

In the meantime the mountaineers, contented with their success against Ferguson, had gone home and dispersed; but the northeast parts of the province were infested by the depredations of an enterprising partisan of the name *Marion*. This man, previous to the defeat of General Gates, had been active stirring up the inhabitants upon the Black River to revolt ...[154]

... *Sumter* again made his appearance in the northwest part of the province . . . he was indefatigable in stirring them up to take arms; and the reputation he had already acquired, with his particular talent for enterprise, in a short time procured him a number of followers . . . [155]

The loyalists assembled, and on the twenty-fifth of February (1781) were proceeding to Tarleton's encampment, inapprehensive of dangers, when they were met in a lane by Lee, with his legion. The loyalists, unfortunately mistaking the American cavalry for Tarleton's dragoons, allowed themselves to be surrounded before they discovered the error. When it at last became manifest, they called out for quarter; but no quarter was granted, and between two and three hundred of them were *inhumanely butchered, while in the act of begging for mercy.*

Humanity shudders at the recital of so foul a massacre. But cold and unfeeling policy avows it as the most effectual means of intimidating the friends of royal government. . . . If the loyalists were before cautious and slow, they now became timid to the excess, and *dreaded taking any active measure whatsoever on behalf of the king's government.*[156]

SIR HENRY CLINTON

The account of King's Mountain given in Stedman's *History*, harrowing as it is, will be challenged by none other than former Commander Henry Clinton, as if any more evidence was needed of the military and psychological value of that little battle in the overall war.

Clinton's second volume arrived fifteen years after Major Ferguson was slain alongside British hopes for a popular counter-uprising in support of the crown. Eleven years after the final evacuation of the colonies, Clinton was compelled to wade into the historical arena yet again. This time his work was titled, *Observations on Stedman's History of the American War,* and he went after Stedman, in some cases line by line:

> Sir. H. Clinton cannot help being of opinion, that the loss of Colonel Ferguson was owing, with great measure, to Lord Cornwallis' (decision) having detached Ferguson with a body of militia without any support of regular troops . . . [157]
>
> The Unfortunate affair of Cowpens . . . hearing his lordship (Cornwallis) had lost all of his light troops at Cowpens . . . [158]
>
> (On) Page 352, Vol ii. Mr. Stedman says, "three days after the action at Guilford Courthouse, Lord Cornwallis began to retire by easy days marches, towards Cross Creeks (Fayetteville)." Nobody can give Lord Cornwallis more credit for his zealous exertions at the battle of Guilford Courthouse, Sir H. Clinton (me); but alas! That victory had every consequence of defeat.[159]
>
> . . . it is very true, that his Lordship (Cornwallis) did offer to return to South Carolina. If his Lordship had never left it, His majesty (King George) might have remained Sovereign of that great Continent.[160]

British soldiers, from Private to General, who were there and who know, told us where they lost the war, and to whom. Did the political class share those opinions?

SHOTS HEARD 'ROUND THE COURT:
North, Pitt, Fox, and the King

Today, after a major defeat the headlines would be blistering: "KING GETS ROYALLY FLUSHED," "COLONIZE THIS!!!," or "AMERICA'S RESET." But that was not the case in the cold winter of 1781. The cover of *The London Gazette*, typically two columns of text without any of the exaggerated tabloid style one-liners we have come to expect, instead opened simply with the following dateline:

Westminster, November 27, 1781,
This day His Majesty came to the House of Peers, and being in his Royal Robes, seated on the Throne with the usual Solemnity, Sir Francis Molyneux, Gentleman Usher of the Black Rod, was sent with a message from His Majesty to the House of Commons, commanding their attendance in the House of Peers. The Commons being come hither accordingly, His Majesty was pleased to make the following Most Gracious Speech:

My Lords, and Gentlemen,
When I last met you in Parliament, I acquainted you with the arduous situation of public affairs at that time, and I represented to you the objects which I had in view and the resolution with which I was determined to persevere in the defense of my Dominions against the combined power of my enemies, until such a pacification could be made as might consist with the honor of my crown and the permanent interest and security of my people. The war is still unhappily

prolonged by the restless ambition which first excited our enemies to commence it, and which still continues to disappoint my earnest desire and diligent exertion to restore public tranquility . . .

In the course of this year, my assiduous endeavours to guard the extensive Dominions of my crown, have not been attended with success equal to the justice and uprightness of my views; and it is with great concern that I inform you, that the events of war have been very unfortunate to my arms in Virginia, having ended in the loss of my forces in that province . . .

The King's speech concluded and in the adjacent column, the long running drama of letters back and forth between the colonies and the Secretary of State, Lord Germain resumed. There was no color commentary. No contextualizing. Just the bare naked correspondences of commanders who were in the midst of getting their teeth kicked in at a place called Yorktown, or crushing insurgencies in the East Indies. There were notices of debts to be collected and goods for sale.

On the same page as one of Cornwallis's many colorful combat diaries, in an adjacent column, was a classified advertisement for sugar and ginger from Barbados, St. Kitts, Antigua, Nevis and Montserrat. *"Samples will be viewed in Wycherley's-yard, opposite Bear Quay, on Tuesday the 11th, Wednesday the 12th, and Thursday the 13th, of December, 1781."* After all the business of the empire was business.

The datelines of the letters varied with the travel times by sea. In the case of the loss of the colonies, the British press would report events almost backwards: Three weeks after the King's speech of acquiescence was printed, Cornwallis's famous letter of October 20th, indicting Clinton in his surrender at Yorktown, would grace the pages of *The London Gazette* on December 18.

Cornwallis's letter would ultimately run in newspapers up and down the American coast, and we know that King George read those papers too.[161] News of the defeat echoed and opposition members of parliament went to work, as their efforts to end the war were seemingly paying off. One can almost feel sorry for King George as his world turned upside down.

The subject of a modern book titled *Lord North: The Prime Minister who lost America*, Frederick North became a casualty of public opinion soured by the war: North was the first minister to be forced out by a no confidence vote of parliament. North and King George shared a frustration with political opposition undermining the effort not uncommon in war fighting today, "parliament showing a reluctance to them must encourage the rebels, and make them plan offensive expeditions on our posts . . . "[162]

Former Whig politician and chronicler of the period, Horace Walpole noted, "The newspapers on the Court side had been crammed with paragraphs for a fortnight, saying that Lord Cornwallis had declared he would never pile up his arms like Burgoyne; that is, he would rather die sword in hand. He had probably made no such declaration, or if he had, it was not known here. However, it cast a deeper shade on his surrender."[163]

Leading up to that fateful surrender were the continuous tallies of British casualties, the horror stories of unexpected defeats and barbarism at King's Mountain, and then again at Cowpens. But it was the Pyrrhic victory at Guilford courthouse that laid bare the vulnerability of Cornwallis's bedraggled army, and enemies of the crown on both sides of the Atlantic seized the opportunity. Charles "James" Fox, as vocal a critic of King George as Parliament had ever seen, was moved to action shortly after the published press accounts of Cornwallis at Guilford Courthouse. As published in *the Memoirs of the Public Life of the Late Right Honourable James Fox (1808):*

On June 12, (1781) Mr. Fox brought forward a motion, the object which was, "That the house should resolve itself into a committee, to consider the American War." He particularly urged, as a strong reason for entering at that time into an inquiry on the subject, that it was evident, from the very circumstances which attended our victories over the Americans, that the final subjugation of them was impracticable.

It appeared, he said, *by the recent dispatches which had arrived from America,* that though Lord Cornwallis had done everything he proposed, by penetrating into North Carolina; though he had been fortunate enough to come up with General Greene, had engaged, and defeated him, he had not found one good consequence result from his success, not being joined by any body of Americans, as he expected, nor even retaining the ground upon which he conquered.

It was therefore manifest that the war in which we were engaged was at once impracticable in its object, and ruinous in its progress ... It was his intention, he said: "That his majesty's ministers ought immediately to take every possible measure for concluding peace with our American Colonies ... "[164]

"But the war was still too favourite an object with the crown to be relinquished, and the majority of the house were not yet convinced of its iniquity and folly. The motion was consequently rejected by a majority of 172 to 99."[165]

NOTHING BUT A SERIES OF INEFFECTIVE VICTORIES, OR SEVERE DEFEATS

While the opposition lacked the votes, it didn't lack the voice. Fox was joined by another politician, moved by news of Guildford Courthouse. At the ripe old age of 21, it was only William Pitt's first year in attendance. Like Fox, he came from a political pedigree, but this occasion would be one of the few when the two men agreed. Surprising many with his force and power, Pitt laid the groundwork for a long political career in these moments captured by his biographer, Henry Cleland:

Some gentlemen had passed the highest eulogisms on the American war. Its justice was defended in the most warm and fervent manner indeed. A noble Lord who spoke early, in the heat of his zeal had called it a 'holy war'. For his part, though the honorable gentleman, who made the motion, and some other gentleman, had been more than once in the course of the debate severely reprehended for calling it a wicked and accursed war, he (Pitt) was persuaded and would affirm, that it was a most accursed, wicked barbarous, unnatural, unjust, and diabolical war! It was conceived in injustice; it was nurtured and brought forth in folly; its footsteps were marked with blood slaughter, persecution, and devastation; in truth everything which constitute moral depravity and human turpitude were to be found in it. It was pregnant with misery of every kind ...

The nation was drained of its best blood; and of its vital resources of men and money.

The expense of it was enormous, much beyond any former experience; and yet what had the British received in Return?

Nothing but a series of ineffective victories, or severe defeats.[166]

VICTORY AT CAMDEN LED TO THE DEFEAT AT YORKTOWN.

The Crown's ineffective victories and severe defeats in the South achieved a tipping point. It would take a few more months until news of Cornwallis's defeat at Yorktown, which King George was compelled to address in Parliament on November 27, 1781, triggered a final cascade of dissent. Fox's *Memoirs* describe the scene and some of the speeches:

Previous the ensuing session of parliament, which met on the 27th of November 1781, government received the mortifying intelligence, that the royal army in Virginia, under command of Earl Cornwallis, had been obliged to surrender prisoners of war. This event convinced the sober and reflecting part of the nation of the utter impracticability of prosecuting the war in America with any prospect of success, and served to cure many, who had been sanguine in their hopes of colonial subjugation, and that mad and extravagant delusion.[167]

It was observed . . . in the last session, that if the capture of Charleston produced no sensible effect, he should grow sick of the American War! This was the time to inquire what the capture of Charlestown had really produced. It had produced a victory over seven thousand men, the flower of British troops, all becoming prisoners of war [Yorktown]. It was natural then to expect that the right honourable gentleman would raise his voice against the continuance of this destructive war, since even our victories were nothing more than the forerunners of hopeless defeats. *The victory at Camden led to the defeat at Yorktown.*[168]

"YOUR ARMIES ARE CAPTURED . . . YOUR DOMINIONS ARE LOST."

Horace Walpole's *Journal of the Reign of King George* summed up the consequences of defeat thusly, "(Dec 4, 1781) The Livery of London voted an admirable and most severe remonstrance to the King against the continuation of the American war, which they said the speech threatened. They besought the King to remove his public and private counselors and used these stunning and memorable words: '*Your Armies are captured; the wonted superiority of your navies is annihilated, your dominions are lost.*'"

"*No King had ever lost so much, without losing it all.*"[169]

EXHIBIT B

Early American Histories

THE REBELS

"There is one party of the work in which I have been very minute; this is in the occurrences in the south . . . I found there was no history existing of that period . . . It exhibits the outlines of our partisan war . . .

But, let not him who carries his researches into the regions of historical truth, receive with too much fastidiousness the narrative of minor events. While men govern the world, their passions govern men and trifles act upon the passions, trifles will have much to do in the affairs of mankind."

—William Johnson, Biographer of
General Nathanael Greene[170]

The American records of the Revolutionary War in the South are far thinner than Britain's for four reasons. First, the always moving national government-in-flight meant limited record keeping. For example, even the Constitutional Convention of 1787 would have been sparsely recorded if not for the personal efforts of one individual—James Madison. Second, those parties whose records we have most of (Washington) were farthest from the Southern action and naturally favor a Northeastern "Continental Army" narrative versus the patriot militia (Sumter, Francis Marion, William Campbell, etc.). Third, local Southern partisan militia actions were spontaneous and often ill recorded; keeping records, or even paper itself, was a luxury and could implicate one in "treason" if detected by Tory Loyalists. Fourth, many early southern records, journals and properties were burnt or otherwise destroyed in the Civil War.

Another challenge of the Americas was its vast impenetrable landmass. Time and terrain made seaborne communiqués more efficient, which of course favored the British fleet. In fact, many of the Northeastern newspapers (*Pennsylvania Gazette*, *New England Chronicle*, etc.) featured English correspondence (Cornwallis, Clinton, etc.) that had originally appeared in the European press or that was distributed directly to American papers for propaganda purposes.

> "I remember well the deep and grateful impression made in the minds of every one by that memorable victory. [King's Mountain] was the joyful annunciation of the turn of the tide of success which terminated the Revolutionary War, with the Seal of our independence."
>
> —Thomas Jefferson
> November 10 1822, recalling of the Battle of King's Mountain
> in a letter to the one of the descendants of Col. Campbell, the
> lead militia commander[171]

General George Washington praised the Southern victories at King's Mountain and Cowpens. Calculating an "Enemy, pretty severely shaken by the two successful strokes upon Ferguson and Tarleton," Washington knew the effects would "awaken more bravery," in the South and the rest of the Colonies.[172] Washington acknowledged that King's Mountain was a "Total Defeat" for the British, a line *The London Gazette* would echo.[173]

Likewise, Washington considered the upset at Cowpens a "victory so decisive and glorious gained with an inferior force." The commander and chief knew it "must have an important influence on the South." Washington's letters in 1780 don't only praise the South, they admonish the Northern colonies for profiteering and disloyalty. Specifically chastising New York, New Jersey, and Connecticut merchants and loyalists, Washington has "No bread, no blankets," leaving him to write the President of Congress that "our prospects are infinitely worse than they have been at any period of the war, and that unless some expedient can be instantly adopted a dissolution of the Army for want of subsistence is unavoidable."[174]

Coming on the heels of food shortages, mutinies, and the horrifying discovery of Benedict Arnold's plot to surrender West Point, one can imagine the relief that the victory at King's Mountain brought to flagging spirits of tired revolutionaries. General Washington confided to Thomas Jefferson, that Arnold's treasonous plot had almost worked.

> On the 25th of September [Arnold] went to the enemy. He entered very deeply into a combination with them, as far as we can judge . . . the primary and principal design of the embarkation they were making was to take West Point, which through preconcerted arrangements between them and Mr. Arnold, in all human probability would have inevitably fallen into their hands . . . [175]

Washington Irving, in his 1859 biography of General Washington, noted that the battle of King's Mountain was small in number but big in effects and it turned the tide of the war.

> The army of mountaineers and frontier men, thus fortuitously congregated, did not attempt to follow up their signal blow. They had no general scheme, no plan of campaign; it was a spontaneous rising of the sons of the soil, to revenge it on its invaders, and having effected their purpose, they returned in triumph to their homes. They were little aware of their achievement. The battle of King's Mountain, inconsiderable as it was in the numbers engaged, turned the tide of Southern warfare. The destruction of Ferguson and his corps gave a complete check to Cornwallis.[176]

The Continental Congress thought King's Mountain and Cowpens were important, as these two resolutions indicate:

Monday November 13, 1780
Resolved, that Congress entertain a high sense of the spirited and military conduct of Col. Campbell, and the officers and privates of the militia under his command, displayed in action of the 7 of October, in which a compleat victory was obtained over superior

numbers of the enemy, advantageously posted on King's Mountain, in the State of North Carolina; and that this resolution be published by the commanding officer of the southern army, in general orders.[177]

Friday March 9, 1781

That the thanks of the Unites States in Congress assembled, be given to Brigadier General Morgan, and the officers and men under his command, for their fortitude and good conduct, displayed in the action at Cowpens, in the state of South Carolina . . . (medals of Gold for Morgan: Virtus Unita Valet—"Virtue is powerful when United" and silver to Lt. Col. Washington—Virtute non Numeris—"as well as swords.")[178]

WILLIAM MOULTRIE

Eyewitness accounts from participants who observed the combat, or perhaps more important, the British and Loyalist reactions to the impact of those actions, provide insight. For example, William Moultrie, the successful commander of the palmetto-log Fort defense of Sullivan's Island (1776) published his memoirs in 1802. Like so many before and after him, he borrowed liberally from *The Annual Register*, but that is no reason to dismiss Moultrie or his memoirs. He was a soldier in the struggle. He knew well the value of psychology in command. (I credit much of his success at Sullivan's Island in 1776 to his personal demeanor of tranquility under fire.)

Moultrie's *Memoirs*, which would educate early Americans for generations on the conduct of the war, describes the scene back in Charleston, as he witnessed the despair of the British when word of their defeat at Cowpens trickled in. He deduced that the actions at King's Mountain and Cowpens, in which the British lost 2,000 troops they cannot replace, turned the war.

Moultrie on King's Mountain and Cowpens

This defeat of Colonel Tarleton's at the battle of the Cowpens, chagrined and disappointed the British Officers and Tories in Charlestown exceedingly. I happened to be in Charlestown at the time when the news arrived. I saw them standing in the streets in small circles, talking over the affair with very grave faces. I knew the particulars as soon as they did. Governor Rutledge sent in person on some pretence with a flag; but in fact it was to inform the American prisoners of our success: the person informed me of the whole affair, which I communicated to the officers at Haddrell's-point, on my return in the evening.

The news gave great joy, and put us all in high spirits. Some of the old British officers who were made prisoners, and paroled to Charlestown, when they came down, were exceedingly angry indeed, at their defeat, and were heard to say, 'that was the consequence of trusting such a command to a boy like 'Tarleton . . . '[179]

The great victory at the Cowpens changed the face of American affairs, and raised the drooping spirits of her desponding friends. In two actions soon after each other, the British lost about two thousand men: that at King's Mountain, on the seventh of October, and that at the Cowpens of the seventeenth of January, 1781: the latter was of more serious consequence to Lord Cornwallis, because it deprived him of nine hundred of his best troops. (*An account of the affair at Cowpens, I had from an American officer of great veracity and high rank, and one that was very conspicuous on that day in the action) . . . [180]

What must his [Cornwallis's] feelings have been, when he received this account of his favorite officer [Tarleton], and one in whom he had the greatest opinion, in regard to his military abilities, and who had with him upwards of twelve hundred of the pick of his army, that he should be defeated by about one thousand men, and half of them militia?

His chagrin and his disappointment must have been great indeed upon this occasion.[181]

Moultrie on Guilford Courthouse

Though some of the British said that such another victory would ruin them. *Lord Cornwallis' conduct after this affair proves that this victory gave him no advantage, and that it left him in a much worse situation than before it happened* . . .

On that day, his lordship destroyed all his baggage, left his hospital and seventy-five wounded men, with a great number of loyalists in the neighborhood of Guilford, and marched off for the sea coast, which shows that he thought himself in no condition to keep the field; and thirteen days before the expiration of his act of grace he reached his shipping at Wilmington, and left the whole of the upper country in the power of General Greene's army.

Lord Cornwallis was extremely mortified at not receiving some support from the Scotch Highlanders, settled at Cross-creek: although he marched through their settlements, and they were opposed to the American measures, yet they kept aloof from the British.[182]

NATHANAEL GREENE

General Nathanael Greene became Commander of the Southern Department after much of the backcountry action that actually turned the war in the Fall of 1780 (Musgrove's Mills, Huck's Plantation, and of course King's Mountain). Those guerilla actions, coming as they did on the heels of British victories at Charleston and Camden, occurred under the watch of the disgraced General Gates, prior to Greene's arrival.

Gates was widely discredited after his humiliating defeat and flight from Camden. Anything Gates was associated with diminished. Thus the Southern partisan actions prior to Greene assuming command have been minimized, especially by chroniclers of George Washington and the camp of historians that favors the Continental army over the backcountry "banditti."

Subsequent southern historians (e.g. Edward McCrady, who we will look at later) would choose to focus on homegrown heroes and question the Rhode Islander General Greene's impact. We will leave the divergent histories and the militia vs. Continental army schism for later as it pertains to modern day Second Amendment issues. Now, let us appreciate that Greene and his supporters will naturally look to the year of 1781 to measure his impact and success focusing on his Army's victories at Cowpens and Guilford Courthouse.

General Greene, a favorite of General Washington's, brought not just his tremendous capabilities but also drew the historical spotlight. With the wagon train of a real army, there were better records/correspondence (i.e. British exhibits), but Greene came armed with something else: General Daniel Morgan, one of the toughest and most inspiring commanders in American military history, who on January 17th gave Tarleton "one devil of a whipping."

Greene's biographer William Johnson admits the dearth of a record on the early Southern fight, and he also crystallizes the role of emotion, and the seemingly small actions that become large in the mind's eye, "men govern worlds, but their passions govern men."

In *Sketches of the Life and Correspondence of Nathanael Greene, Major General of the Armies of the United States In the War of the Revolution,* published in 1822, Johnson offers:

The Battle of Cowpens was fought on the 17th of January 1781. It cannot be passed over without due attention as it was the first link in the chain of events that led even to the capture of Cornwallis and the successful termination of the revolutionary war.[183]

Interesting perspective, since Johnson, is pro-Greene and pro-Continentals, and naturally will focus on a decision made by Greene. Others (McCrady, pro-militia) say King's Mountain was the first link or even Huck's Defeat at Williamson's plantation. Regardless which link you choose, the chain to the end begins in the South.

HENRY "LIGHT HORSE HARRY" LEE

No work on Southern military history could be complete without mentioning the venerated name Robert E. Lee. Lee's connection to the Revolution is legion. Not only did he marry George Washington's step-granddaughter but Lee, the only general ever to be asked to command the armies of both sides of a war (the Union and the Confederate), was the son of Henry "Light Horse Harry" Lee.

"Light Horse Harry" became Governor of Virginia and represented its citizens as a member of Congress, but before all that he had a war to win. From New Jersey to South Carolina, at almost every battle of the entire Revolution, "Light Horse Harry" witnessed and fought like few others of his time. King's Mountain, Lee tells us, deprived the British of one quarter of their army. It also forced Cornwallis's retreat out of North Carolina, after entering as "conquerors."

"Light Horse Harry" was a hero of the Southern Campaigns fighting beside Greene, Marion, and Pickens in actions both conventional and guerilla, and yet he saves his greatest praise for Daniel Morgan. The insights of a witness with such broad perspective, edited by his son, one of the greatest military thinkers in history is instructive and definitive:

> The victory of the Cowpens was to the South what that of Bennington (Saratoga Campaign) had been to the North, General Morgan, whose former services had placed him high in public estimation, was now deservedly ranked among the most illustrious defenders of his country ; . . In military reputation the conqueror of the Cowpens must stand before the hero of Bennington (Starke).[184]

Early American historians would challenge each other over which Southern battle, King's Mountain or Cowpens, most turned the tide of the war. The irony is that today's contemporary historians ignore both those battles and the South altogether.

RAMSAY, *THE ANNUAL REGISTER*, AND CHARGES OF PLAGIARISM

One of the first contemporary histories that had a local and national point of view was David Ramsay's *History of South Carolina* (1785). Ramsay served in the State legislature, the Continental Congress and as a field surgeon during the bloody year of 1780, until his capture by the British. While he has been criticized for drawing heavily from British sources, many of his observations of action in South Carolina have in turn been quoted by British officers who actually fought in the battles Ramsay describes.

"Like all the historians of the Revolutionary era, Ramsay saw historical writing as a vehicle for fostering nationhood, an instrument for promoting the kind of unity, even homogeneity, that the cultural nationalists desired," wrote Lester Cohen, editor of a recent reprinting of Ramsay's work. Ramsay tells us to "consider the people of all the thirteen states, as a band of brethren, speaking the same language, professing the same religion, inhabiting one undivided country, and designed by heaven to be one people."[185]

"Ramsay as Plagiarist," was the title of an article by O.G. Libby in *The American Historical Review* of 1902. Libby concluded Ramsay and others were "no longer authorities at first hand, but merely discredited and doubtful contemporaries, whose accounts . . . were taking unverified material from a British magazine (*Annual Register*) wholly without credit, copying not facts but the very phrases and wording of whole paragraphs and pages."

Cohen's foreword which appeared in a 1990 edition of Ramsay's might have had some degree of self-interest at stake, but I concur with the sentiment that:

"Ramsay did in fact lift passages verbatim form *The Annual Register* but even if all the examples are conceded . . . the plagiarism has no substantial impact on its value to modern readers."[186]

■

Plagiarism appears to invoke varying degrees of outrage, depending on the political agenda at hand. In the course of the six years I have been researching this case, I have been struck by the hypocrisy of the academic left, in this instance as it relates to plagiarism or other labels, such as racism, which spurn a contributor and discredit their version of events. The "labeling" attack affords a cynical tool for obliterating actual facts by destroying the messenger. This is the case not only of historians, but of historical figures more broadly (Washington and Jefferson as slave owners, etc.) as their 18th century actions are brought to focus in a 21st century politically correct environment.

We will explore the left's employment of selective outrage and personal destruction in later sections, but for now let us look at two instances of plagiarism that should be considered before the work of Ramsay or others are dismissed out of turn.

In an article titled "Why Biden's Plagiarism Shouldn't be Forgotten," David Greenberg notes that during his 1988 quest for the White House, Vice President Joe Biden "borrowed" someone else's life. In this case the donor was a British Labor Party Leader with a compelling life story named Neil Kinnock. After watching a video tape of the British politician, Greenberg writes, "Biden lifted Kinnock's precise turn of phrase and his sequence of ideas . . . But the even greater sin was to borrow biological facts from Kinnock, that, although true about Kinnock, didn't apply to Biden. Unlike Kinnock, Biden wasn't the first person in his family history to attend college, as he asserted; nor were his ancestor coal miners, as he claimed when he used Kinnock's words."[187]

Perhaps you can give a politician the benefit of the doubt, especially when one is as gaffe prone and verbose as Joe Biden. But what happens when a carefully crafted work that elicits deep emotional responses is found to be a fake? Do we forsake its cultural value? Or is there some implicit truth which can or should still be salvaged?

After novelist Harold Courlander presented evidence to a Manhattan judge that Alex Haley's *Roots* plagiarized his novel *The African* eighty-one times, Haley agreed to pay $500,000 to settle the case. The statement read: "The suit has been amicably settled out of court. Alex Haley acknowledges and regrets that various materials from the *The African* by Harold Courlander found their way into his book *Roots*." Furthermore, the *Washington Post* story recounts several of the eighty-one plagiarized scenes that Haley incorporated into *Roots*, supposedly about his own family ancestry, that were originally penned by a white novelist. The $500,000 dollar settlement in 1978 dollars adjusted for inflation would be worth $1.7 million today.[188]

■

Despite the controversy, I have chosen to sample from Ramsay's accounts because British officers who fought in the Southern Campaigns of '80-'81 thought it credible and important. Ramsay's history was generally accepted and widely sold for more than 130 years following the revolution. As one of the first American history books written by an American, Ramsay (and in fairness *The Annual Register*) influenced millions via the scores of historians who would reference his work. One note of irony before we delve into the material: Ramsay, despite later being branded a plagiarist, was the first American to file for a copyright.[189]

In *The History of South Carolina*, Ramsay faulted the heavy hand of the British in the occupation of the South Carolina backcountry with igniting the civil war. Specifically Ramsay cited the burning of bibles and Psalms belonging to the Scots Irish backwoodsman as a point of no return which "causes unusual animation" and led to Huck's Defeat, a precursor to King's Mountain, one of the first, albeit small, American victories in the South.

Ramsay was in the camp that credited Cowpens as the turning point of the war, calling it the first link in the chain of events, a literary chain that would become well-worn by historians to follow. But regardless of your point of view of the primacy of King's Mountain in

October 1780 or Cowpens, three months later in January 1781, the fact remains that those two battles interrupted the British plan to roll up the colonies and as Ramsay tells us, their "glory and importance spread from one end of continent to the other."[190]

Huck's Defeat

The friends of Independence having once more taken the field in South Carolina a party of corps commanded by Colonel Sumter, consisting of one hundred and thirty three men, on the 12th of July 1780 engaged at Williamson's Plantation in the upper parts of South Carolina with a detachment of British troops and a large body of Tories commanded by Captain Huck. They were posted in a lane, both ends of which were entered by the Americans. In this unfavorable position they were speedily routed and dispersed. Capt. Huck and several others were killed. This was the first advantage gained over royal forces since their landing at the beginning of the year.

At the very moment this unexpected attack was made, a number of women were on their knees, vainly soliciting Captain Huck for his mercy on behalf of their families and property. During his command he had distressed the inhabitants by every species of insult and injury. He had also shocked them with profanity. In a very particular manner he displayed his enmity to the Presbyterians, by burning the library and the dwelling house of their clergyman, the Rev. Mr. Simpson, and all Bibles which contained the Scots translation of the Psalms. These proceedings, no less impolitic than impious, inspired the numerous devout people of that district with unusual animation. *A warm love for independence blended itself with a religious fervor, and these two passions reciprocally added strength to each other* . . . [191]

Elated with their victory, the conquerors became more insolent and rapacious, while the real friends of independence, thoroughly alarmed at their danger became resolute and determined . . . Unfurnished with the means of defence [Marion] was obliged to take possession of the saws at the sawmills, and to convert them to into horsemen's swords. So much was he distressed with ammunition, that he was engaged when he had not but three rounds to each man of his party. At other times he brought his men into view, though without ammunition, that he might make a show of numbers to the enemy.

Major Wemyss burned scores of houses belonging to the inhabitants living on the Pedee, Lynch Creek and Black River, who were supposed to do duty with him, or to be subservient to his views. This measure had an effect contrary to what was expected. Revenge and despair cooperated with patriotism to make these ruined men keep the field. The devouring flames sent on defenseless habitations by blind rage and brutal policy, increased not only the zeal but the number of [Marion's] followers.[192]

King's Mountain

This unexpected advantage gave new spirits to the despondent Americans, and in a great degree frustrated a well-concerted scheme for strengthening the British Army by the cooperation of the inhabitants who were disaffected to the cause of America. It was scarcely possible for any event to have happened, in the present juncture of affairs, more unfavorable to the views of Lord Cornwallis than this reverse of fortune.

The total route of the royalists, who had joined Maj. Ferguson, operated as a check on their future exertions. The same timid caution which made them averse from joining their countrymen, in opposing the claims of Great Britain, restrained them from risking anymore in support of the royal cause.[193]

The panic occasioned by the reduction of Charlestown, and the defeat of General Gates, began to wear off. The defeat of Maj. Ferguson, and the consequent retreat of Lord Cornwallis from Charlotte to Winnsborough, encouraged the American militia to repair to the camps of their respective commanders.[194]

Cowpens

The Glory and importance of this action [Cowpens] resounded from one end of the continent to the other. It re-animated the desponding friends of America, and seemed to be like a resurrection from the dead to the southern states.

Tarleton's defeat [Cowpens] was the first link in a grand chain of causes which finally drew down ruin, both in North and South Carolina, on the royal interest.[195]

Guilford Courthouse

[Guilford] though called a victory by the British operated against them like a defeat. Lord Cornwallis was reduced to the alternative of retracing his footsteps to South Carolina, or advancing to Virginia, while the country behind him was left open to Green, at the head of a respectable force . . .

Lord Cornwallis advanced northwardly, and seated himself in York Town, Virginia, where in October following he was reduced to the necessity of surrendering his whole army prisoners of war.[196]

REGIONALISM:
Diverging Histories of North and South

I n post-Revolution victory, Ramsay had a goal of national unifica-
tion. Given his concern for copyright infringement, he also had an
eye on book sales. His initial foray was a *History of South Carolina*. Later he would seek a larger audience with a *History of the
United States*, one of the first efforts. Others would join him and the
market began to grow. Ramsay's efforts, as well as those other early
historians, were inventoried by historiographer Daniel Boorstin, who
authored dozens of books, held dozens of degrees, and spent a dozen
years as the Librarian of the United States Congress. Boorstin earned
the Pulitzer Prize for his work in American History. *The Americans:
The National Experience*, published in 1965 is a treasure for anyone
seeking a deeper understanding of how our history was crafted and
by whom.

The Librarian of Congress gives a thorough accounting of the early
writers and the scandals that plagued them, often with roots in . . .
The Annual Register. Boorstin tells us the first volume of American
History was written by William Gordon and as you can imagine is
heavily laden with content from the Register. Ramsay's would follow
shortly after, with some of the same issues.[197]

According to Boorstin, the battle over ownership of the historical
record started off over who first got the label of "traitor" by insti-
gating rebellion, Mr. James Otis of Massachusetts ("Taxation without
representation is tyranny!") vs. Mr. Patrick Henry of Virginia ("Give
me liberty, or give me death!"). John Adams would enter into this

controversy on behalf of Massachusetts. "The question of priority was not trivial," wrote Boorstin:

> It troubled Adams, who was eager to have the record set right, to prevent Virginia from seizing laurels which belonged to others . . . The [Adams] version of Otis and of the origins of the Revolution was perpetuated in Boston's Fourth of July Orations, which were made into a book and given by a patriotic Bostonian to every school in the city, every academy in the state and every college in the United States. [198]

Newly formed state historical societies began to develop with a goal of preserving and promoting a region's role in the fight for independence. These societies started as a northern phenomenon and the South was late to the game. Inter-state rivalry and factionalism would sometimes be reflected in divergent histories.[199]

The Constitutional Convention, presidential elections (Jefferson) and later War of 1812 would create friction between the new states. The divide between the Southern war hawks and the Northern states ready to secede back to English control (Hartford Convention of 1814) would shame the north and strain the political system for decades, in turn deepening the regional fault lines. While Washington D.C. burned, Southern soldiers were once again defeating British forces in the South at places like New Orleans while Northern states were negotiating separate trade and peace deals. Legitimate divisions and animosity smoldered over national loyalty and civic participation. And then there was the diabolical issue of slavery.

As the nullification crisis simmered in the 1830s, Boorstin tells us that the centennial of Washington's birth created a rift over moving the body of our first president to the new capital.

> Southern representatives, foreseeing civil war and their separation from the Union, imagined the resulting indignities. "Remove the remains of our venerated Washington," warned Wiley Thompson of Georgia, "from their association with the remains of his cohort and his ancestors, from Mount Vernon and from his native state, and deposit them in this capitol, and then let a severance of the Union

occur, and behold! *The remains of Washington on a shore foreign to his native soil.*"[200]

By 1850, side-by-side comparisons of Northern (Bostonian) and Southern (Virginian) histories start to show differences. Boston Lawyer Richard Hildreth wrote an anti-slavery novel before penning *The History of the United States of America from the Discovery of the Continent to the Organization of the Federal Constitution,* (1852). Hildreth's pro-Northern account gives short shrift to Southern efforts. While the facts and timelines remain, Hildreth blanches the significance of key events. Subtle omissions of consequence leave readers without an understanding of the South's significance.[201]

On the other hand, George Tucker, a Virginia lawyer who served in the U.S. House in the 1820's, has a heaping buttery serving of pro-Southern factoids in his *The History of The United States From their Colonization to the End of the Twenty-Sixth Congress in 1841* (1856). For example, Tucker calls King's Mountain the turning point of the entire war.[202]

GEORGE BANCROFT

As civil war approached and was consummated, attention would turn to the matters at hand. Three quarters of a million casualties were followed by a harsh period of "reconstruction," as the young nation tended to its wounds. In the years that followed, George Bancroft would write one of the most important and lyrical histories of the United States. His volumes would become the top-sellers and be considered the most important histories produced in the nineteenth century. Historiographer Daniel Boorstin estimated that Bancroft's work wound up in one third of the homes in New England.

Bancroft served as Secretary of the Navy and helped to found the United States Naval Academy. Who does this Massachusetts native give credit to for winning the revolutionary War? The South. What is particularly astonishing is that Bancroft's *Volume 10*, covering the War of Independence was actually written ten years after the Civil War, at a time when the South was particularly unpopular, and yet he persisted in painting an accurate picture, even if disagreeable to some audiences in a grieving nation.

From Bancroft, we learn of Washington's despair in 1779 and 1780. We learn that despite the world being at war with Great Britain, it was the South that caused her defeat. King's Mountain "Changed the Aspect of the War" and at Cowpens, America "won the most special victory of the War." Also, one of the first to remark on the psychological effects of the Southern front's news back on the British parliamentarians, Bancroft connects the cumulative moral effect on the British opposition forces (William Pitt, Charles Fox, Edmund Burke, etc.) in Parliament.

Specifically that the Battle of Guilford Courthouse was like a modern day "Tet Offensive" of the Vietnam war, a battle with political effects far beyond the actual military consequences. Bancroft not only gave the South their due, but the French as well. He noted that if the victory of Saratoga brought in the French, without whom we could not have won, then it was the cumulative effects of the Southern battles of King's Mountain, Cowpens, and Guilford Courthouse that won the war. Specifically that the Battle of Guilford Courthouse led to the British Surrender at Yorktown.

WASHINGTON'S DESPAIR IN 1780

In a "letter sent by private hand," [Washington] drew the earnest thoughts of George Mason to the ruin that was coming upon the country from personal selfishness and provincial separatism in these words: . . . I have beheld no day, since the commencement of hostilities, that I thought her liberties in such eminent danger as at present. Friends and foes seem now to combine to pull down the goodly fabric we have been raising at the expense of so much time, blood, and treasure . . . [203]

On the 8th of May Washington wrote: "I never was, and much less reason have I now to be afraid of the enemy's arms, but I have no scruples in declaring to you, that I have never yet seen the time in which our affairs, in my opinion were at as low an ebb as at the present; and without speedy and capital change, we shall not be able to call out the resources of the country.[204]

CIVIL WAR IN THE BACK COUNTRY

For two years cold-blooded assassinations, often in the house of the victim and in the presence of his wife and little children, were perpetrated by men holding the King's Commission, and they obtained not indemnity merely, but rewards for their zeal. The enemy were determined to break every man's spirit or to ruin him.[205]

KING'S MOUNTAIN

The victory at King's Mountain, which in the spirit of American soldiers was like the rising at Concord, in its effects like the successes at Bennington, changed the aspect of the war. The loyalists of North Carolina dared rise. It fired the patriots of the two Carolinas with fresh zeal. It encouraged the fragments of the defeated and scattered American army to seek each other and organize themselves anew.[206]

COWPENS

The fame of the great victory at the Cowpens spread in every direction. Greene announced in General orders the victory, and his army saluted the victors as "the finest fellows on earth, more worthy than ever of love." . . . Davidson of North Carolina wrote that the victory "gladdened every countenance and paved the way for the Salvation of the country. . . . (Morgan) bore the brunt of every engagement with Burgoyne's army, and now he had won the most extraordinary victory of the war at the Cowpens.[207]

GUILFORD COURTHOUSE

Although the battle at Guilford drew after it, for the British, all the consequences of defeat, and put an end to their power in North Carolina, no praise is too great for the conduct of their officers and troops throughout the day.

... *The battle of King's Mountain drove Cornwallis back to South Carolina; the defeat at the Cowpens made his second invasion of North Carolina a desperate enterprise; the battle of Guilford Courthouse transformed the American army into pursuers, the British into fugitives.*[208]

EFFECTS IN BRITAIN

"From the report of Cornwallis," said Fox on the twelfth of June to the House of Commons, "there is the most conclusive evidence that the war is at once impracticable in its object and ruinous in its progress ..."[209]

"America is lost, irrecoverably lost, to this country," added Fox. "We can lose nothing by a vote declaring America independent."[210]

The first tidings of the surrender of Cornwallis reached England from France about noon on the twenty-fifth of November. *"It is all over,"* said North many times, *under the deepest agitation and distress.*[211]

AFTER THE CIVIL WAR, EVEN PRESIDENTS AGREE ON KING'S MOUNTAIN

"So it was that the battle of Cowpens was fought and won in South Carolina while the Northern army was in mutiny and Virginia overrun and pillaged by Arnold."

—Edward McCrady, *The History of South Carolina in The Revolution 1780-1783*[212]

EDWARD MCCRADY

By 1902 a bold work by Edward McCrady proclaims the role of the South in the American revolution in no uncertain terms. Counting the battles and skirmishes to make the point that the South cannot be dismissed, McCrady's *The History of South Carolina in The Revolution 1780-1783*, reminds the world that Yankees were fighting in the South on behalf of the crown. McCrady is overlooked and deliberately attacked by liberal historians because they don't like his legal work during Reconstruction, and in today's politically correct environment, McCrady's racism is enough to banish a lifetime of work, regardless of the facts. Ironically, McCrady's efforts at minority voter disenfranchisement in South Carolina in the 1870s and '80s mirrored that of Massachusetts's similar efforts to suppress voting rights in 1857.[213]

McCrady claims that if Cornwallis had not been bogged down by Southern partisans, the British would have won the war. He credits

Huck's Defeat (Williamson's Plantation) and King's Mountain with igniting the sparks in combination with the horrendous mistake the British made in attacking the Presbyterian faithful. McCrady also reminds us that the South was more beat up and suffered more damage than anywhere else, listing 137 battles fought in South Carolina in 1780 and 1781.

Drawing heavily from the English writings (*Strictures*, *Campaigns*, Stedman, etc.) he notes that Tarleton turns on Cornwallis and he takes issue with Ramsay in giving too much credit to Greene. For McCrady, Cowpens is not the first link, but is later in a chain that for McCrady started at Huck's Defeat. Finally, he argues that because the South lacked a "commander" (other than Gates) to get the glory for earlier victories, they go unclaimed.

Judge for yourself if McCrady's accounts are inconsistent with the ground truth as we have established it:

Ramsay, the historian, glorying in this American victory, asserts that Tarleton's defeat was the first link in a grand chain of causes that finally drew down ruin both in North and South Carolina on the Royal interests . . .

The battle of Cowpens was much nearer the end of the chain of causes that led to redemption of these states than to its beginning. The material results of the victory at Cowpens bear no comparison to those obtained by the series of partisan actions which culminated at King's Mountain, and which were enlarged and emphasized at Fishdam, Blackstock, and Hammonds' Store. As has been shown in the proceeding volume, the net results of these engagements had been three-to-one in favor of the Americans killed, wounded, and prisoners and had resulted in disconcerting campaign in which the whole American cause was involved.

The victory at King's Mountain had caused the abandonment of the invasion of North Carolina and Virginia at a time most favorable to the royal cause. It had recalled Cornwallis to South Carolina just as he was about to commence a march which but for this cause might have ended in a junction between Leslie and himself in Virginia and their united advance upon Washington in the Jerseys, and this at a time while the British fleet had command of the American waters, blockading the French at Newport.

If a chain is to be drawn from the fall of Charlestown to the Glorious end of the war, its first link will be found at Williamson's Plantation, when Bratton and Lacey rose upon Huck, and its last at the capitulation at Yorktown.[214]

They probably did not know that the French fleet, from the assistance of which so much had been expected, was cooped up at Newport, nor how important it was to delay and prevent the consummation of the British plans until it could be released—in short they did not know what great consequences would flow from their exertion to harass and retard the British on their march through the State; but they acted upon each occasion as it presented itself of striking a blow in behalf of liberty, content with performing small things as the opportunity allowed, they accomplished great results in the cause of their country.

Huck's defeat, Flat Rock, Rocky Mount, Hanging Rock, Musgrove's Mills, Nelson's Ferry, Fishdam, and Blackstock, and even King's Mountain, were small affairs as great wars go, but they counted up to great proportions in the end. It is not, perhaps, too much to say that at a most critical moment they saved the cause of liberty and independence in America.[215]

YANKEES

While South Carolina received but little assistance from any state but North Carolina, and none from the North, her territory was garrisoned by Americans serving in the British army enlisted from Connecticut, from New York, from New Jersey, and Pennsylvania. The British Forces at King's Mountain and at Ninety Six were composed *entirely* of provincials raised in the Northern States (Note: McCrady exaggerates numbers, but a significant percentage were Yankees) . . .

Northern States furnished several excellent Tory officers who operated with the British army in South Carolina. Among these were lieutenant Colonels Turnbull and Cruger and Major Sheridan of New York, Lieutenant Colonel Allen of New Jersey and two brilliant cavalry leaders from Massachusetts, Major John Coffin and Colonel Benjamin Thompson, afterwards Count Rumford. Pennsylvania on the other hand furnished the notorious Huck whose career was, however, soon ended. Connecticut sent the infamous Dunlap, and Maryland the robber Maxwell.[216]

ASPIRING PRESIDENTS WOULD ALSO ACKNOWLEDGE THE SOUTH

> The victory was of far-reaching importance, and ranks among the decisive battles of the revolution. It was the first great success of the Americans in the South, the turning point in the Southern campaign, and it brought cheer to the patriots throughout the union. The loyalists of the Carolinas were utterly cast down and never recovered the blow; and its immediate effect was to cause Cornwallis to retreat from North Carolina, abandoning his first invasion of that state.
>
> —Theodore Roosevelt, *Winning the West*[217]

At the 150th Anniversary celebration of the Battle of King's Mountain, Oct. 7, 1930, President Herbert Hoover addressed a crowd of thousands that had gathered just south of modern day Charlotte. It was the dawn of radio, and Hoover's address was carried far and wide, reminding Americans of a valorous stand that so many since have forgotten:[218]

> It was a little army and a little battle, but it was mighty portent. History has done scant justice to its significances, which rightly should place it beside Lexington and Bunker Hill, Trenton and Yorktown, as one of the crucial engagements in our long struggle for Independence.
>
> The battle of King's Mountain stands out in our national memory not only because of the valor of the men of the Carolinas, Georgia,

Tennessee, Kentucky, and Virginia, who trod here 150 years ago, and because of the brilliant leadership of Colonel Campbell, but also because the devotion of those men revived the courage of the despondent Colonies and set a nation upon the road of final triumph in American independence.[219]

COUNTING STOLEN VALOR

"A defeat so overwhelming as that suffered by Ferguson's command is rare in warfare."

—Historical Section of the U.S. Army War College[220]

Congressman William F. Stevenson who represented South Carolina's 5th Congressional district in the 1920s was a man with a plan. He sponsored House Resolution HR 230 compelling the Historical Section of the U.S. Army War College to produce a report titled *The Battle of King's Mountain, South Carolina, October 7, 1780 & Battle of Cowpens, South Carolina, January 17, 1781* (1928).

My suspicion is that Stevenson wanted official justification for the recognition and hopeful visit of President Herbert Hoover for the upcoming 150th Anniversary event, and he needed an official document to make the case. After all, King's Mountain National Military Park was in Stevenson's Congressional district just southwest of Charlotte. And Cowpens is just a short drive away. Does the influence exerted throw the report into suspicion? Did it make Ferguson's taunts any less serious, or the response of the Overmountain Men, any less heroic?

KING'S MOUNTAIN

While Ferguson was at Gilbert Town he paroled one of his prisoners and sent him into the mountains with a message to the leaders there, *"that if they did not desist from their opposition to the British arms and take protection under his standard, he would march his army over the mountains, hang their leaders and lay their country waste with fire and sword."*[221]

On October 1, 1780 at Denards Ford in Tyron County, Ferguson issued the following taunt to prospective loyalists: *"I say, if you wish to be pinioned, robbed and murdered, and see your wives and daughters, in four days abused by the dregs of mankind—in short if you wish or deserve to live and bear the name of men, grasp your arms in a moment and run to camp."*[222]

Receipt of the news as to how the mountain men overcame Ferguson thrilled the entire country, and Congress showed its appreciation of this magnificent feat . . . In considering the effect of the Battle of King's Mountain upon the situation in the South, it was only this epic tragedy to Ferguson's army that halted Cornwallis in his subjugation of North Carolina. Without this or a similar calamity, he would have reached the northern borders of the Province in December, and with the Chesapeake occupied by the British fleet, Virginia would have suffered the same fate . . . such a situation . . . would have been problematic.

The battle of King's Mountain was the outstanding victory of the Americans in 1780. Following it, Cornwallis was compelled to abandon North Carolina, and for a time assume the defensive . . . It is an exemplification of American aspirations for self-government and *a display of romantic hardihood and bravery well worthy of the careful study of American youth.*[223]

COUNTING STOLEN VALOR

Eighty years after the mandated report by the Army War college, the Congress was at it again. This time, instead of acknowledging Southern heroism and sacrifice, their efforts produced the opposite effect. In 2007, the U.S. Congress commissioned the National Parks Service *Report to Congress on The Historic Preservation of The Revolutionary War and War of 1812 Sites in the United States (NPS Report)*. Do you think the results reflect the facts we knew to be true at an earlier time in our history? No.[224]

Dozens of significant actions in South Carolina are omitted, despite the "referenced" sources listing dozens more southern battles than were included in the NPS list. For example: Huck's Defeat (Williamson's Plantation) the battle that ignited the South was not listed. The NPS Report's methodology lists several "source" references (Mark Boatner, Francis Heitman) but those "sources" tell a different story.[225]

I own the referenced sources, and they list dozens more southern battles than were included in the NPS list. Budget cuts? Northern Battlefields did not get trimmed, only Southern sites did.

In 2007, the NPS Report lists total Revolutionary Battlefields and Related Sites in NY= 90, NJ=37, and in South Carolina . . . 34

The NPS's own sources challenge these numbers. Take Heitman, for example:

In 1914, Francis Heitman published the *Historical Register of Officers of the Continental Army During the War of American Revolution* which lists the actions of the war. Heitman is widely referenced by historians as the "de facto" list of Revolutionary War battles.[226]

According to the study done by Heitman (1914):

1. South Carolina had 40 actions in 1780 alone!
2. SC had more combat than the other 12 colonies combined
3. 1780 had 75 actions, 35 were in the other colonies, and 40 in SC.

In 1914, Heitman (an NPS source document) lists total Revolutionary actions as NY=92, NJ=34, and in South Carolina . . . 86!!

Compare 86 in 1914 with only 34 in 2007. It just doesn't add up.[227]

In 1902, Edward McCrady identified and listed casualties for 137 actions in South Carolina:

In 1779, when the war turned southward, there were nine affairs in South Carolina, and in these none but her own continentals and militia took part. In a proceeding volume, we have shown that in 1780 there had been thirty-four engagements in the state, in eight of which Continental troops had taken part and in the remaining twenty-six only partisan bands.

From the advent of Greene to the end of the war, i.e. during the years 1781-82, it will be seen by the table appended that there were eighty-three battles etc., fought and that in these the Continentals from other southern states, took part in nine; that South Carolinians took part with these Continentals in ten, and that they fought sixty-four without assistance from anyone coming from beyond the borders of the state.

To recapitulate then, of the *one hundred and thirty-seven battles*, actions, and engagements, between the British and Tories and Indians on the one hand and the American Whigs on the other, which took place in South Carolina during the revolution, *one hundred and three were fought by South Carolinians alone.*[228]

No, it's not that there have been some new discoveries or magical vetting that has found only the Northern reporting to be credible and the Southern not so. In fact, the opposite is true. Easier access to historical documents through online scanned original texts from 200 years ago have opened up the study of history to "amateurs" that often have more expertise than the "experts." Take, for example, Sergeant First Class Patrick O'Kelley, a retired U.S. Army Special Forces soldier who has seen action in theaters around the world.

SFC O'Kelley is now a high school teacher, author, and Revolutionary War re-enactor. As much as anyone living today, this expert in partisan and guerilla warfare has retraced the steps of the partisans of the South. SFC O'Kelley, an expert in small unit "hit and run" tactics like those pioneered by Francis Marion in the swamps of the Carolinas, has written a series of books, *Nothing But Blood and Slaughter*, cataloging the conflict in the southern colonies.

SFC O'Kelley identified over 700 actions in the South, and 400 in South Carolina alone.[229]

There used to be a time when Americans revered the contribution of the South. Children's school books like the nineteenth century *Mc-Guffey Readers*, which educated more backcountry Americans than any other single source, openly acknowledged the South. The Readers were often the sole teaching instrument for wagon train families pushing ever farther westward. The use and reuse of these frontier textbooks among siblings and neighbors, coupled with their estimated reach of over 120 million sold, suggests their influence on American historical awareness. In one edition, the only story on the Revolutionary War is that of the Southern guerilla leader Francis Marion, the infamous "Swamp Fox."[230]

■

It wasn't just the children's books that honored the Southern soldier. After the critical victory at King's Mountain, the Continental Congress proclaimed:

> . . . that Congress entertain a high sense of the spirited and military conduct . . . displayed in action of the 7 of October, in which a *compleat victory was obtained over superior numbers of the enemy,* advantageously posted on King's Mountain . . . [231]

The congressional proclamation of Thanksgiving after the victory at Yorktown specifically singled out the Southern soldiers in a prayer of thanks on Friday October 26, 1781.

> . . . We cannot help leading the good people of these states to a retrospect on the events which have taken place since the beginning of the war, so we recommend in a particular manner to their observation, the goodness of God in the year now drawing to conclusion: in which the confederation of the United States has been completed in which there have been so many instances of prowess and success in our armies; *particularly in the Southern States,* where, notwithstanding the difficulties with which they had to struggle, they have recovered the whole country which the enemy had overrun . . . [232]

∎

You've now seen the evidence.

Once upon a time, Britain expressed admiration for their Southern adversaries, and Americans themselves thanked God for the South.

So how did we get to the prevailing attitude of "God Damn the South" that exists today?

CLOSING
ARGUMENT

Crooks, Cronies, and Consequences of the War on God, Guns, and Guts

---

MOTIVES:
"Long March" to Culture War

The debris had not settled from two bombs ripping through spectators at the Boston Marathon when it began. That day, April 15, 2013, two successive CNN analysts asked what millions of Americans had been conditioned to think: "Were the bombers Islamic radicals or Right wing extremists?" NPR and others joined in speculating on the identities and motivations of the terrorists. But on that April day, thirty of the thirty-one terrorists on the FBI's "Most Wanted" list were Muslims. The one non-Muslim on the list was a Leftist with "ties to animal rights extremist groups," wanted for blowing up pharmaceutical companies. Why then did the media assume the Boston bombers were likely "Right wing" Americans?[233]

April 15th might have been tax day, but the only Americans conducting attacks were at the Internal Revenue Service (IRS). Far from being the aggressors, the members of the Taxed Enough Already (TEA) Party were the victims. In a scandal that would break less than a month after the bombing, it was discovered that conservative TEA Party groups were being specifically profiled for scrutiny and harassment. USA Today reported that while Right wing organizations were "sitting in limbo," Leftist groups with names including words like "Progress" or "Progressive," were being approved relatively quickly for non-profit status. Both the conservative and the liberal groups were "engaged in the same kinds" of 501(c)(4) political activity, but only the conservatives faced the scrutiny of the taxman.[234]

Was it because President Barack Obama ridiculed the TEA Party as "Tea Baggers"? Or as Kimberley Strassel at the Wall Street Journal

asked pointedly, was it because Vice President Joe Biden compared the
TEA Party to "terrorists"?[235]

Boston would not be the first rush to judgment at the expense
of conservatives or their cause. In another tragic April, this one in
2011, the founder of the Left wing website *The Daily Kos* blamed
Governor Sarah Palin for the tragic shooting of Congresswoman Ga-
brielle Giffords, her staff, and her constituents. His tweet, "Mission
accomplished, Sarah Palin," has come to signify the vitriolic depths of
modern American political discourse.[236]

By speculating that the Boston bombers were either Jihadists or
"Right wing extremists," the mainstream media was reinforcing negative stereotypes, not against Muslims but against conservative Americans, to its viewing audience. The Department of Homeland Security
(DHS) apparently agreed with the negative stereotyping according to
a report published in 2009 titled "Right wing Extremism: Current
Economic and Political Climate Fueling Resurgence in Radicalization
and Recruitment."[237] A highlight from the report singled out veterans:

*"The possible passage of new restrictions on firearms and the return
of military veterans facing significant challenges reintegrating into
their communities could lead to the potential emergence of terrorist groups or lone wolf extremists capable of carrying out violent
attacks."*[238]

Conservative author Michelle Malkin called the report a "piece of
crap."[239]

The political left in the United States that now controls the Democratic party and the liberal media that supports their cause have
worked relentlessly to sow disdain and distrust of conservatives who
value the three tenets of American Exceptionalism identified by the
nineteenth century French writer Alexis de Tocqueville:[240] 1) A faith
driven sense of family and morality [God], 2) a fierce sense of patriotism and willingness to fight for their limited government [Guns]
and, 3) a sense of dynamic support for individuality, states' rights and
entrepreneurial risk-taking [Guts]. In an effort to "radically transform" America, all three of these pillars are under attack by the Left

according to the paradigm developed one hundred years ago by an Italian communist.[241]

Antonio Gramsci, a militant atheist who wrote his manifestos in Italian jails while his family was in Moscow during the 1920s, is the father of a school of thought by which the Marxists attack the culture and institutions of Western society in order to facilitate the revolution of the oppressed. Gramsci gave the name of "cultural hegemony" to the control exerted by the privileged classes over the masses through vehicles like popular culture and religion. In order to overturn the capitalist society and fulfill the Marxist vision, the established culture must be discredited and countered with an "alternative." Lee Congdon, Professor Emeritus of History at James Madison University spelled out Gramsci's influence in the Culture Wars in these terms: "Gramsci counseled his side to begin a 'long march through the institutions,' by which he meant the capture of the cinema, theater, schools, universities, seminaries, newspapers, magazines, radio, television, and courts."[242]

The effects of the "long march" in what is now a multi-generational indoctrination across campuses and newsrooms is reflected in the exponential speed with which public opinion is moving from traditional conservative positions to "alternative" views on major social issues including the Iraq War, drug legalization, illegal immigration, gun control, gay marriage, and even religious faith, with atheism spreading rapidly.[243] A comparison of attitudes on the Vietnam and Iraq wars illustrate the point: "while it took over three years for a majority of Americans to call Vietnam a mistake, a majority of Americans began to call Iraq a mistake within about a year and three months," according to Gallup which has tracked the polls in both wars.[244]

Popular TV shows with prominent gay characters, such as ABC's *Modern Family*, have helped to move public opinion on gay marriage from 37 percent support in 2004 to a new high of 58 percent support in 2013. Conversely, Hollywood morality and other secular influences, including the public school system, have led to a new low in America: in 2012 Protestant Christians became a minority for the first time since the founding of the nation.[245] That trend goes hand in hand with a surge in atheism as folks leave the church.[246]

One in five adults now claim no religious beliefs, and that number balloons to one in three for young adults under thirty. A consequence of this downward spiral is the closing of 3,500 churches every year. While America's faith dwindles, there is a not-so-coincidental silver lining for the Left: that fast growing group of non-believers voted 70 percent for Obama and heavily identifies with liberal positions.[247]

"Why Obama Should Seek to Destroy the Republican Party," was the title of an article that John Dickerson wrote for *Slate.com*. Dickerson isn't just a private citizen or columnist. Dickerson is the political director at CBS News. While the media elites shout their disdain of conservatives from the bully pulpit, conservatives are letting their voices be heard in different ways.[248]

Within weeks of Barack Obama winning a second term in the November 2012 presidential election, online petitions began flooding the White House's *We the People* website. All fifty states had angry citizens who filed them, but it was eight former confederate states that each amassed the 25,000 signatures necessary for the White House to respond. The Obama administration was not amused by the petitions seeking to "Peacefully grant the State of (Texas, for example) to withdraw from the United States of America and create its own NEW government" and pushed back that "600,000 Americans died in a long and bloody civil war."[249]

■

Twenty years earlier, at the 1992 Republican National Convention, Pat Buchanan sought to define the phenomenon he was witnessing on the campaign trail in the heartland of America: "There is a religious war going on in this country. It is a cultural war, as critical to the kind of nation we shall be as the Cold War itself. For this war is for the Soul of America," said Buchanan.[250]

A year prior, in 1991, sociologist James Davison Hunter published *Culture Wars: The Struggle to Define America*. The book was relatively unknown until Buchanan's battle cry, like the horns at Jericho, shook millions of American homes. The acknowledgment of cultural conflict took wings propelling the Republicans to a historic victory in the 1994 midterm elections. A lesser known but significant event of 1994 was the publication of Hunter's follow up to *Culture Wars*, cryptically titled *Before the Shooting Starts: Searching for Democracy in America's Culture War.*[251]

Like the Holocaust, there are even culture war deniers, who are working to enable the Left's usurping of American culture by contesting that it is even under attack. Stanford professor Morris Fiorina argues that the electorate is not polarized in his book *Culture War? The Myth of a Polarized America*. Other leftists however have been more forthright in their plans and goals in reshaping America. Liberal icons like Henry Louis Gates, Jr. and Todd Gitlin have both attacked into the culture war maelstrom respectively with *Loose Canons: Notes on the Culture Wars* and *Twilight of Common Dreams: Why America is Wracked by Culture Wars.*[252]

In his newest book, professor Gates puts the battle in perspective: "When Buchanan said that the war was for the soul of America, he misspoke. This war, as it continues even at length and in forms that we could not have possibly imagined in the early 1990's, is not for the Soul of America. The war *is* the Soul of America."

Is the sectional and ideological hatred that George Washington warned us about in his 1796 farewell address really so intense?

I have already intimated to you the danger of parties in the State, with particular reference to the founding of them on geographical discriminations . . . The alternate domination of one faction over another, sharpened by the spirit of revenge, natural to party dissension, which in different ages and countries has perpetrated the most horrid enormities, is itself a frightful despotism.[253]

In response to trending phenomena, The United States Military Academy at West Point published a Counter Terrorism Center Brief in 2013 focusing on Right wing extremism as a reactionary response to the "natural and logical progressive movement." Yes, even at West Point, the battle lines are being drawn.[254]

An April 2013 poll conducted by Fairleigh Dickenson University with a sample size of 823 registered voters sought to take a snap shot of America's attitudes about guns. Polling two weeks after the

Boston bombing, and four months after the Sandy Hook Elementary School shooting that left twenty-six dead, the poll revealed a huge political divide: 65 percent of Republicans opposed new gun laws while a "completely opposite" view was given by 73 percent of Democrats who say that Congress should pass more laws to stop gun violence.[255]

Polarization around guns and faith are nothing new, but this poll went to the heart of what different groups in America believe their guns are actually for: "Overall, the poll finds that 29 percent of Americans think that an armed revolution in order to protect liberties might be necessary in the next few years, with another five percent unsure."

An analyst for the poll, political science professor Dan Cassino, observed, "The differences in views of gun legislation are really a function of differences in what people believe guns are for," said Cassino in a press release announcing the polls results. "If you truly believe an armed revolution is possible in the near future, you need weapons and you're going to be wary about the government taking them away."[256]

Suspecting that there were regional differences that the original reporting had not revealed, I called Professor Cassino for clarification. "How did the South and Midwest perform?" I asked, knowing this was the heart of conservative America. He said, as I expected, they were the most likely to agree and that correlated with higher party identifications of Republicans, 44 percent of whom agreed with the necessity for revolution.

James Davison Hunter, author of the previously mentioned *Culture Wars* and *Before the Shooting Starts*, was part of a panel convened to discuss just such matters, in May 2006 for the Pew Forum's Biannual "Faith Angle Conference on Religion, Politics and Public Life." American history tells us that small minorities do the agitating and the fighting, but what was Hunter's response when challenged if there could be a "proper war" when two-thirds of the population are unengaged and the issues are only driven by the extremes?[257]

Hunter answers: "In fact, you can. In fact, total war is a fairly recent and a rare phenomenon in history. Through most of history, war has been a minority affair, and there are all sorts of illustrations one could call attention to." In closing, he noted: "Conservatives have done extremely well in mobilizing within the Republican party . . . And while they have gained in politics, they have lost in the culture, and it is precisely for that reason that (conservatives) will lose politics eventually as well."[258]

Did conservatives lose the culture, or was it stolen?

ACCOMPLICES:
Marxism Goes Mainstream

F our presidents (Lincoln, Garfield, McKinley, and Kennedy) were assassinated in the 100 years from 1865 to 1965. There have been numerous attempts on others including two on Gerald Ford within weeks of each other. In 1968, The Rev. Dr. Martin Luther King Jr. was murdered in Memphis, triggering nationwide rioting and a callout of Federal troops. Senator Robert F. Kennedy was murdered two months later. Shortly after, the Democratic National Convention was rocked by riotous protests. More than 500 riots rocked the United States from 1960-1970. All that against a backdrop of the War in Vietnam, which in 1968 took its deadliest turn, fueling even more protests back home.[259]

The point of this timeline is to contextualize the perspective of former president Jimmy Carter who took office on the heels of the aforementioned trauma, including a truckers' strike in 1974 that killed men in eight states and required the National Guard to keep highways open. Yet having lived through all of that strife, former President Jimmy Carter still sees the situation today as worse than at any time since the Civil War.

While promoting his 25th book, Carter told Brian Williams at NBC Nightly News that: "this country has become so . . . polarized that its almost astonishing . . . I think President Obama suffers from the most polarized situation in Washington that we have ever seen—even maybe in the time of Abraham Lincoln and the initiation of the war between the states."[260]

Who did president Carter blame for the extreme hostility and polarization in Washington? "Fox News."

Former President Carter got it wrong. Fox News, while the most watched cable news channel, still only has a fraction of the viewership of mainstream media. Fox News is not merely in competition with cable news outlets for mindshare such as MSNBC and CNN, but also with ABC, NBC, and CBS, as well as Comedy Central, Discovery, National Geographic, Bravo, HBO, and the liberally programmed ancillary networks that populate the 500-channel universe.[261]

In a moment of candor, captured on tape by the Media Research Center, Mark Halperin who at that time in 2004 was Political Director for ABC News, confessed: "Most members of the establishment media live in Washington and New York. Most of them don't drive pickup trucks, most of them don't have guns, most of them don't go to NASCAR, and every day we're not out in areas that care about those things and deal with those things as part of their daily lives; we are out of touch with a lot of America . . . "[262]

This is the same Mark Halperin who co-wrote the political blockbuster *Game Change* about the 2008 presidential campaign. Between his book and the subsequent HBO film which skewers Governor Sarah Palin, Halperin's tome is considered by many to be the de facto political history of the 2008 elections. Halperin is now at TIME magazine and a contributor on MSNBC where his cohorts share his ignorance of the heartland culture of God, Guns, and Guts. While his biases are evident, they are mild compared to others.

▪

"Anti-intellectual cultures, like that of the fundamentalist South do not produce world class or even national-class intellectuals."

—Michael Lind, *Made in Texas: George W. Bush and the Southern Takeover of American Politics*[263]

North vs. South is not a new phenomenon. Nor is it limited to America. Without exploring theories of climate, fertility, or governance, regional differences have existed since the dawn of time. The "hard-working-North versus lazy-South" narrative persists around the world from Germany to Greece and Northern California to South Beach in Miami and even Boston's maligned "Southies." But nothing is as profound as America's struggle with "the North" and "the South."[264]

Some, including the hosts of the MSNBC network, like Chris Matthews, have gone so far as to say the Civil War, which cost three-quarters of a million lives, is still going on.

Today's civil war is a culture war with territorial distinctions. Film and television programming with its blatant liberal bias is produced in coastal blue states. While books can be written anywhere, the pipeline of authors and agents shaping public opinion is concentrated in New York City, as are the gatekeepers who select topics "worthy" of print, television or internet editorial support (or "buzz). For our purposes, the authors and publishers who have had the greatest impact in distorting the truth of our Revolutionary history are liberals concentrated in New York and Massachusetts as evidenced by their commentaries or political contributions, or both. The battle is for mindshare. The terrain is cerebral and conquest is ultimately political. And in that nexus of politics and history, geography plays an important part.[265]

If you doubt the role of politics in the regional bias question, consider some of the anti-Southern books written shortly after the Republican Surge of the mid '90s, which, like the Tea Party gains in 2010, was led by the South:

Confederates in the Attic: Dispatches from the Unfinished Civil War was a 1998 best seller that identified a clergyman by his "pastor's dog-collar." I'm not much for judging books by their cover, but the cross-eyed confederate with slicked hair, a bow-tie, and a humongous meat cleaver of a knife screams "in-bred-genetic-bizarro." In this instance, the art department captured the author's hatred of the South perfectly.[266]

As a Union organizer in the 1980's, Tony Horwitz had already traveled the south with an unpopular product to sell. The South's unrelenting rejection of "organized labor" (some agrarians overtly connected unions to communism, others eschewed the creep of industrialization, and many rejected the implied atheism in the communist ideologies that drove early union efforts) clearly left a bad taste in

Horwitz's mouth. When he returned in the nineties to write *Confederates in the Attic,* he got his revenge. Beyond skewering the usual stereotypes and suggesting Confederate war re-enactors had latent homosexual tendencies, he claimed a "striking consonance between the GOP's Contract with America and the Confederate Constitution; both called for term limits, budget balancing, curbs on taxation and other restraints on the state."[267]

Peter Applebome, a reporter for *The New York Times,* skewers the South in *Dixie Rising: How the South Shapes American Values Politics and Culture.* It's not just the rehashing of tired anti-southern vitriol like H.L. Mencken's rant: "the (South) bunghole of the United States—a cesspool of Baptists, a miasma of Methodism, Snake Charmers, phony real-estate operators, and syphilitic evangelists." There are more insidious connections that might be lost on the casual reader. For example, the subtle blending of Neo-Conservative with Neo-Confederate leaves a loaded impression of the term neo-cons.[268]

Applebome links Oklahoma bomber Timothy McVeigh to the South because " . . . his favorite t-shirt was one you could buy from the Southern partisan General Store by calling 1-800-23Dixie." As it happens, McVeigh's favorite shirt featured a quote of Thomas Jefferson's, "The tree of liberty must be refreshed from time to time with the blood of patriots and tyrants," which you can also buy at Amazon .com.[269]

Here are some more anti-southern titles:

Better off Without'Em: A Northern Manifesto for Southern Secession was so lousy I couldn't get past the three references to male genitalia in four pages of introduction, so I put the book down. The author was an editorial director of *CNNgo.com.*[270]

Attack of the Theocrats: How the Religious Right Harms Us All and What We Can Do About It was written by an atheist activist. The author scrutinizes fifty members of the U.S. House and U.S. Senate. Can you guess their political affiliations?

Forty-seven are Republicans. Three are Democrats.[271]

What's the Matter with Kansas? How Conservatives Won the Heart of America. The New York Times's most liberal editorialist called it the "year's most prescient political book." Naturally, that year, 2004, was an election year that featured a Massachusetts liberal, John Kerry, trying to unseat Texas republican George Bush. The book touches on some of the well-worn dog whistles for liberals with references to Alger Hiss, a convicted Communist spy that the left has never stopped apologizing for, and Whitaker Chambers, the former atheist spy turned Christian conservative who betrayed the KGB-spy ring, and as such has remained a target for liberals for a half century. Did I mention Chambers was radicalized at Columbia University? And another battlefield on the culture war landscape—the Scopes Trial, which provided the break-out moment for the ACLU.[272]

RETURN TO HISTORY

While the mass market anti-southern bigotry flourishes, the focus of this presentation is the Grand Theft History of the South's role in the Revolutionary War. We have seen the texts of the prior centuries but what do the modern texts tell us?

In 1972, Briton Michael Pearson recreated the American Revolution exclusively through the contemporary British Point of view in a wonderful work aptly titled, *Those Damned Rebels*. Pearson references the material we have just spent chapters pouring over and gets it right:

> Then in October had come the trauma of King's Mountain . . . the effect of King's Mountain was disastrous to the British. "No sooner had the news of it spread through the country," Clinton related, "than the multitudes of disaffected flew to arms from all parts and menaced every British post on both frontiers."[273]

Twenty-two years later another English author would cover the war from the British perspective. *The Long Fuse* by Don Cook was published in 1995. This time a more contemporary telling of the same story would completely omit a key Southern battle, Cowpens.

CLOSING ARGUMENT: ACCOMPLICES ■ 159

Furthermore, the author deliberately scrubbed the impact that Cowpens had on the elite and the public back in Britain where the "total defeat" was front page above the fold news.

Naval Academy Historian Robert Bass even went so far as to suggest the battle of Cowpens, fought on Jan. 17, 1781, may have been the single root cause of the undoing of the American adventure for the British. In the *Green Dragoon* (1957), Bass asserts, "As the controversialists continued to roll off the phrase 'the unfortunate day of Cowpens,' the impression grew stronger that the 17th day of January, 1781 Lieutenant Colonel Banastre Tarleton lost the battle that lost the campaign that lost the war that lost the American Colonies!"[274]

Certainly, every American and British author of the period and for the next 100 years would take the South seriously. But a phenomenon, exemplified by Don Cook, started with the gradual omission of the role and import of the South in American history.

Cook's blatant mistake is not only omitting Cowpens, a battle so significant that Congress decorated the victorious general, but furthermore Cook writes history that is incorrect. For example:

> The news of Yorktown fell on London as a complete surprise. There had been neither warnings nor signs of what was coming . . . At least at Saratoga four years before, there had been a chain of events that foreshadowed surrender. But this time, as far as London knew General Cornwallis had marched from Charleston to the Virginia Coast on a virtually unbroken trail of successes.[275]

The evidence we have presented clearly shows Cook's statement to be false. Recall, we already established the awareness of Cowpens and Guilford through the opposition speeches of Pitt and Fox. While Cook does provide the opposition speech of Pitt, he again fails to give the background on why and where it came from (e.g. news of Guilford has been in the papers, Cowpens, King's Mountain, etc.).

As a former Deputy Sheriff, this theft of history intrigued me. I began my investigation with a comparative analysis of American historiography of the last two centuries. The results were shocking, but the editorial malfeasance or historical malpractice was only a symptom of a larger political phenomenon that the history thieves, the offending authors, and some prominent ones too, did not necessarily create but were complicit in. Their slanting of history corresponded with their web of competing economic and political loyalties that often have been to Marxist communist ideologies that oppose our own Republican ideals.

I was stunned to learn that the vast majority of acclaimed, award-winning, professionally successful historians of the South were in fact admitted unapologetic Marxists and communists. This goes a long way in explaining the next question, that of motive for Grand Theft History.

■

What are some of the cultural and political triggers and motivations behind this concerted effort to deny America its history? What forces aligned to profit from the demonization of the South? What role has the "welfare industrial complex," a $20 trillion dollar leviathan created by Lyndon Johnson's failed "war on poverty" in1965, played on revising down Southern history in order to revise up the dollars that must be paid to keep the underclass from rioting?[276]

CROOKS & CRONIES:
Historical Malpractice Sells Books

The South has become ground zero to the opposition of liberal tax and spend policies. Today the "TEA Party" caucus in the U.S. Congress is predominantly a Southern phenomenon without one member from the original Northeastern colonies despite its namesake Boston roots. Most of its conservative adherents and liberal detractors would be surprised to learn that the *signature* yellow banner "with a lively representation of a rattlesnake in the middle with the attitude of being about to strike, and these words underneath, "Don't tread on me!"" was of Dixie origin. It was a Southerner, Col. Christopher Gadsden, who immortalized the image. Out of his own pocket, Gadsden made it a standard on America's fledgling Navy and hung it in the South Carolina Legislature in February of 1776.[277]

Consider how perceptions and labels have changed over time. Today we see a rattlesnake as a nuisance—more of a threat to our house pets than a fearsome monster. In the mid 18th century, however, it struck real fear of sudden death. In Europe, folks "tremble only at the name of Rattle-Snake, imagining that the Country of Carolina is so full of them, that there is no going into the woods without Danger of Life."[278] This change in perception is true of how we view the American Revolution and who fought it, as well as the political alignment of the South, which has shifted significantly in the past twenty years.

"It is easy to forget how thoroughly the Democratic Party once dominated southern congressional elections. In 1950 there were no Republican senators from the South and only two Republican representatives out of 105 in the Southern House Delegation." The significant reversal from centuries-long Democrat domination of southern state legislatures and federal representation is the theme of *The Rise of the Southern Republicans* by political scientists Earl and Merle Black.[279]

Politics and populations have changed, thanks to everything from air-conditioning to the attractive business climate provided by the Southern rejection of the Northeastern formula for stagnation: labor unions, high taxes, and excessive regulation.

By 1990, 71 million Americans lived in the eleven states of the former confederacy comprising 28 percent of the U.S. population. Composition of the Southern congressional delegation to the House of Representatives favored Democrats two-to-one over Republicans. Remember, Democrats were a majority in the House from 1955 to 1995.[280]

However twenty years of economic and population growth coupled with a conservative realignment over faith issues like abortion and Don't Ask Don't Tell (DADT) would change the face of the South. In 2010, the 98 million Americans living in the South would represent 32 percent of the U.S. population and generate a Gross Domestic Product (GDP) ranked fourth in the world, ahead of Germany and just behind Japan, China, and the U.S. as a whole. Another startling fact is that in 2010, in a complete reversal from twenty years prior, the South was represented by 2.5 Republicans for every Democrat![281]

The new Republican ascendancy of the last few decades has given the South a unique opposition voice for the first time since the Civil War. During most of the last century the South was tucked inside the fold of the larger democratic majority which controlled both the House and Senate. The recent rise of Southern Republicans co-incided with a leftward radicalization of the Democratic party that began purging conservative Democrats in favor of a more radically socialist orientation typified by the leadership of San Francisco congresswoman, Nancy Pelosi.[282]

Pelosi's district and agenda are polar opposites from the waning coalition of Southern Blue Dog Democrats, many of whom lost their seats under her tenure. The liberal policies of Pelosi and Obama were not appreciated in conservative Southern communities that had maintained their democratic representation more out of a historical hatred of the GOP (the "party of Lincoln") then of shared Washington and urban elitist values. I know these truths first hand as a veteran of that chapter of the 2010 political-culture wars.[283]

I worked hard with the help of Senator Tim Scott, Lt. Col. Allen West, Governor Sarah Palin, Herman Cain, Mayor Rudy Giuliani, National Republican Committee Chairman Pete Sessions (R-TX), Rep. Paul Ryan, and Speaker John Boehner to take out a Carolina Blue Dog. While my run for congress came up short, our conservative efforts in southeastern North Carolina were part of a historical wave election that wiped out twenty-eight of the fifty-four members of the Blue Dog coalition no longer able to reconcile their personal "conservative viewpoints" with a national party radicalized by the Pelosi/Reid/Obama agenda. My former opponent, democrat Mike McIntyre, unable in good faith to advocate for the liberal policies of his national party, finally chose to retire. Today the seat is held by a Republican for the first time since 1870's Reconstruction. As TIME columnist Joe Klein griped, the Blue Dogs "were cut in half."[284]

It is worth noting that the inverse is also true: moderate republicans in the Northeast have likewise become an increasingly rare breed. Encumbered by the growing conservatism of their Southern leadership, GOP members from the northern states are losing ground with the liberal electorates there.[285]

POLITICS

What has this concentration of opposition to Leftist policies in the Southern states done to make it a political target of Liberal attacks? Is the historical revisionism reflexive or part of a broader strategy to diminish Southern cultural identity and the character that makes the region unique? Or, is it simply "American Culture" that is under attack and the rural South and Midwest are the last bastions? Is the renewed political focus of Democrat politicians intent on targeting Texas for its thirty-five electoral votes indicative of the South becoming the key political battleground as President Obama's victories in Virginia, Florida, and North Carolina in 2008 portend?[286]

The Republican Revolution of 1994 gave rise to a conservative Republican brand of "Culture Warriors" that spawned forth from the

South. Newt Gingrich of Georgia, Dick Armey of Texas, Trent Lott of Mississippi, Tom Delay of Texas. The South was ascendant in the 1990s with Bill Clinton from Arkansas and Al Gore from Tennessee rounding out a decade in which the Olympics were held in Atlanta, Georgia (1996). For many liberals, the war on the Southern brand of conservatism came to a fever pitch with the 2000 election of George W. Bush from the great state of Texas. The narrowly decided election put the liberal attack machine into overdrive with active measures to delegitimize President Bush every step of the way.[287]

As in past clashes, when external threats have brought national unity, the terrorist attacks of 9/11 slowed the erosion of our national fabric for a time, launching Bush's approval rating to the highest ever recorded in the seventy years of Gallup history, a whopping 90 percent. But the successive wars in Afghanistan and Iraq would deeply polarize the country, resulting in electoral upsets in 2006. The cratering economy would continue the Democratic landslides and in 2008, on the eve of Barack Obama's historic election, George W. Bush had the lowest approval rating of any president in history. Just 20 percent of Americans approved of the job he was doing.

How did a president who engendered the highest approval leave office with the lowest and what role did the liberal media play in this reversal?[288] I survived and was scarred by the media's effort to destroy support for the Iraq War and I know firsthand how actively the Left sought to turn the war against the president. But the real roots go back deeper. One hundred years deeper, at least.

The conflict between the Progressive "Gramscian" worldview that seeks to upend existing culture and the Traditionalists that seek to adhere to the model described by de Tocqueville was frightfully articulated by John Fonte, Senior Fellow and Director of the Center for American Common Culture at the Hudson Institute. Fonte describes the stakes in the conflict as "no less than what kind of country the United States will be in decades to come."[289]

Gramsci recognized that Marx's ideal of revolution could not happen unless the existing culture was "delegitimized" and a "new system of values" was created. Fonte goes on to detail Gramsci's theory that, "values permeate all spheres of civil society—schools, churches, the media, voluntary associations—civil society itself,

[Gramsci] argued, is the great battleground in the struggle for hegemony, the 'war of position.'" Fonte concludes that, "private life, the work place, religion, philosophy, art, and literature, and civil society, in general, are contested battlegrounds in the struggle to achieve societal transformation" and that the only thing stopping the "progressive" conquest of Gramsci's ideologies are those born of the traditional or founding culture. Thus the criticality of controlling the cultural and learning institutions and in turn the history books one page at a time.[290]

ALISTAIR COOKE

Alistair Cooke's *America* was the first #1 *New York Times* bestselling American history book since World War Two and ultimately sold more than 2 million copies. Taxpayer supported Public Broadcasting System (PBS) television put Cooke's version of history into millions more homes. Cooke even addressed the United States Congress as part of a 1976 bicentennial celebration.

Curiously missing from his book, TV show, and address, was the role of the South in the War for Independence. There is no mention of Southern valor and contribution at all. In fact, Cooke jumps from Saratoga in 1777 to the victory at Yorktown in 1781. Four years of hard fighting and the historical contributions of the South are cast into oblivion. Was it an accident? Or did it reflect the liberal sentiments of the 1970s?[291]

The strongest evidence of Cooke's outright bias, other than the facts of the historical record so clearly documented by the British in the 1780s, and put forth here in Exhibits A and B, comes from fellow best-selling British author Winston Churchill. The contributions of the South are explored with great detail, vigor, and admiration in Churchill's *History of the English Speaking People* (1957)[292]. And we established that lesser known British authors like Michael Pearson were writing heartily about the South in 1972. Editorial space was not an issue as Cooke devotes ninety pages to pre-Revolution colonization. Cooke knew the facts because his countrymen, peers, and predecessors, laying them out clearly, yet Cooke chose to omit them.[293]

KEN BURNS

Alistair Cooke protégé Ken Burns would likewise enjoy commercial success with selective editing at taxpayer expense. Burns's PBS series *Civil War* with a book/TV tie-in would repeat Alistair Cooke's #1 best-selling performance with a sweeping version of American history. Burns, who once gave a speech titled "Why I am a Yellow Dog Democrat," has given over $75,000 dollars to liberal groups or candidates like John Kerry and Barack Obama.

When not a "regular contributor" to Keith Olbermann's *Countdown* program on MSNBC with fellow Leftist Michael Moore, Burns was collaborating with another one of America's best-selling "history" authors, David McCullough, for several taxpayer-supported PBS projects including Burns's version of the Civil War which McCullough agreed to narrate.[294]

You might spot the trend here since David McCullough who, like Alistair Cooke, hosted a show on PBS for over a decade, joined Burns and Moore in contributing the maximum level allowed by federal law to Barrack Obama in 2008. PBS, The Public Broadcasting Service, itself is a contributor to Bill and Hillary Clinton's Clinton Foundation according to a 2015 Politico report. Other media entities Politico identified as contributors to the Clintons include: NewsMax, Thomson (Reuters News Service), Google, Twitter, News Corporation Foundation (Fox News), Houghton Mifflin Harcourt (publisher), Bloomberg Philanthropies, Bloomberg LP, Discovery Communications, AOL, HBO, Viacom, NBC Universal (parent of NBC, MSNBC, and CNBC), Time Warner (CNN owner), Turner Broadcasting (CNN pParent), Hollywood Foreign Press Association, Public Radio International, The Washington Post, Huffington Post, Hearst Corporation, Howard Stringer (Former CBS, CBS News and Sony Executive) and ABC News anchor George Stephanopoulos.[295]

DAVID MCCULLOUGH

In March 2008, David McCullough told Charlie Rose on a PBS interview that, "we don't spend enough [time] in seeing the connectedness of each individual to the people who influence them." Prescient, given McCullough's work for President Jimmy Carter.

In 1977, McCullough wrote a book on the Panama Canal, *The Path Between the Seas*, that President Jimmy Carter credited with getting his transfer of ownership and control of the Canal through the U.S. Senate. President Carter used McCullough's book extensively, and McCullough himself lobbied lawmakers on behalf of President Carter's agenda.

More important than McCullough's personal history of supporting liberal causes are his intentional omissions of the historical record. Specifically, McCullough's two #1 *New York Times* bestsellers, *1776* and *John Adams*, both sold millions of copies, and both omit or downplay the importance of the South in the Revolutionary War, even in the context of the narrow subject matter of their titles' focus.

McCullough's *1776* omits an important action of that year that stimulated North Carolina to press for independence: the Battle of Moores Creek Bridge. Also, he only gives a passing nod to the British defeat at Charleston (Sullivan's Island), without any of the valor of that battle nor the significance of the British abandoning the South for years and then their subsequent defeat there when they returned. Nine British warships, which significantly outgunned the Fort's defenders, were damaged and or destroyed in the attack on Sullivan's Island. There were more than one hundred combined casualties and a number of ruined vessels from the world's greatest navy, but the Palmetto fort held. McCullough offers not a single mention of Moores Creek, and only three sentences on Charleston in a 370-page book.

In *John Adams*, again the coverage of the South is lopsided. The southern delegates are caricatures, and the urgency for independence born of the Halifax Resolves, which were a consequence of the Battle of Moores Creek Bridge, goes unmentioned. With the Halifax Resolves, North Carolina was one of the first states to declare independence, but you wouldn't have gathered that from watching the

9-hour mini-series produced by Tom Hanks. A Northeastern bias is understandable in a story of war viewed through the eyes of one New Englander, written by a fellow New Englander (McCullough), but the letters of Adams and his wife in 1781 reflect an awareness of the South's contribution that the book and subsequent HBO series do not.

To My Dearest Friend (Abigail), Amsterdam, 2 Dec, 1781:
General Washington has done me great honor and much public service by sending me authentic accounts of his own and General Greene's last great actions. They are on the way to negotiate peace. It lies wholly with them. No other ministers but they and their colleagues in the army can accomplish the great event . . . [296]

To My Dearest Friend (Abigail), Amsterdam, 18 Dec, 1781:
I fancy the Southern States will hold their heads very high. They have a right. They will scarcely be overrun again, I believe, even in the hasty manner of Cornwallis. (Adams knew of Gen. Greene's activities in the South. (See 2 Dec. letter, above)[297]

Perhaps a defense can be made that McCullough was taking poetic license to focus his narrative, which is understandable. But a troubling fact remains, even for a selective editor: In 1781, John and Abigail Adams had very little correspondence, and what they did have, as presented above, mentioned the South. Abigail Adams actually complains to John about this lack of correspondence in 1781. "I know you must have written many times since I had the pleasure of a receiving a line from you, for this month completes a year since the date of your last letter," she wrote in May of 1781. She wouldn't get a response back from John until December and his only two letters to her in the year of the British defeat at Yorktown (1781) both refer to the South (above).[298]

JOSEPH ELLIS

If McCullough's flexibility with the truth can be forgiven, that of his friend and fellow Massachusetts professor Joseph Ellis cannot. It is one thing to plagiarize from another writer because they write better, or you are lazy or maybe just make a mistake, like Steven Ambrose and Doris Kearns Goodwin have admitted to doing.[299] But how should the public, the press and academia respond when a supposed historian is exposed as a serial liar? How much credibility should be afforded someone who not only distorts events, but even worse, deliberately fabricates events that never even happened?[300]

Yet another contemporary pop historian has been caught lying, in this case about serving in the Vietnam war. The lies about his fabricated service did not cost him his job, nor hurt his standing in the liberal press. *The New York Times* waited just two years after it discovered Joseph Ellis was a liar before it started rehabilitating Ellis's reputation by featuring his book reviews.[301]

Leftists clamored to defend Ellis, a professor who for decades spun a web of lies to his students. Looking young women and men deeply in the eyes, Ellis would recount the horrors of war. A war he never saw, and some suggest he took pains to avoid. Fellow historian David Garrow attacked hard: "Ellis's confession that he has larded his classes about the Vietnam war with fraudulent falsehood about his own utterly spurious military service there ought to preclude Ellis from ever again taking the podium in a college classroom."[302]

"So he lied! Foolish thing to do, but his work holds up anyway," said *The New York Times*.[303] A flip dismissal for a far reaching author who the *Washington Post* described as, "doubtless (Ellis) is now the most widely read scholar of the Revolutionary period, and thus probably the most influential as well." His books are largely about the Revolutionary period and founders such as George Washington, John and Abigail Adams, and Thomas Jefferson.[304]

In the wake of the lying scandal discovered by *The Boston Globe* while researching Ellis's 2001 Pulitzer prize win, not a single mainstream media report connected Professor Ellis with commentary he provided on behalf of beleaguered President Bill Clinton in 1998. Was he lying then?

It was the height of the Lewinsky imbroglio and a DNA study had erroneously suggested that Thomas Jefferson had in fact fathered children with one of his slaves. The report was retracted weeks later with no fanfare, but the damage to Thomas Jefferson's legacy was permanent. So was the smoke screen for Bill Clinton. Professor Joseph Ellis, who had penned a Jefferson biography several years prior and at the time suggested it "highly unlikely" that Jefferson fathered the slave's child, was now changing his tune when it was politically expedient.[305]

In short, Ellis sold out his "impartial" scholarship in order to provide cover for a philandering president with a defense that there was indeed a historical precedent of "great men" with weak self-restraint.

Today, having shredded the professional academic standard of objectivity, Ellis flaunts his partisanship. His professor profile page at Mount Holy Oakes celebrates his anti-TEA Party, anti-Bush, and pro-Obama editorials. "*The teaching side of my life and the writing side of my life are part of the same collective whole,*" he admitted. Ellis was instrumental in his college employer hiring fellow liberal Anthony Lake, a Clinton appointee who is also an Alger Hiss apologist.[306]

The pattern of Ellis's lies are instructive about the things the professor finds worthy of opposing. In the case of Vietnam, he was against the war, and so he lied about his credentials to embellish his position as an objector "with medals." In the case of the South, he exaggerated his role as a Freedom Rider, in order to embellish his role in the Civil Rights struggles, leaving one to conclude that he saw the South as he saw Vietnam: a morally repugnant battlefield.[307]

Ellis's deliberate omissions of Southern battles and the importance of the South in America's victory in the revolution, while simultaneously focusing almost exclusively on the Southern culpability for the national stain of slavery, demonstrate a bias that has shortchanged his readers and painted an inaccurate and unrealistic view of history. Later, we will explore the impact of Ellis's overemphasis on Washington's army of continentals as compared to his delegitimizing of partisan militia.[308]

For proponents of gun control, this false narrative of a rebel "Army" works to undermine the intent of "well armed citizenry," able to band together for their defense, as they did at King's Mountain, a battle Ellis's books fail to acknowledge. But what can be expected from a professor who claimed to score the winning touchdown on his football team, when he never played football?[309]

Ellis's efforts at historical revisionism have not gone entirely unchallenged. David Barton, the founder and president of WallBuilders, has written *The Jefferson Lies* in defense of the third president's character.

WallBuilders is a "national pro-family organization that presents America's forgotten history and heroes, with an emphasis on America's moral, religious and constitutional heritage." In a methodical and well-researched narrative, David Barton strips away the fabrications and the agendas behind the attacks on America's founding history and exposes the perpetrators and their motivations. Barton reveals one of the first and most persistent defamers of Jefferson and his character is the liberal Democrat UCLA professor Fawn Brodie.[310]

FAWN BRODIE

The scandalous *Thomas Jefferson: An intimate History* was not Fawn Brodie's first book, but it catapulted her to fame. To one historian, disdainful of Brodie's runaway speculation on the former president's sex life, the book "strives to picture Jefferson as a secret swinger." In the wake of Watergate and the revelations of FDR's and JFK's mistresses the public appetite for scandal was stoked. *An Intimate History* was called "the most controversial life story of the year" (1974). [311]

If Brodie's theories of Jefferson's serial infidelity were controversial, her methodology was more so. Brodie incorporated techniques of a Freudian "psychohistory" in which she analyzed the writings of her subjects and juxtaposed her own experiences. In the case of Jefferson, the Brodie family's personal misfortune proves ruinous for the late president. Just years before she wrote the book on Jefferson's alleged affairs, Brodie learned of her own husband's infidelity, which would not be worth mentioning if her method of historical interpretation had not drawn so openly on her own personal experiences, and her history of Jefferson wasn't so keenly focused on his libido.[312]

Fawn Brodie's tragic past would influence her writings in other ways. Brodie was raised as a Mormon in the Church of Latter Day Saints (LDS). She left the church in college and became an atheist and would later write a book attempting to debunk her family's faith. Brodie's mother tried three times to kill herself and ultimately succeeded by burning herself alive. But the time prior, her second attempt, Brodie's mother stabbed herself with a crucifix. Whether her views of faith influenced the secular projections she would put on her subjects, one thing is certain: her rebellion against her past influenced her work and her feelings about the South.

"Like other Mormon kids I had been taught that Reconstruction was a brutal period of revenge on the South . . . " Brodie's quest to debunk her own education led her to develop a new theory of reconstruction by rehabilitating the historical villains, the radical Republicans, and demonizing the Southerners. Channeling psychohistory, she projected her thoughts into the minds of her heroes, and also the villains, as the South would become.[313]

In 1959 she wrote *Thaddeus Stevens: Scourge of the South* which was among the first efforts at liberal revisionist history of Reconstruction, the decade-long phase of occupation after the Civil War.[314] In a book of essays on slavery where her work appeared with Howard Zinn, Brodie lamented that: "The reputation of abolitionists . . . has suffered also by their being warmly embraced in recent times by the American Communists, who heralded them as forerunners of the Second American Revolution. The resulting damage by association has been deadly."[315]

CROOKS & CRONIES:
The Ivory Tower is Really Red

How the history of the American Revolution has been stolen has much to do with the transition of the Old Left to the New Left and how communist subversives undermined the legitimate champions of the civil rights movement and co-opted a youth culture with ideas of radicalism that were bought and paid for by agents out of Moscow, not in an effort to enhance or improve American society, but to destroy it. We will consider how non-violence morphed into open rebellion and rioting in the 60s and the 70s in the fight for civil rights and against the Vietnam War with the deployment of federal troops, which happened again during the Los Angeles riots in 1992, bombings, assassinations, and a capitol literally set aflame.[316]

"ACID, AMNESTY, ABORTION!" went the chants of the 1970s.[317] Where have these bomb throwers and rabble-rousers gone? They now teach your children. As former leftist leader and campus radical, Todd Gitlin, gloated: "we may have lost some elections but we won the textbooks."[318] The Marxist war on the Southern culture and history may play out across media and best sellers, but the intellectual heft to power the movement, and the critical and academic top-cover to avoid sales crushing criticisms or professional embarrassment at being exposed as a fraud is provided by the academics: the "Ivory Tower" radicals.

"Mounts a clarion Defense of the Principles of Marxism"
—*Los Angeles Times*, Review of Howard Zinn's
Marx in Soho[319]

HOWARD ZINN

No more vivid example of the "Gramscian" mode in popular American culture exists than a *New York Times* columnist lamenting the 2010 passing of Zinn. Bob Herbert was winking to the liberal yet decidedly influential readership of the paper in choosing this passage from Zinn's *A People's History of the United States* guessing most of his audience would know it by heart:

> If you look through high school textbooks and elementary school textbooks in American history, you will find (Andrew) Jackson the frontiersman, soldier, democrat, man of the people—*not Jackson the slaveholder, land speculator, executioner of dissident soldiers, exterminator of Indians.*[320]

Does having an FBI file make you a more credible historian to the left?

In the case of Howard Zinn it would seem so.

FBI File No. 100-360217 has translated into sales of more than 2,000,000 copies since the first publication in 1980 of *A People's History of the United States.*[321]

When Zinn wasn't attending Communist Party meetings "five nights a week," as he claimed, Zinn was teaching classes on communism in the early 1950s, marching to boycott removal of Russian missiles from Cuba in 1962 or visiting Ho Chi Minh in Vietnam in 1969.[322]

Claiming to be "Something of an anarchist. Something of a socialist, "Zinn has also proven to be a writer with an impact. It is estimated that his sales continue at over 100,000 volumes a year, giving his books more reach into college and high school classrooms than any other history text.

Besides his obvious revulsion of the South, which he called "the most terrible place in the world" in his first book, *The Southern Mystique* (1959), Zinn also has a palpable disdain for America and its founders, which he is transmitting to young readers. *A People's History* starts by decrying Columbus as a murderer and goes on to claim that the founding fathers agitated for war to distract people from their own economic problems and stop popular movements, a strategy he claims the country's leaders would use in the future. In the process, Zinn completely ignores the role and nature of the South in the Revolutionary War.[323]

> "The generation of the Sixties started out with its "discoveries" about the tragedy of the Vietnam War and the deficiencies of America in general. From that dramatic moment, when ideals clashed hard against reality, the generation proceeded to its analysis of the causes of things, and as the Sixties New Left evolved into the Academic Left, it began to hand down to a subsequent generation its delusions about the meaning of America and the nature of history, delusions for which there seems to be no means of correction."
>
> —John Patrick Diggins,
> the National Interest, September 1, 2002[324]

BREEDING GROUND

The radicalization of our nation's colleges is a well-trod turf. William Buckley's *God and Man at Yale* ignited the modern conservative movement when he questioned the marginalization of faith on campus in 1950. Buckley paved the way for contemporary luminaries like David Horowitz and Dinesh D'Souza. Horowitz, himself a former 60's radical and self-proclaimed "red diaper baby" offers a particularly trenchant look at the communist machinations of the '60s campus organizations that were far from benign vehicles of student self-expression, but were in fact actively fomenting revolutionary violence. Horowitz's books and website, www.discoverthenetworks.org, are invaluable tools for culture warriors.[325]

According to Milton Friedman, FDR drew most of the brain trust for the New Deal from Columbia University.[326] LBJ did too. It's where Whitaker Chambers was radicalized and it was home to Frances Fox Piven and Richard Cloward.[327] Their infamous "Cloward and Piven" strategy to topple the federal government by flooding the welfare rolls in order to trigger massive wealth redistribution became the backbone of LBJ's War on Poverty.[328] Community organizer adherents of their strategy have helped the Left grow a $20 trillion dollar entitlement machine that has cost the nation three times more than all of its real wars combined, from the Revolution to Afghanistan.[329] It's also worth noting that Professors Cloward and Piven engineered the same welfare surge in New York City which led to its bankruptcy in 1975.[330]

Columbia University, a hot bed of radicalism for almost 100 years[331]—enough to fill its own volume—recently hired left wing terrorist Kathy Boudin, after she served twenty-two years for the murder of two police officers.[332] Boudin was a member of the Black Panthers, a group that Eric Holder's Justice Department refused to investigate.

Like the Communist Party and the ACLU, the Leftist movement began as a largely Northeastern liberal phenomenon centered around "cosmopolitan" intellectuals in New York City and Columbia University. It is safe to say Columbia has turned out more radicals, anarchists, and communists than any other single American institution.

RICHARD HOFSTADTER

At Columbia University's History Department for example, Richard Hofstadter, himself a communist, replaced a communist and in turn was replaced by communist Eric Foner, who continues to head the Department today. Richard Hofstadter was the guide and arbiter of hundreds of Columbia University's PhDs through the '50s and '60s and his peers at the university were none other than Frances Fox Piven and Richard Cloward. His acolytes, none other than Howard Zinn and Eric Foner.

Hofstadter's early work on Social Darwinism highlighted the problem of "dog-eat-dog" economics that Ayn Rand would mock ten years later. Hofstadter had a knack for calling conservatives "paranoid" in his breezy literary style, which was always long on prose and short on footnotes. Consider this charge of conservative paranoia from a communist academic, one of a series of communist deans

CLOSING ARGUMENT: CROOKS & CRONIES / THE IVORY TOWER . . . ■ 177

at Columbia University graduate schools. "America has been largely taken away from them and their kind, though they are determined to try to repossess it and to prevent the final destructive act of subversion. The old American virtues have already been eaten away by cosmopolitans and intellectuals; the old competitive capitalism has been gradually undermined by socialistic and communistic schemers," wrote Hofstadter.[333]

As the saying goes: Just because you're paranoid it doesn't mean they're not out to get you.

The distinctly anti-Southern bias of the Columbia communists was shared by Karl Marx and is recorded in his congratulatory correspondence to Abraham Lincoln. That is not hyperbole.[334] Marxist Labor historians have dominated the study of Southern history. Before Eric Foner, who replaced Hofstadter and now sits atop the perch of academic preeminence, was another Columbia Marxist PhD named Eugene Genovese.[335]

EUGENE GENOVESE

Like Foner and Zinn, Eugene Genovese studied under Hofstadter and was an open communist. In fact, Genovese became the first openly Marxist President of the Organization of American Historians and his book *Roll Jordan Roll: the World the Slaves Made (1974)* established Genovese as the lead thinker on Southern history for decades. That is, until he found Jesus, and his academic star faded.[336]

When Genovese had a spiritual awakening and embraced Jesus Christ, he naturally dropped the atheist ideology of the left and in turn was "excommunicated" from the club of media and academic elites that shill each other's work on air and in print and assure tenured positions at universities around the country. The shame is that Genovese continued to produce important work on the South, but his audience was accordingly decimated as he became a dreaded "conservative."

Many of Genovese's detractors, and the critics that will attack my position, would benefit from his wisdom on the South. In *The Southern Tradition (1993)* Genovese, a native New Yorker, reformed Communist, and born again Southerner, writes:

Those of us who spent our lives in a political (leftist) movement that piled up tens of millions of corpses to sustain its futile cause and hideous political regimes have a few questions to answer . . . [337]

Consider these next passages from a professor and educator trained as a Marxist at Columbia, who broke free of that mindset and would become a professor at a number of colleges in Georgia:

The Northern Victory in 1865 silenced a discretely southern interpretation of American History and National identity, and it promoted a contemptuous dismissal of all things Southern as nasty, racist, immoral and intellectually inferior. . . Rarely these days, even on southern campuses, is it possible to acknowledge the achievements of the white people of the South . . .

We are witnessing a cultural and political atrocity-an increasingly stressful campaign by the media and academic elite to strip young white Southerners, and arguably black Southerners as well, of their heritage, and therefore, their identity . . . [338]

ERIC FONER

Howard Zinn was praised by Eric Foner: "The idea that historians have to be neutral about everything is the death of history. Every historian has beliefs and feelings about what they're studying. Howard made them very explicit."[339]

With that invitation we will take a closer look at the beliefs and feelings of the current Dean of the History Department at Columbia University. Who is the man that bestows a coveted "doctorate in history" from a prestigious university to those seeking to publish and teach future generations American history?

"Eric Foner of Columbia University is one of our nation's most acclaimed historians . . . *He is also one of the foremost exponents of what has become known as "radical history":* the euphemism of choice for Marxist and neo-Marxist historians who seek to overturn the old mainstream political history."

—Ronald Radosh, *The National Review*, 2002[340]

Some have called Eric Foner "the most professionally successful academic historian of our time." So if you haven't heard of him, it doesn't mean he hasn't been busy shaping the national debate on the South, Slavery, Affirmative Action, and recently, restitution payments to former slaves. Foner's work reenvisions Reconstruction to fit a Marxist narrative while omitting credible evidence of contrarian views in order to advance his agenda and denigrate the South.[341]

"Foner's vision of American history comports with the political correctness favored by the left today—indeed at times he seems less interested in Reconstruction than in reconstructing latter day American Society, " according to Paul Gottfried, writing for *the American Conservative*.[342]

Foner winks and taunts when he acknowledges that "the context within which a historian lives and writes affects his choice of subject and approach to the past." He begins a collection of essays with one titled "My life as a Historian," in which he seeks to put his own work in the context of his political and personal life according to a review of Foner's book, *Who owns History? Rethinking the Past in a changing World*.[343]

But does this make his history suspect? Not necessarily.

It is Foner's politically loaded reinterpretation of history that makes his history suspect. My research of his work on the post-Civil War period of Reconstruction (1865-77) has turned up a number of instances where, like his idol Howard Zinn, Foner has either minimized or omitted sources critical in contextualizing the period in order to achieve his political objectives. I have obtained original hundred-year-old volumes Foner has noted as sources in his work and his selective editing is significant.[344] But given our focus on the Revolutionary War, let us be satisfied that as a "thought leader" in the space of Southern History, Foner is very much a co-conspirator in fostering an atmosphere of academic hostility towards the South, at Columbia and beyond.

"Liberal America it seems must remain forever corrupted by slavery while Bolshevik Russia remains even in the historical past tense, forever free of Tyranny. Foner . . . is both an unabashed apologist for the Soviet system and an unforgiving historian of America."

—John Patrick Diggins, *the National Interest,*
September, 2002[345]

THE FONER FAMILY TIES

Since Professor Eric Foner attributes much to his familial influences, so will I.

Professor Foner's father and three uncles all lost their jobs in the New York educational system "as a result of an investigation into Communist activity at the City Colleges, according to a *New York Times* obituary (1994). Professor Foner's uncle, Philip Foner, was called an "eminent Marxist labor historian" by the *Times*, and they should know one when they see one.[346]

Philip Foner's books were published by International Publishers, the propaganda arm of the Communist Party USA. International Publishers was started with Soviet seed money. Its leadership was actively connected to Soviet subversion operations as has been established in House Committee hearings as well as the Venona decrypts (captured Soviet communiqués declassified in 1995. More on that shortly). Uncle Philip Foner's books are still available on the International Publishers catalog. To this day Philip Foner's work represents the bulk of material (eighteen titles) sold by this communist outlet based on 23rd Street in New York City.[347]

The only author that International Publishers carries more works from is Karl Marx. Between Marx and Foner they represent 50 percent of the entire offering of the Soviet front operation's propaganda. See for yourself at their website, www.intpubnyc.com, where the home page will direct you to the Communist Party USA, and even better, the Young Communist League USA.

Eric Foner's uncle, Moe Foner, was a communist who was forced out of one Union in 1951 for his communism and quickly joined another where he enlisted Rev. Dr. Martin Luther King in the fight to unionize hospital workers. According to *The New York Times*, "In the late 1960s, he became a key leader in rallying union opposition against the Vietnam War."[348]

Professor Foner's other uncle, Henry Foner, fought in WWII. In 1961, Henry became president of the Fur Dressers and Dryers union, and held that position for twenty-seven years. According to his official biography "[Henry Foner] helped to involve that union in a wide range of social issues, including the struggle for civil rights, helping to mobilize other unions in opposition to the war in Vietnam and joining the early efforts to achieve universal healthcare coverage." These activities continue to be mainstays of Democratic political efforts championed by Hillary Clinton and later Barack Obama.[349]

> "We cannot build a mass communist Party unless we use one of our best weapons—Literature. We cannot reach the masses in America without agitational and propaganda literature of our party."
>
> —Alex Trachtenberg, Soviet operative and
> publisher of Philip Foner[350]

FONER FAMILY AND THE KGB

Brace yourself, because this next discussion will feel surreal, but the pitch and fever of my critics will confirm its veracity. All of these accusations of Marxism and communist connections are substantiated well beyond articles and website book sales. They are part of the historical record of the Cold War in which foreign governments were actively working to undermine the culture and government of the United States. A war that through proxies turned hot in a number of flashpoints, most notably the Korean and Vietnam Wars. Overseas the bullets flew while agents here in America did the methodical work of undermining cultural institutions.

This is not hyperbole. Rather, it is the unpopular acknowledgement of an issue that continues to be politically contentious because the old

Left has metamorphosed into the new Left and now wields influence through the Democratic party, academia, and the media. Soviet front groups, the Foner family, spies like Alger Hiss and the Rosenbergs, or even the communist connection to the ACLU are real and only the tip of the iceberg. Their collective influence on our culture and educational system cannot be overlooked so we will do one last deep dive to authenticate this foreign influence hurting our country.

International Publishers, the publisher and current distributor of Philip Foner's books, was founded and run by Alexander Trachtenberg who Whittaker Chambers, himself a reformed spy, called "the party's cultural commissar," and a member of the "Central Control Commission" that orchestrated Chamber's membership to the Communist party. The 1949 Annual Report of the Committee of Un-American Activities labeled Trachtenberg as the "leading official of the communist party of the United States."[351]

Alexander Trachtenberg associate Rudy Baker ran the "secret apparatus" for the Communist Party USA from 1938 to the end of WWII at which point he slipped out of the county and disappeared. Baker operated under a number of aliases, and one of his tasks was "to ensure communications with the Soviet Union." Baker ran operatives and a covert short wave radio network with links from Canada to Latin America. The decrypted code word for these radio operations was "Automobile."

Rudy Baker communicated with Moscow using microdots. One communiqué with the "Comintern"* read: "Letters in future examine all envelopes, some of them will have micro under flaps or postage stamps." As John Earl Haynes and Harvey Klehr intricately detail in *Venona: Decoding Secret Espionage in America.* Haynes and Klehr have researched this era exhaustively and their texts are building blocks of counterintelligence professional education to this day. Haynes and Klehr even traveled to Russia during the brief post-Cold War window when Russian authorities made the formerly classified

---

* "Comintern" is an abbreviation of the Communist International whose goal was to use "all available means, including armed force, for the overthrow of the international bourgeoisie and for the creation of an international Soviet republic as a transition stage to the complete abolition of the State."

KGB files accessible to scholars. In many cases their sources are the former Soviet spymasters themselves.[352]

"Moscow absorbed a significant share of the cost of the Communist Party USA's secret apparatus," and sent thousands of dollars in cash mail drops. In 1941 alone, Haynes and Klehr note, "$35,000 had gone to Alexander Trachtenberg, head of International Publishers ($600,000 in 2013 dollars)."

The same Trachtenberg who received Soviet money in mail drops is also the publisher of Philip Foner's books.

These dots were connected in an important expose by David Lincove, "Radical Publishing to 'Reach the Million Masses': Alexander L. Trachtenberg and International Publishers." Lincove records that during the Communist Party's 10th Anniversary convention in New York, May 1938, Alex Trachtenberg said, "We cannot build a mass communist Party unless we use one of our best weapons—Literature. We cannot reach the masses in America without agitational and propaganda literature of our party."[353]

This same Trachtenberg who published Foner also published Stalin's *History of the Communist Party of the Soviet Union* (Short Course)—a 100,000 copy print run was to be distributed across the country and heavily discounted for youth. Today the Marxists Internet Archive invites you to "freely copy, distribute, display and perform this work; as well as make derivative and commercial works." It appears there are those still eager to spread the message.[354]

The last Stalin books sold by International Publishers were reportedly in the early 1970s. Today, references to Stalin have been scrubbed from the website's inventory and young readers might be forgiven for asking "so, what's the big deal?" But the historical record, where it is still able to shine through, gives us an insight into the true goals of this dark movement.

David Lincove describes a troubling book distributed by International Publisher that was penned in 1934 titled *Religion in the USSR*. Written by E. Yaroslavsky, a leader of the militant atheists, *Religion* argues for the superiority and greater importance of building socialism compared with wasting time on superstition in religion. Unfortunately, this Soviet state-sponsored effort to spread propaganda undermining faith was not an isolated incident.

> "*[Religion] is the opium of the people.* The abolition of re-
> ligion as the illusory happiness of the people is required for
> their real happiness. The demand to give up the illusion about
> its condition is the demand to give up a condition which needs
> illusions."
>
> —Karl Marx, A contribution to the *Critique of Hegel's
> Philosophy of Right*, 1844[355]

ROGER BALDWIN

Alex Trachtenberg was a delegate to the Fourth Congress of the Comintern in Petrograd and Moscow, December 5, 1922. In 1927, the Comintern organized the World Congress Against Colonial Oppression
and Imperialism in Brussels, Feb. 10-15, 1927. Massachusetts born
and Harvard educated, Roger Baldwin attended that Congress.

Roger Baldwin traveled to Moscow several months later in June
of 1927. While in the Soviet Union, Baldwin was inspired to write a
virulently anti-American diatribe, that he would do much apologizing
for later in his life: "While the State exists there will be no freedom.
Where there is freedom, there can be no state." Several years later, in
1934, Baldwin wrote, "Freedom in the USA and the USSR."[356]

> The class struggle is the central conflict of the world; all others are
> incidental. When that power of the working class is once achieved,
> as it has been only in the Soviet Union, *I am for maintaining it by
> any means whatever. Dictatorship is the obvious means in a world
> of enemies* at home and abroad. I dislike it in principle as dangerous
> to its own objects. But the Soviet Union has already created liberties
> far greater than exist elsewhere in the world . . . [357]

Roger Baldwin would go on to do much more than attend Comintern events, or merely pen anti-American propaganda while in
the capital of America's existential nemesis. Baldwin would build the
American Civil Liberties Union (ACLU) and in so doing set in motion

the machinery that has been working for almost 100 years to dismantle America from the inside.

Baldwin was its first Executive Director and ran the ACLU until 1950, pioneering the use of American courts to effectively turn the longstanding cultural norms on their head, just as fellow Marxist Antonio Gramsci had envisioned.

In a well-researched work in this space, *Original Intent: The Courts, the Constitution, and Religion,* David Barton details the many abuses over time of our legal system at the hands of the ACLU and their affiliates.

Barton notes that with the advent of judicial activism, Modern courts have struck down many long-standing religious practices and expressions. The attack on the original intent of our founders in framing the Constitution and our rights, often hinges on the expression "Separation of Church and State." Many believe it to be part of the constitution. It is not.[358]

"Separation of Church and State," is language from a legal decision in 1947. According to Barton, the expression of "Separation of Church and State," was used two times in the first 150 years of our founding, but in the past decades has been used (and abused) literally thousands of times. State and local officials, often pushed and prodded by the ACLU, have gone even farther.

"In Minnesota, a state employee was barred from parking his car in the state parking lot because he had a religious sticker on his bumper," according to Barton. It is tragically ironic that President Jimmy Carter, a former preacher, awarded the Presidential Medal of Freedom to Baldwin in 1981.[359]

CROOKS & CRONIES:
ACLU, from Tennessee to Hollywood

I n order to truly tear down our society, or more aptly destroy it from within, the Left must kill God. They have waged a war on faith and the common culture that at one time had defined Americans with shared hopes, dreams and heroes. As Pat Buchanan warned, "When the faith dies the culture dies. When the culture dies the people die."[360] Rates of atheism accelerate and we wonder why suicide has overtaken car accidents as the number one cause of death by injury, according to the Centers for Disease Control and Prevention.[361]

More veterans kill themselves than die in combat, and politicians act surprised after we have chased God out of the classroom, the courtroom, and the foxhole. One place where that "old time religion" retains the strongest grip is in the South, which is another reason the cultural Marxists have been pointing their guns at the Bible Belt for hundreds of years. Today the Left tells us that Christianity and adhering to biblical values is tantamount to hate speech, as the tyranny of "tolerance" is the new vogue. The South was being attacked for its faith before it was cool.[362]

The fabricated spectacle of the 1925 Scopes Trial was bought and paid for by the ACLU, a decidedly atheist and anti-American union, with the goal of subverting Christianity in America.[363] When the ACLU wasn't defending communist bombers trying to trigger the American chapter of the global workers revolution, they were running ads in the Tennessee newspapers seeking a plaintiff to help them overturn Tennessee state law.[364]

The ACLU's real goal was to attack faith all the way to the Supreme Court, and while the case helped them raise "enormous sums" of money from Northeastern liberals eager to upset the cultural norms and laws of Tennessee, the case itself was bogus.[365]

John T. Scopes, the defendant, was a substitute gym teacher who later admitted he had never even taught evolution, as the sham case alleged. My great aunt, Blanche C. Gregory, was the literary agent for his post-trial tell-all. I have a signed copy of Scopes's "confession."

But at the time, it was the trial of the century. Hundreds of thousands of words were beamed around the world on newly wired telegraph lines and radio waves. Noted defense attorney and atheist Clarence Darrow represented Scopes for the ACLU, and three-time presidential candidate and evangelical leader William Jennings Bryan represented the State of Tennessee in the landmark case in which the Holy Bible was literally put on trial.[366]

The ACLU didn't just create the case and then provide attorneys. They outfitted a mansion in Dayton for press and "experts" to give interviews despite being banned from testifying. The ACLU was running a full-fledged press campaign in their effort to debunk Christianity. In the 1920s fundamentalist Christianity was on the rise, in response to industrialization, urbanization and Darwinism. The Scopes trial laid those differences bare. And new technological developments conspired to assist the ACLU's efforts.

I was exposed to the play supposedly based on the trial, when I was in the seventh grade at the Horace Mann School in Riverdale New York. My teacher was a kind and compassionate man who had a bit of '60s activism still coursing his veins. When, in the height of the 1980s Cold War, he taught our class that the Rosenbergs were innocent of atomic espionage for Stalin, how could we as young children not believe him? We were convinced by this earnest liberal that the Rosenbergs had been scapegoated during the Red Scare.[367]

When my teacher used the play *Inherit the Wind* to teach a classroom full of lily-white New York children of privilege—with a few "scholarship" (financial aid) cases mixed in—that the South was bigoted, of course we believed him. Who were we as thirteen-year-olds to challenge our textbooks? These were characters in a play, and later a film, but they were based on a true story right? The preacher who condemns his daughter to hell just because she loved Scopes, that really happened, didn't it? It sure was shocking. Thirty years after being exposed to *Inherit the Wind*, I remember how it made me feel, and how it caused me to doubt my faith for many, many years. Mission Accomplished, Roger Baldwin.[368]

It didn't matter that what the teacher taught us was wrong, had never happened, or were complete fabrications. There was no retraction of the searing impressions of religious bigotry that the play and film conveyed, despite being fabricated out of whole cloth, just like the case. There was no mention for example that the playwrights, with personal biases of their own, were using a court case from the 1920s to fight a battle for social justice against conservatism in the 1950s.[369]

My old teacher no longer works in the classroom. He has been promoted to running an entire school division.

By the time Hollywood got in on the act, there was very little semblance left of the actual case, but plenty of innuendo and condemnation of the Southern people. The 1960 film *Inherit the Wind* was nominated for four Academy Awards and continues to be widely seen. I caught it on cable just a few months ago. After the Hollywood treatment, the movie is even more overtly liberal (and more inaccurate) than the play. But you wouldn't guess that from the promo: "Based on a real-life case in 1925, two great lawyers argue the case for and against a science teacher accused of the crime of teaching evolution."

The atheist reporter/narrator was a composite of real life atheist H.L. Mencken. He had some pithy one-liners, "Be kind to bigots week" or the "bible beating bunko artists," and naturally gets the last word. He was the same H.L. Mencken who described the South as, "the bunghole of the United States, a cesspool of Baptists . . . ", whose magazine, the *American Mercury*, launched self-loathing southerner W.J. Cash.[370]

W.J. Cash's searing *Mind of the South* is conveniently referenced as the de facto window into the Southern consciousness by authors, professors, and critics of the South looking for low hanging fruit. While Cash's writing is crisp, not enough effort is made by users of this resource to understand Cash's identity crisis or inherent biases.[371] Some have even alleged that Cash killed himself out of guilt for turning on his southern homeland. Elements of anti-southern guilt or shame are evidenced by many other southern literary and academic figures from William Faulkner and Tennessee Williams, who both drank themselves to death, to Southern university faculty who have trended more and more liberal and anti-South.[372] For example, University of North Carolina at Chapel Hill Professor Don Higginbotham has written the only book on the American Revolution that is on the U.S. Military Academy (West Point) reading list. Higginbotham's *The War of American Independence* is subtly anti-Southern and does not accurately reflect the role or import of Southern partisan activities.[373] While there can be no doubt about the readability of these anti-Southern works, it is also true that there has not been any room afforded to writers or historians with a more pro-Southern point of view.

HOLLYWOOD

The Marxist tradition in Hollywood is loud and proud, and by all accounts is still thriving. Consider the way forces have conspired to portray the South in popular culture from *Smokey and the Bandit*, to *The Dukes of Hazzard*, to the Bible-quoting sniper played by Barry Pepper in Steven Spielberg's *Saving Private Ryan*. Or for a different generation, *Deliverance* and *Cool Hand Luke*.

"What we've got here is a failure to communicate . . . "

Howard Zinn's infamous *People's History* has been made into a film that, like *Inherit the Wind*, makes its way into thousands of classrooms across the country. The Zinn film, *The People Speak*, was executive produced and narrated by Matt Damon, a long time Zinn fan who even went so far as to feature Zinn's book in the movie he co-wrote with Ben Affleck, *Goodwill Hunting* (1997). Other notable Hollywood liberals such as Morgan Freeman, Danny Glover, and Hugo Chavez embracing anti-American Sean Penn give credence to Zinn's *History*. Sadly, *The People Speak* has aired on the History channel, leaving uninformed viewers to assume it is credible.[374]

Abraham Lincoln: Vampire Hunter is a 2012 film produced by Tim Burton. It blames the Civil War on the premise that Vampires were Southerners. Leaving aside for the moment the inherently anti-Christian messaging of the vampire genre, let's focus on the anti-Southern regionalism. President Lincoln is forced to melt down the silverware in the White House for silver bullets in order to defeat the army of vampires that is the confederacy. In one more stab at Southern traditions of Christianity, the lead vampire character is named, "Adam, the first."[375]

Lincoln, the film adaptation of Doris Kearns Goodwin's book, was directed by Steven Spielberg, just in time to commemorate the 150th Anniversary of the Civil War. The screenplay introducing America to President Abraham Lincoln was written by Tony Kushner. Kushner's previous claim to fame is his smash hit play *Angels in America: A Gay Fantasia on National Themes*. In Kushner's play, executed Soviet atomic bomb spy Ethel Rosenberg is portrayed as an angel, a literal angel.

While there are myriad anti-Christian themes, I call your attention to Kushner's choice of Rosenberg to demonstrate the recurring battles playing out in the culture war across a number of intellectual terrains. A movie of the play was produced by HBO Films, the same people who brought you the nine-hour McCullough mini-series, *John Adams*.

■

Almost one hundred years after the case, the ACLU achieved its goal as the Scopes Trial continues to leave a wake of false assumptions about the "separation of Church and State." Questions of America's origins as a Christian nation abound as the Left continues to delete references of faith from our founders' pasts. Even a new edition of Alexis de Tocqueville's *Democracy in America* has been selectively scrubbed of his observations on American piety by unscrupulous editors.

The answer to the question "Is nothing sacred?" is clearly no. The Left attempts to define the Constitution, and by extension America, as "Godless." This interpretation glosses over the original intent of our founders as well as the recorded constitutions of the thirteen colonies. Each of the thirteen were deeply religious and their constitutions spoke in great detail about what kinds of believers could or could not hold office.

A Christian God is referenced nineteen separate times in Samuel Adams's 1772 declaration of "The Rights of the Colonists", a precursor to the Declaration of Independence, and yet skeptics like President Obama have the gall to claim America is not a Christian nation?[376] To non-believers this point seems trivial, almost farcical. But to Christians that believe that the Bible is the word of God and that our founders placed their lives, fortune, and sacred honor in the protection of the Providence of a Christian creator, the very act of watching the continued stripping of our Christian heritage out of the national fabric is deeply sickening.

"I am a Southerner, a churchgoer, and a swing voter in presidential elections.. . . I have no automatic faith in government's capacity to solve problems. I share these details to make clear that I am not a reflexive lefty. Far from it."[377] At the time Jon Meacham was promoting his book on America's faith, while trying to keep the now defunct left-leaning *Newsweek* magazine, afloat. He failed at the magazine, and while his book *American Gospel* may have been successful monetarily, it fails in conveying America's true founding principles. We will look at Meacham as we conclude our exploration because in two separate works Meacham manages to not only minimize faith, but also the role and importance of the South in our founding.

In *American Gospel*, Meacham incorrectly suggests America was not founded as a Christian nation. "The right's contention that we are a Christian nation," he writes, "that has fallen from pure origins and can achieve redemption by some kind of return to Christian values is based on wishful thinking, not convincing historical argument."

While Meacham is wrong, no challenges to his scholarship have broken through the mainstream media filters because all of the Columbia School of Journalism trained newsroom producers agree, or even worse, don't know better.

To Mr. Meacham, and to you my judge and jury, my response is simple: read what the founders left behind, for yourselves. A look at the constitutions of all the colonies and their subsequent statehoods will tell any discerning reader all they need to know. While Meacham has chosen to cherry-pick a few references, I would recommend that you invest in a book by William J. Federer titled *The Original 13: A Documentary History of Religion in America's First Thirteen States.*

It painstakingly lists all the documents associated with the founding of a colony to its most recent version of statehood.

For example, the chapter on the State of New Jersey includes twelve documents starting with the 1614 "Charter for those who Discover," up to the most recent 1947 "Constitution of New Jersey." For Massachusetts, Federer's book lists twenty-three original documents, from the "Petition for New England Charter," and "the Mayflower Compact" in 1619 and 1620 respectively through the 1917 "Constitution of Massachusetts."[378]

After reviewing all of these state or colony specific guidelines on faith, I came to a deeper understanding of why the U.S. Constitution is purposely silent on faith. Not because our founders were Godless, but because the states were very explicit on the expectations of religious character, for citizens and office holders. For example, many went so far as to bar atheists from holding any kind of office, or swearing oaths. To whom does an atheist swear? And if they don't fear God, does their oath have any meaning?

In *The Original 13*, Federer notes that a contemporary of Frenchman Alexis de Tocqueville published a work describing the various constitutions of America's states. In 1835 de Tocqueville's peer observed, "All of the American constitutions exhort the citizens to practice religious worship as a safeguard both to good morals and to public liberties. In the United States, the law is never atheistic . . . " After detailing the religious mandates of each state, starting with Massachusetts, the French scholar concludes, "There is not a single state where public opinion and the customs of the inhabitants do not forcefully constrain an obligation to these beliefs."[379]

In response to the recent pop history fad of denying Christianity in America's founding, David Barton has explored the methodology and research of many of these works like Meacham's only to conclude, "Scholars purported to investigate whether America really did have a Christian founding . . . While allegedly examining the Founding Era, strikingly 88 percent of the "historical sources on which they rely postdate 1900, and 80 percent postdate 1950!"[380]

Today, too many authors are relying on contemporary "histories" or interpretations instead of going to the sources. Barton and Federer are both preservationists of the original documents and while their works are comprehensive, both would extol to you as I do, to look at these original works for yourself. Remove the filter.

EPILOGUE:

"Cling to Your Guns and Your Religion"

"It is Idle to talk about preventing the wreck of Western Civilization. It is already a wreck from within. That is why we can hope to do little more now than scratch a fingernail of a saint from the rack or a handful of ashes from the faggots, and bury them secretly in a flowerpot against the day, ages hence when a few men begin again to dare to believe that there was once something else, that something else is thinkable, and need some evidence of what it was, and the fortifying knowledge that there were those who at the great nightfall, took loving thought to preserve the tokens of hope and truth."

—Ronald Reagan recited these words by
Whittaker Chambers, author of *Witness,* one of Reagan's
favorite books, in 1975

Barack Obama and his supporters warned us that they wanted to "fundamentally transform America," and they meant it. Only when we are powerless to defend ourselves from tyranny will their transformation be complete. New York's former Mayor, Michael Bloomberg, not satisfied with trying to limit the size of your soda cup is now channeling his personal fortune to strip away your Second Amendment rights.[381]

Bloomberg has joined Obama and the liberals in a massive nationwide effort to target political candidates that support your right to bear arms. Patrick Henry spoke forcefully about a people "three million armed" and ready to resist at a time when 3,000,000 was the entire population of the colonies. Jefferson, Adams, and our other founders felt strongly about our need for arms as well, but that interpretation isn't good enough for Joe Biden and his liberal partners in the media advising you to "just buy a shotgun."

■

Mao Tse-Tung famously said "power flows from the barrel of a gun," and Senator Diane Feinstein seems to agree. Feinstein was planning gun grab legislation to coincide with Obama's second term long before the tragic 2012 school shooting in Newtown, Connecticut. Sadly, all of the hand ringing and public outrage by the liberals has produced no meaningful deterrent to future attacks. Since the Newtown school was technically a "gun-free zone," no law-abiding citizens were armed, but those liberal rules didn't stop the deranged psychopath who moments after murdering his own mother in her bed stormed the school building, hell bent on destruction.[382]

The New York Times reported that the Newtown shooter, twenty-year-old Adam Lanza, spent most of his time in his basement playing video games like the hyper-realistic *Call of Duty*, a "first-person shooter" video game that visualizes modern warfare better than any government simulator I have ever trained on. In fact, the realism of the digital "blood" splattering on the game's "virtual goggles" is too gruesome for me.[383]

Meanwhile the video game, movie, and music industries that the liberal Democrats rely on for campaign contributions have offered zero solutions to an epidemic they are integral to creating. The military has long known the value of operant conditioning in simulators. I trained my men on them before we went to Iraq. In fact the video game/simulation stimuli is one of the reasons that today's modern soldiers are more effective and shoot their weapons to kill the enemy more often than soldiers in any other preceding war.[384]

Songs work, too. Violent music helps desensitize and build an appetite for destruction, which is one of the reasons that as a Marine platoon commander I had my men sing songs about wartime exploits and "stomping out Al Qaeda guts." Why has the focus of these post-shooting recriminations been the 2nd amendment rights of law-abiding citizens? Why has no member of Congress asked for an investigation into the violence-provoking lyrics that are prevalent in all the communities with the worst murder rates?

Why is it that rap-star Curtis Jackson, who goes by the name "Fifty Cent," can sell eleven million copies of an album called *The Massacre* that makes overt comparisons to the Columbine High School shootings (1999) in which twelve students and a teacher were murdered and twenty-one students were wounded? Why has no media organization or legislative body asked why Curtis Jackson assaults the listener with over forty gunshots in the opening seconds of the album while a mixture of screaming children and nursery rhymes are drowned out in the gunfire?[385]

Why was Curtis Jackson, the purveyor of this forty-round "assault music" paid $100 million dollars when Coca-Cola bought a company that Jackson pitched for? Where were the protesting parents? Where was the perennially boycotting "Reverend" Al Sharpton?[386]

■

Recognizing how deeply Guns and God historically have figured into American culture, the left is employing multi-pronged efforts to dismantle these belief systems. Another recent salvo comes from Michael Bellesiles who has tried valiantly to rewrite American history, and almost got away with it. The goal of his book, *Arming America: The Origins of a National Gun Culture,* was to downplay the role of the militia and deny the existence of Revolutionary era American gun culture.[387]

If, as Bellesiles claimed, our gun culture was an "invented tradition," well then all the easier to dismantle it. As it turns out very little in Bellesiles' book is true. His publisher, Knopf, was forced to recall the remaining copies and destroy them after numerous historians identified flawed and misleading research. In some cases he rearranged the wording in source documents to accommodate his worldview. In other instances, Bellesiles created figures and sources out of whole cloth.[388]

It should be no surprise that *The New York Times* was salivating about this book and its political implications in the Second

Amendment argument months before it even hit the stand. If one prong of the left's attack on gun rights is to deny the existence of a revolutionary gun culture, the other prong of the same argument is that the militia was largely irrelevant and it was the continental army under Washington that did all the fighting and all the winning of the Revolutionary War.[389]

This is a key part of Ellis's thesis, and in turn McCullough, who has looked to his fellow new Englander for historical top-cover. Under that paradigm, the "well-regulated militia" of the Second Amendment is really limited to uniformed soldiers and has nothing to do with the population writ large. The Bellesiles model would have given the left the ammo needed to roll up our rights. That version of history didn't actually exist, so he fabricated it.

The founders went beyond establishing that one of our most basic God-given rights was the right to life, which in turn means the right to self-defense. They also, in an aversion to standing armies, felt strongly that citizens of a Republic, much like the Romans, had a duty to participate in the defense of the republic. And when that duty is shirked, as Rome would discover after outsourcing its defense to mercenaries, the citizenry would lose respect for the value of a Government they no longer fought to protect. The Vietnam War didn't just train a generation of draft dodgers and campus radicals, it also exposed the draft and the deferment system to renewed scrutiny which ultimately led to our all-volunteer military force.

What the left has recognized is that in the wake of selective service, the volunteer military has created a Sparta-Gap that enlists more conservatives and more Christians than the rest of the country at large. Thomas Ricks of *The Washington Post* has explored this phenomena in terms of a civil-military divide. I see it more regionally, after having witnessed three wars up close and have a first-hand feel for who actually makes the choices to serve in the front line combat arms and the infantry.

After analyzing the enlistment and casualty data myself, I can confidently declare that red states send more of their sons and daughters to fight and die in our nation's wars than the blue state liberals—from the Alamo to Vietnam to Iraq and Afghanistan today. Southerners don't just give more of their money to charities, when compared to other parts of the country; they give more of their blood, as their faith tells them to.[390]

This Sparta-Gap, as I have coined it, is viewed differently by the Conservative and the liberal ideologies as one might imagine. Conservatives see the military and its culture as normal but view the country at large as too morally lax. Alternatively, Liberals see the "progress" of modern society as normal and the military as an antiquated throwback organization whose male leadership, which is disproportionately Southern and conservative, as in need of an extreme makeover.[391]

Thus the Obama Administration's electorally calculated emphasis on women in the Infantry units and open homosexuality with the repeal of DADT which has zero to do with the needs of the military or combat effectiveness and everything to do with pandering to special interests and weakening the conservative backbone of our military leadership. If you doubt the damage caused by political correctness in the military, familiarize yourself with the story of Operation Redwing as chronicled by Marcus Luttrell in the book and film, *Lone Survivor* (2007). Luttrell and his fellow U.S. Navy SEALs feared prosecution for killing on the battlefield and as a result they allowed their position to be compromised, which ultimately led to the death of nineteen service members. Luttrell references the SEAL's fear of prosecution five different times in his book as he recounts the tragic loss of his valiant brothers in arms who were as much casualties of political correctness as the Taliban.[392] I have firsthand experience with these tragic consequences and I grieve for the families of these heroes.

The Left sees the civil military divide or Sparta-Gap as something that must be cured with more tolerance, revisionist history and quota-driven diversity at the expense of combat power. Conservatives on the other hand see the military as an organization with a single purpose, fighting and winning wars. If we tinkered with our professional sports teams the way we do with our military, we would immediately regret it as performance suffered. For example, no one is calling for more short fat old white guys on the basketball court, even though that would be "fair" and better "reflect" society. Unlike sports, there are no do-overs in war.

■

Today, the war that Conservatives need to concern themselves with winning is the culture war. The Left has enlisted the century old doctrine of communists like Antonio Gramsci to overturn the existing culture in order to establish counterculture conditions for their accumulation of power. Gramsci's "long march" into the institutions of media, academia, and the pulpit, is succeeding in remaking American society into something unrecognizable to most traditionalists and this is causing immense friction. By tapping into and even stoking social unrest, the political organizing principles of radicals like Saul Alinksy are driving the American electorate towards ever greater levels of societal transformation and redistribution.

On the first page of *Rules For Radicals*, Alinksy credits "Lucifer" as the "the first radical known to man." The book, which has taken on legendary status among the ranks of campus and community organizers—including Barack Obama and Hillary Clinton—seeks to foment revolution.[393] It opens with an over-the-shoulder acknowledgement of Satan while simultaneously denigrating Christianity as mere "mythology."[394]

Alinksy's oft referenced work is chock-full of the building blocks of rebellion: "[Lenin]said that the Bolsheviks stood for getting power through the ballot but would reconsider after they got the guns!"

When addressing "young radicals" in the wake of the violent protests of the late sixties, Alinsky instructed, "Remember: once you organize people around something as commonly agreed upon as pollution, then an organized people is on the move. From there it's a short and natural step to political pollution, to Pentagon pollution."

The political motivations and machinations behind this historical revisionism should by now be clear. I expect after hundreds of pages of directly sourced correspondence from British officers and American Presidents you are convinced that a crime of historical omission has indeed been perpetrated with deliberate intent. Finally, it is my sincere hope that this brief exploration has not only led you to an indictment of the perpetrators of this historical theft, but that you are hungry to explore the original sources for yourselves. The transformative power of the internet has opened up a vast expanse of human knowledge at your finger tips. Use this opportunity to arm yourself with the truth in advance of the struggles that are yet to come. As the

Book of Jude notes, now is the time to contend for your faith, in God and in America.

> You go into these small towns . . . And it's not surprising then they get bitter, they cling to guns or religion or antipathy toward people who aren't like them or anti-immigrant sentiment or anti-trade sentiment as a way to explain their frustrations.[395]

Barack Obama said these things because he believes them and he is correct.

Traditional Americans *do* cling to our God, our Guns, and our Guts.

If we didn't, we wouldn't have won our freedom. If we don't, we won't keep it.

I rest my case.

ACKNOWLEDGMENTS

After thanking God for using all things for good, according to his purpose, for those that believe in him (Rom. 8:28), I must acknowledge a true friend and mentor who has left us here on earth to reside with the angels, my beloved friend Jack Hawke.

Like me, Jack was a Yankee transplant born again Southern who had dabbled in electoral politics. Jack ran for Congress, served as chairman of the North Carolina Republican party, and ultimately paved the way for North Carolina's terrific Governor, Pat McCrory. The list and ways that Jack Hawke influenced my life are legion, but his simple humanity, his laugh, his happy warrior joy, always left those in his presence feeling "Faanntaastic!"

Jack, I miss you, and like so many of us that you left behind, I think about you every day. More than anyone else, you gave me a chance at redemption and helped me to reclaim my own stolen valor. Along the way you introduced me to other happy warriors, men of character, vision and principle who love the South like Carl Venters, Parks Griffin, Cecil Worsley, Mike McCarley, and Senator George Rountree whose great grandfather, George Davis, was the Attorney General of the Confederacy. Representatives Walter Jones and Pete Sessions have both touched my life in different ways at different times, but their graciousness and genuine affection has left an indelible mark, and I am forever grateful. Keep fighting hard for America!

The love and warmth of Carl and Linda Venters has yielded many dear friends, men like Frank Corcoran and Adair Graham. Frank and

I have shared many adventures and many tears. Like Carl and me, Frank is a former Marine officer who doesn't take himself too seriously even though he knows better than most how unforgiving life can be. Frank and I have laughed and cried, drunk wine, shot guns, and eaten steaks, though not always in that order. Our adventures together are just getting started but it already feels as comfortable as a lifetime.

Adair Graham, his wife Louise, and children Rachel, Adair Jr., Jean, and Hilda and their families have embraced mine, and given us refuge from the storms of life. I am grateful for the love, friendship, and fellowship that we have shared and will for many more years to come. Whether it was touring battlefields, from Gettysburg to Normandy, or sharing a cigar on a lazy Carolina afternoon, or watching election returns at midnight, I am proud to call the Chief my sparring partner. The Chief has helped me to refine ideas and prose with his instinct for blood and mind for political maneuver. I look forward to all the battlefields yet to come, Chief!

This book would certainly not exist if it weren't for the unwavering belief and perseverance of my agent, Mel Berger at William Morris Entertainment. I am quite literally the least significant client on Mel's impressive roster, and yet he has toiled for years to help me find my voice. I can't thank Mel enough, but if you'd like to, you can always buy a second copy of this book for a friend! My editor Kevin Smith, like Mel, worked hard to make my first book, *Warlord*, a reality and now he has lent his time and talents to this book. Thank you, Kevin for keeping me on track. Anthony Ziccardi, you too walked with me on my first book, and now here we are with Michael L. Wilson at Post Hill Press, thank you for having the courage and the faith to walk with me, once more unto the breech.

As I turn to my family, there is my "Brother from Another Mother," JR McKechnie. JR has been steadfast and loyal from our first days bartending together while getting our various degrees in New York City. JR and I witnessed the attacks of 9/11 together so it is appropriate, here, to honor the loss of Kevin Cleary and all of our friends who perished on 9/11. I'll never forget my first "big" dinner with JR as he was a fast track lawyer and I was at Goldman Sachs. His efforts to help me shape my arguments, read the drafts and challenge my assumptions made this book what it is. Thank you, Jay.

The only person who has done more to bring this book to fruition is my mother, Merry. My mom is one of those happy warriors that this book is dedicated to. Because of her fierce example, and Scotch-Irish bloodline that dates back to the revolution itself, I am the warrior that I am. My father and his gentle example shaped me and I can only hope to repay him by being half the father to my children that he has been to me. Grazie, Papa!

To my boys, so precocious and full of wonder, I can only ask for their patience and understanding as I have worked on this book at great personal cost to them. They both inspire me daily, to be a better example as a Christian, as a professional, as a Crossfit athlete, father, and husband. 'Merica!

To my wife Jill, who has weathered many of my storms, from Al Qaeda death threats to political attack websites that slander her and my mother. I can't think of anyone who could have shouldered your burdens with so much grace and poise, and all the while growing into the amazingly successful woman that you have become. You are a diamond that has emerged from many trials and pressures stronger and more radiant than ever. Jill, you are my Wonder Woman: a superior professional, a committed Crossfit athlete, a nurturing mother, and a beautiful and dedicated wife who loves the Lord. I love you, Lil' honey.

Wow! Thank you God for all my many, many blessings, most importantly the gift of your son. I ask your blessings on all the men and women who keep us safe and their families here at home, and I ask this in the name of Jesus Christ. Amen.

MEET THE AUTHOR: ILARIO PANTANO

A Marine Sniper who once faced the death penalty for killing terrorists in Iraq, no one knows the theft of history better than Ilario Pantano. Unlike most so-called culture warriors, Pantano actually has the scars and he "knows what it's like to be caught in a crossfire," said Colonel Oliver North.

MSNBC host Chris Matthews has said Pantano is "a guy who knows what he's talking about." Fox's Sean Hannity told America that Pantano "belongs in Congress," and Sarah Palin, Donald Rumsfeld, Paul Ryan and Allen West have all agreed.

Pantano is a tireless advocate for our nation's veterans. He has raised money for their legal defenses and has provided military commentary on Fox News, CNN, and MSNBC. His numerous articles, profiles, and interviews have appeared in American Legion Magazine, The Wall Street Journal, Soldier of Fortune, and TIME magazine.

APPENDIX

The Battlefields

y goal is that you get up, go out and see some of these Southern battlefields for yourself. Walk the ground. This is history you can touch and it can be done in just a few days. Do so, before it's too late. Kings Mountain State Park has become one of my family's favorite campsites, and Cowpens is not even thirty minutes away. Guilford Courthouse is just a two-hour drive from Kings Mountain. Information provided is courtesy of each respective park operator. Additional books and reference sources are provided in Endnotes and Bibliography. Enjoy!

BATTLE OF MOORES CREEK, NC
Website: http: //www.nps.gov/mocr
Site Location: 40 Patriots Hall Drive, Currie, NC 28435
(910) 283-5591

BATTLE OF SULLIVAN'S ISLAND (Ft. Moultrie/Charleston, SC)
Website: www.nps.gov/fosu/historyculture/fort_moultrie.htm
Site location: 1214 Middle Street, Sullivan's Island, SC 29482
(843) 883-3123

BATTLE OF CAMDEN, SC
Website: http://www.battleofcamden.org/camden_trail_brochure.pdf
Site Location: Historic Camden Revolutionary War Site is located at
    222 Broad Street, Camden, SC, 29020, 1.4 miles from Exit 98/I-20
    on US Highway 521 North heading towards Camden.
(803) 432-9841

BUFORD'S SLAUGHTER (Battle of the Waxhaws)
Website: http://nationalregister.sc.gov/SurveyReports/HC29002.pdf
Site Location: Historical marker is located about 9 miles east of
    Lancaster on SC Highway 522, a quarter of a mile south of
    Highway 9. Lancaster County, South Carolina.

HUCK'S DEFEAT (Williamson's Plantation at Historic Brattonsville, SC)
Website: http://www.chmuseums.org/battle-of-hucks-defeat-hb/
Site Location: 1444 Brattonsville Rd, McConnells, SC 29726
(803) 684-2327

BATTLE OF MUSGROVE'S MILLS, SC

Website: http://www.southcarolinaparks.com/musgrovemill/
introduction.aspx
Site Location: 398 State Park RD, Clinton, SC 29325
(864) 938-0100

BATTLE OF KING'S MOUNTAIN, SC

Website: http://www.nps.gov/kimo
Site Location: 2625 Park Road, Blacksburg, SC 29702
(Exit #2 off of Highway 85)
(864) 936-7921

OVERMOUNTAIN VICTORY TRAIL

Website: http://www.nps.gov/ovvi

Trail Starts:
Abingdon Muster Grounds: 1780 Muster Place Abingdon, VA 24210;
(276) 525-1050; (www.abingdonmustergrounds.com)
Sycamore Shoals: 1651 West Elk Avenue, Elizabethton TN 37643
(423) 543-5808 (www.sycamoreshoalstn.org)

Trail Finish:
Kings Mountain: 2625 Park Road, Blacksburg, SC 29702
(864) 936-7921 (www.nps.gov/kimo)

BATTLE OF COWPENS, SC

Website: http://www.nps.gov/cowp
Site Location: 4001 Chesnee Highway, Gaffney, SC 29341
(864) 461-2828

BATTLE OF GUILFORD COURTHOUSE, NC

Website: http://www.nps.gov/guco
Site Location: Guilford Courthouse National Military Park, 2332 New
Garden Road, Greensboro, NC 27410-2355
(336) 288-1776

BATTLE OF YORKTOWN, VA

Website: http://www.nps.gov/york
Website: http://www.nps.gov/nisi
Site Location: Colonial National Historical Park, Yorktown,
VA 23690
(757) 898-2410

APPENDIX: THE BATTLEFIELDS ■ 211

NINETY SIX, SC
Site Location:1103 Highway 248 S,Ninety Six, SC 29666
(864) 543-4068

SYCAMORE SHOALS, TN
Website: http://www.sycamoreshoalstn.org
http://tnstateparks.com/parks/about/sycamore-shoals
Site Location: 1651 West Elk Avenue, Elizabethton TN 37643
(423) 543-5808

ADDITIONAL REVOLUTIONARY WAR SITES OF INTEREST

GEORGIA

The Georgia Society Sons of the American Revolution focuses on primarily eight major battle sites and has produced brochures concerning these "campaigns" which are available here. Most notable is the Battle of Kettle Creek. http://www.georgiasocietysar.org/revtrail/pdf/brochure_kettlecreek.pdf

The Battle of Kettle Creek was one of Georgia's most memorable victories during the American Revolution. The Kettle Creek Battleground is located ten miles from Washington off SR 44 in Wilkes County, GA. An exhibit of artifacts is displayed at the Washington Historical Museum, Washington, GA. http://www.nps.gov/nr/feature/july/2011/ Kettle_Creek_Battlefield.htm

NORTH CAROLINA
More Revolutionary War in Southeastern North Carolina

Download the official guide to Revolutionary War era sites in Southeastern North Carolina here: http://www.nps.gov/mocr/historyculture/upload/NC-Rev-War-Sites.pdf or http://www.nchistoricsites.org/

Alamance Battleground:
Here in 1771, an armed rebellion of backcountry farmers called Regulators battled with royal governor William Tryon's militia. The spark for this conflict was growing resentment in the Carolina colony against the taxes, dishonest sheriffs, and illegal fees imposed by the British Crown. In response, the Regulators were formed and began to fight back. Though the rebellion was crushed, a few years later their tactics

became a model for the colonists fighting the British in the American Revolutionary War.
Site Location: 5803 N.C. 62 S, Burlington, NC 27215
(336) 227-4785

Tryon Palace:
North Carolina's first capitol—where governors ruled, legislators debated, patriots gathered, and George Washington danced.
Site Location: 610 Pollock Street, New Bern, NC 28562
(252) 514-4900

Fort Johnston:
In 1775, fearing attack from the rebellious citizens of North Carolina, Royal Governor Josiah Martin fled Tryon Palace and sought refuge at Fort Johnston. When Patriot forces attacked the fort, Governor Martin fled to the safety of a British ship.
Site Location: Intersection of Davis and Bay Streets, Southport, NC 28461
(910) 457-7927

Brunswick Town:
In 1765 the colonists challenged the Crown's authority to distribute hated tax stamps. That action, eight years before the Boston Tea Party, halted collection of the tax along the Cape Fear River.
Site Location: 8884 St. Philips Road SE, Winnabow, NC 28479
(910) 371-6613

Burgwin-Wright House:
In 1781, "the most considerable house in town" was occupied by Lord Cornwallis as his headquarters shortly before his defeat and surrender at Yorktown, Virginia.
Site Location: 224 Market Street Wilmington, NC 28401
(910) 762-0570

SOUTH CAROLINA
From the South Carolina State Parks website:

Andrew Jackson State Park:
This park and museum tell of the Seventh President's life in the Waxhaws of the South Carolina backcountry during the Revolutionary War.
Site Location: 196 Andrew Jackson Park RD, Lancaster, SC 29720
(803) 285-3344

Hampton Plantation State Historic Site

This plantation served as a place of refuge for women and children during the Revolutionary War. The rice fields surrounding the property hid Francis Marion from British troops searching for him.
Site Location: 1950 Rutledge RD, McClellanville, SC 29458
(843) 546-9361

Landsford Canal State Park

This Catawba River crossing was used by both Patriot and British troops on their way to Revolutionary War battles in South Carolina.
Site Location: 610 Pollock Street, New Bern, NC 28562
(252) 514-4900

NOTES

Preface

1. Crockett, David, *Narrative of the Life of David Crockett of the State of Tennessee*, Carey, Hart & Co., Baltimore. MD: 1834.

OPENING ARGUMENT:
How the Liberal War on Southern Culture is
Rewriting America's Past

2. Black, Earl & Black, Merle, *The Rise Of The Southern Republicans*, Harvard University Press, Cambridge, MA: 2002, p. 14.
3. Cohen, Stefanie, "Fourscore and 16,000 Books," *Wall Street Journal*, 12 Oct. 2012, Dec. 2012, http://online.wsj.com/article/SB10000872396390444024204578044403434070838.html
4. McCrady, Edward, *The History of South Carolina in The Revolution 1780-1783*, Macmillan Company, New York: 1902.
5. Ibid.
6. The Writings of George Washington, Ed. Ford, 1891, To The President of the Congress, HQ, 7 November, 1780, p. 24
7. Wilson, Woodrow, *A History of The American People, Volume 2*, Harper and Brothers, New York: 1907
8. Revolutionary Orders of Gen. Washington, ed. Whiting, 1844 #90, KINGS MTN HQ, Totoway Oct 27 1780, p. 123
9. Clinton, Henry, *Narrative of Lieutenant General Sir Henry Clinton, K.B. Relative to His Conduct During Part of His Command of the King's Troops in North America, Particularly That Which Respects the Unfortunate Issue of the Campaign of 1781*, J. Debrett, Burlington House, Picadilly, UK: 1783
10. Roosevelt, Theodore, *Winning the West, Volume 2*, G.P. Putnam's Sons, New York: 1889
11. Herbert Hoover: "Address on the 150th Anniversary of the Battle of Kings Mountain", October 7, 1930. Online by Gerhard Peters and John T. Woolley, *The American Presidency Project*. http://www.presidency.ucsb.edu/ws/?pid=22379
12. Churchill, Winston S., *A History of the English Speaking Peoples, Volume 3: The Age of Revolution*, Dodd, Mead & Company, London: 1957
13. American Battlefield Protection Program, "Report to Congress on The Historic Preservation of The Revolutionary War and War of 1812 Sites in the United States," *National Park Service, U.S. Department of the*

Interior, Sep. 2007, Dec. 2012, http://www.nps.gov/hps/abpp/Rev1812_ Final_ Report.pdf

14. *Journals of the Continental Congress, 1774-1789, (Vol. 18,19 & 21)*, Thirty Four Volumes Published by the Library of Congress, 1904-1937, http://memory.loc.gov/ammem/amlaw/lwjclink.html

15. Webb, Jim, *Born Fighting: How The Scots-Irish Shaped America*, Broadway Books, New York: 2004; Gardner, Amy, "Webb Withdraws as Possible Vice President Pick for Obama," *The Washington Post*, 8 Jul. 2008, Mar. 2013, http://articles.washingtonpost.com/2008-07-08/ news/36803525_1_virginia-democrats-webb-gi-bill; Ellerson, Lindsey, "Webb to Remain in Senate, No longer VP Candidate," *ABC News*, 7 Jul. 2008, Mar. 2013, http://abcnews.go.com/blogs/politics/2008/07/ webb-to-remain/

16. Horowitz, David, *Indoctrination U: The Left's War Against Academic Freedom*, Encounter Books, New York: 2007; Horowitz, David, Re-forming Our universities: The Campaign for an Academic Bill of Rights, Regnery Publishing, Washington DC: 2010

17. Ibid.

18. Carmel Clay High School, IN, 'Inherit the Wind' Curriculum, Dec 2012, http://www1.ccs.k12.in.us/teachers/esalona1/ITW ; NYC Department of Education, NY, 'Inherit the Wind' Curriculum, Dec 2012, <http://schools. nyc.gov/offices/teacherlearn/arts/americanvoices.html>

19. Zakarin, Jordan, "Tarantino's 'Django Unchained' Reignites Debate Over N-Word in Movies," *The Hollywood Reporter*, 15 Dec. 2012, Mar. 2013, http://www.hollywoodreporter.com/news/tarantino-django -unchained-reignites-debate-402445

20. Drennen, Kyle, "Jamie Foxx Defends SNL 'Kill All the White People' Joke on NBC's 'Today': 'I'm a Comedian'" Newsbusters.org, 12 Dec. 2012, Mar 2013, http://newsbusters.org/blogs/kyle-drennen/2012/12/12/ jamie-foxx-defends-snl-kill-all-white-people-joke-nbcs-today-im-comedi

21. Farndale, Nigel, "Josh Brolin on Playing George W. Bush in Oliver Stone's New Film," The Telegraph, 23 Oct. 2008, Mar. 2013, http:// www.telegraph.co.uk/culture/film/3562496/Josh-Brolin-on-playing-George-W.-Bush-in-Oliver-Stones-new-film.html; O'Connell, Libby, "The People Speak-Democracy is Not a Spectator Sport," *HISTORY Channel*, Mar. 2013, http://www.history.com/shows/the-people-speak/articles/ the-people-speak-story

22. Gitlin, Todd, "Choosing our better history," *Social Science Research Council*, 1 Jun. 2009, Apr. 2013, http://blogs.ssrc.org/tif/2009/06/01/ choosing-our-better-history/?disp=print

23. Schraffenberger, Donny, "Karl Marx and the American Civil War Espionage," *International Socialist Review*, Nov-Dec. 2011, Mar. 2013, http:// www.isreview.org/issues/80/feat-civilwar.shtml

24. McWhirther, Cameron, "Southern Baptists Pick Black Leader," *Wall Street Journal*, 20 Jun. 2012, Dec. 2012, http://online.wsj.com/article/SB1000142 405270230337920457747696237009268.html; Rusin, David, "Hate-Crime Stats Deflate 'Islamophobia' Myth,", *National Review Online*, 11 Jan. 2013, Jan. 2013, http://www.nationalreview.com/articles/337417/ hate-crime-stats-deflate-islamophobia-myth-david-j-rusin# ; Meese,

Edwin and Marshall, Jennifer, "A Summer of Intolerance," *Heritage Foundation Editorial featured in USA Today*, 7 Oct. 2012, Jan. 2013, http://www.heritage.org/research/commentary/2012/10/a-summer-of-in-toleranceDorell, Oren and Grossman, Cathy Lynn, "Boy Scouts May Soon Welcome Gay Youths, Leaders,"*USA Today*, 29 Jan. 2013, Jan. 2013, http://www.usatoday.com/story/news/nation/2013/01/28/boy-scouts-gay-united-way/1870919/; Tomasky, Michael, "The Boy Scouts and the South," *The Daily Beast*, 29 Jan. 2013, Jan. 2013, http://www.thedaily-beast.com/articles/2013/01/29/the-boy-scouts-and-the-south.html

25. Farrow, Anne; Lang, Joel; and Frank, Jennifer, *Complicity: How the North Promoted, Prolonged and Profited from Slavery*, Ballantine Books, New York: 2006, p. xvi
26. Ibid.
27. Lind Michael, "The Tea Party, the debt ceiling, and white Southern extremism," *Salon.com*, 2 Aug. 2011, Mar. 2013, http://www.salon.com/2011/08/02/lind_tea_party/; Lind, Michael, *Made In Texas: George W. Bush and the Southern Takeover of American Politics*, Basic Books, New York: 2003

EXHIBIT A.1 **History as Headlines:**
The London *Gazette* and *The Annual Register*

28. *The London Gazette*, Issue, 12251, 15 Dec. 1781, Dec, 2012, https://www.thegazette.co.uk/London/issue/12251/page/1
29. Ibid.
30. *The London Gazette*, "History of the Gazette," Dec, 2012, https://www.thegazette.co.uk/history
31. *The London Gazette*, Issue, 12162, 13 Feb. 1781, Dec, 2012, https://www.thegazette.co.uk/London/issue/12162/page/1
32. Edited by Burke, Edmund, *The Annual Register or a View of the History, Politics and Literature for the Year 1781*, Robert Dodsley, London, England: 1782, p.52-53
33. Boorstin, Daniel, *The Americans: The National Experience*, Vintage Books, New York: 1965 p. 366
34. Botta, Charles, *History of the War of Independence of the United States of America*, 1809 –Italian 1820 English, p. 312
35. Sarason, Bertram D., "Edmund Burke and the Two Annual Registers," *PMLA, Published by Modern Language Association*, Vol. 68, No. 3, Jun. 1953
36. Ibid.
37. Feulner, Edwin, J., "The Roots of Modern Conservative Thought from Burke to Kirk," First Principles Series Report #19, The Heritage Foundation, Jun, 8, 2008, Mar, 2014
38. Sarason, Bertram D., "Edmund Burke and the Two Annual Registers," *PMLA, Published by Modern Language Association*, Vol. 68, No. 3, Jun. 1953
39. Edited by Burke, Edmund, *The Annual Register or a View of the History, Politics and Literature for the Year 1781*, Robert Dodsley, London, England: 1782, p. 55

40. Ibid, pp. 69-70
41. Ibid, p. 70-71
42. Ibid, p. 71
43. Ibid, p. 129
44. Ibid.
45. Ibid, p. 130

EXHIBIT A.2 Commander as Correspondent: General Cornwallis

46. Edited by Ross, Charles, *Correspondence of Charles, First Marquis Cornwallis*, John Murray, London, England: 1859, p. 56
47. Ibid, p. 58
48. Ibid, p. 58
49. Ibid, p. 59
50. Ibid, p. 62
51. Ibid, p. 62
52. Ibid, p. 67
53. Ibid, p. 68
54. Ibid, p. 69
55. Ibid, p. 70
56. Ibid, p. 71
57. Ibid.
58. Ibid, p. 72-73
59. Ibid, p. 76
60. Ibid, p. 90
61. Ibid, p. 83
62. Edited By Ian Saberton, *The Cornwallis (Marquis Charles Cornwallis) Papers: The Campaigns of 1780 and 1781*, Vol. 4, Naval & Military Press, East Sussex, England: 2010, p. 45
63. Ibid. pp. 47, 49

EXHIBIT A.3 Stephen Jarvis and the Connecticut Yankees Invade Dixie

64. Jarvis, Stephen, "An American's Experience in the British Army," *The Connecticut Magazine*, Volume XI, Number 2, Summer of 1907
65. Ibid.
66. Ibid.
67. Ibid.
68. Ibid.
69. Ibid.
70. Ibid.
71. Ibid.
72. Ibid.
73. Ibid.
74. Ibid.
75. Ibid.

76. Ibid.
77. Stryker, William S, Adjutant-General of New Jersey, New Jersey Volunteers (LOYALISTS), In the Revolutionary War, Naah, Day & Naah, Book and Job Printers, Trenton, NJ: 1887, p. 41
78. Moss, Bobby Gilmer, *Uzal Johnson, Loyalist Surgeon: A Revolutionary War Diary*, Scotia Hibernia Press, Blacksburg, SC: 2000, p. 65,66
79. Ibid, p. 77 (U84)
80. Ibid.

EXHIBIT A.4 Commander as Correspondent: Cornwallis at Guilford

81. Schenck, David, LL.D., *North Carolina 1780-1781: Being a History of the Invasion of the Carolinas by the British Army Under Lord Cornwallis in 1780-1781*, Heritage Books, Westminster, MD: 2007 (1889)
82. Edited by Ross, Charles, *Correspondence of Charles, First Marquis Cornwallis*, John Murray, London, England: 1859, p. 83
83. Edited By Ian Saberton, *The Cornwallis (Marquis Charles Cornwallis) Papers: The Campaigns of 1780 and 1781*, Vol. 4, Naval & Military Press, East Sussex, England: 2010, p. 12
84. Edited by Ross, Charles, *Correspondence of Charles, First Marquis Cornwallis*, John Murray, London, England: 1859, p. 85
85. Ibid, p. 87
86. Edited By Ian Saberton, *The Cornwallis (Marquis Charles Cornwallis) Papers: The Campaigns of 1780 and 1781*, Vol. 4, Naval & Military Press, East Sussex, England: 2010, p. 110
87. Ibid, p. 104
88. Ibid, p. 107
89. Edited by Ross, Charles, *Correspondence of Charles, First Marquis Cornwallis*, John Murray, London, England: 1859, p. 93
90. Ibid, p. 94
91. Edited By Ian Saberton, *The Cornwallis (Marquis Charles Cornwallis) Papers: The Campaigns of 1780 and 1781*, Vol. 4, Naval & Military Press, East Sussex, England: 2010, p. 116
92. Edited by Ross, Charles, *Correspondence of Charles, First Marquis Cornwallis*, John Murray, London, England: 1859, p. 97
93. Ibid.
94. Ibid, p. 99
95. Ibid, p. 101
96. Edited by Benjamin Franklin Stevens, *The Campaign in Virginia, 1781: An Exact Reprint of Six Rare Pamphlets On the Clinton-Cornwallis Controversy, With Very Numerous Unpublished Manuscript Notes By Sir Henry Clinton, and the Omitted and Hitherto Unpublished Portions of the Letters in Their Appendixes and from the Original Manuscripts*, London: 1887, p. 10
97. Edited by Ross, Charles, *Correspondence of Charles, First Marquis Cornwallis*, John Murray, London, England: 1859, p. 105
98. Ibid, p. 106

EXHIBIT A.5 **Clinton v. Cornwallis: "Who Lost the War?**

99. Book Review, "The Clinton Cornwallis Controversy," *The New York Times*, 8 Jul. 1888, Jan. 2013, http://query.nytimes.com/mem/archive-free/pdf?res=F30F17F63F5E15738DDDA10894DF405B8884F0D3

100. Ibid.

101. Edited by Ross, Charles, *Correspondence of Charles, First Marquis Cornwallis*, John Murray, London, England: 1859, p.130

102. Ibid.

103. Ibid, p.132

104. Ibid, p.135

105. Edited by Benjamin Franklin Stevens, *The Campaign in Virginia, 1781: An Exact Reprint of Six Rare Pamphlets On the Clinton-Cornwallis Controversy, With Very Numerous Unpublished Manuscript Notes By Sir Henry Clinton, and the Omitted and Hitherto Unpublished Portions of the Letters in Their Appendixes and from the Original Manuscripts*, London: 1887 p. 33

106. Ibid, p. 85

107. Ibid, p. 88

108. Ibid, p. 93

109. Ibid, p.121

110. Ibid, p.180

111. Clinton, Henry, *Narrative of Lieutenant General Sir Henry Clinton, K.B. Relative to His Conduct During Part of His Command of the King's Troops in North America, Particularly That Which Respects the Unfortunate Issue of the Campaign of 1781*, J. Debrett, Burlington House, Picadilly, UK:1783, p. 1

112. Ibid, p. 5

113. Ibid, p. 30-31

114. Ibid, p. 36

EXHIBIT A.6 **"Bloody" Banastre Tarleton and His "Unfortunate" Day**

115. Tarleton, Banastre, *A History of the Campaigns of 1780 and 1781 in the Southern Provinces of North America*, Colles, Exshaw, White, H.Whitestone, Burton, Byrne, Moore, Jones, and Dornin, Dublin, Ireland, 1787, p. 24

116. Ibid, pg. 29-32

117. Ibid, pg. 26

118. Ibid, pg. 167

119. Edited by Ross, Charles, *Correspondence of Charles, First Marquis Cornwallis*, John Murray, London, England: 1859, p.59

120. Tarleton, Banastre, *A History of the Campaigns of 1780 and 1781 in the Southern Provinces of North America*, Colles, Exshaw, White, H.Whitestone, Burton, Byrne, Moore, Jones, and Dornin, Dublin, Ireland, 1787, p. 167-169

121. Edited by E. Alfred Jones, *The Journal of Alexander Chesney, a South Carolina Loyalist in the Revolution and After*, The Ohio State University Bulletin, Volume XXVI October 30, 1921, Number 4

122. Ibid, p. 16
123. Ibid, p. 17
124. Ibid, p. 40
125. Tarleton, Banastre, *A History of the Campaigns of 1780 and 1781 in the Southern Provinces of North America*, Colles, Exshaw, White, H.Whitestone, Burton, Byrne, Moore, Jones, and Dornin, Dublin, Ireland, 1787, p. 24
126. Ibid, p. 214
127. Ibid, pp. 215, 216
128. Ibid , p. 216
129. Edited by E. Alfred Jones, *The Journal of Alexander Chesney, a South Carolina Loyalist in the Revolution and After,* The Ohio State University Bulletin, Volume XXVI October 30, 1921, Number 4, p. 21
130. Ibid, p.22-23
131. Tarleton, Banastre, *A History of the Campaigns of 1780 and 1781 in the Southern Provinces of North America*, Colles, Exshaw, White, H. Whitestone, Burton, Byrne, Moore, Jones, and Dornin, Dublin, Ireland, 1787, p. 224
132. Ibid, p. 225
133. Ibid, p. 24
134. Ibid, p. 227
135. Ibid, p. 24
136. Ibid.
137. Ibid, p. 122-23
138. Ibid, p. 405

EXHIBIT A.7 Glory Seekers, Finger Pointers, and the Chorus of Critics

139. Mackenzie, Roderick, *Strictures on Lt Col. Tarleton's "History of the Campaigns of 1780 and 1781, in the Southern Provinces of North America,"* Strand, et al., London, England: 1787, p. 3
140. Ibid, p.41
141. Ibid, p. 88
142. Ibid, p.107
143. Ibid, p. 108
144. Ibid, p. 117
145. Ibid, p. 118
146. Ibid, p. 122-23
147. Ibid, p. 137
148. Hanger, George, *Address to the Army in Reply to Strictures by Roderick Mackenzie on Tarleton's "History of the Campaigns of 1780 and 1781,"* Ridgway, London, England: 1789, p. 122
149. Ibid, p. 127
150. Walpole, Horace, *Journal of the Reign of King George The Third from the Year 1771 to 1783*, Volume 2, Richard Bentley, London, England: 1859, p. 473
151. Stedman, Charles, *The History of the Origin, Progress, And Termination of the American War*, Volume 2, J. Murray, London, England: 1794, p. 217-218

152. Ibid, p. 222
153. Ibid, p. 224
154. Ibid, p. 226
155. Ibid.
156. Ibid, p. 333
157. Clinton, Henry K. B., *Observations on Stedman's History of the American War*, J. Derbett, London, England: 1794, p.15
158. Ibid, p. 16
159. Ibid, p. 17
160. Ibid, p. 23

EXHIBIT A.8 Shots Heard 'Round the Court: North, Pitt, Fox, and the King

161. Edited by Donne, W. Bodham, *The Correspondence of King George The Third with Lord North from 1768 to 1783*, John Murray, London, England: 1867 letter 664, p. 358
162. Edited by Donne, W. Bodham, *The Correspondence of King George The Third with Lord North from 1768 to 1783*, John Murray, London, England: 1867 letter 700, p. 395
163. Walpole, Horace, *Journal of the Reign of King George The Third from the Year 1771 to 1783*, Volume 2, Richard Bentley, London, England: 1859, p. 475
164. Fell, Ralph, *Memoirs of the Public Life of the Late Right Honourable James Fox, Volume 1*, D.N. Shury, London, 1808, p. 191
165. Ibid, p. 194
166. Cleland, Henry, *Memoirs of the Life of the Right Honourable William Pitt*, Albion Press, London England, 1807, p. 34-36
167. Fell, Ralph, *Memoirs of the Public Life of the Late Right Honourable James Fox, Volume 1*, D.N. Shury, London, 1808, p. 199
168. Fell, Ralph, *Memoirs of the Public Life of the Late Right Honourable James Fox, Volume 1*, D.N. Shury, London, 1808, p. 205
169. Walpole, Horace, *Journal of the Reign of King George The Third from the Year 1771 to 1783*, Volume 2, Richard Bentley, London, England: 1859, p. 475

EXHIBIT B.1 The Rebels

170. William Johnson, *Sketches of the Life and Correspondence of Nathanael Greene, Major General of the Armies of the United States In the War of the Revolution*, A. E. Miller, Charleston, SC: 1822, p. ix
171. Letter, 1822 November 10, of Thomas Jefferson, to John Campbell, Tucker-Coleman Collection, Jefferson Papers, Special Collections Research Center, Swem Library, College of William and Mary, http://hdl.handle.net/10288/15385
172. George Washington, The Writings of George Washington, collected and edited by Worthington Chauncey Ford (New York and London: G. P. Putnam's Sons, 1890). Vol. IX (1780-1782). May 21, 2015. <http://oll.libertyfund.org/titles/2413>

173. Edited by Whiting, Henry, *Revolutionary Orders of General Washington Issued During the Years 1778, '80,'81, & '82*, Wiley & Putnam, New York: 1844

174. George Washington, The Writings of George Washington, collected and edited by Worthington Chauncey Ford (New York and London: G. P. Putnam's Sons, 1890). Vol. IX (1780-1782). May 21, 2015. <http://oll.libertyfund.org/titles/2413>

175. Edited by Fitzpatrick, John C., *The Writings of George Washington from Original Manuscript Sources, 1745-1799, Volume 20*, United States Government Printing Office, Washington, DC: 1939

176. Irving, Washington, *The Works of Washington Irving, Volume 14: Life of Washington, Part Four*, The Jenson Society, New York: (1859) 1907, p. 231

177. The Journals of the Continental Congress, Vol. XVIII, 1780, ed. 1910

178. The Journals of the Continental Congress, Vol. XIX, 1781, ed. 1912

179. Moultrie, William, *Memoirs of the American Revolution, Volume 2*, 1802, (Reprinted by Applewood Books, Bedford, MA), p. 255

180. Ibid, p. 258

181. Ibid, p. 259

182. Ibid, p. 271

183. Johnson, William, *Sketches of the Life and Correspondence of Nathanael Greene, Major General of the Armies of the United States In the War of the Revolution*, A. E. Miller, Charleston, SC: 1822, p. 48

184. Lee, Henry, *Memoirs of the War in The Southern Department of the United States*, University Publishing, New York: 1869 (1827), p. 230

EXHIBIT B.2 Ramsay, *The Annual Register*, and Charges of Plagiarism

185. Ramsay, David, *The History of the American Revolution Vol. 1*, Foreword by Lester H. Cohen (Indianapolis: Liberty Fund 1990). Vol. 1., Jan. 2013

186. Libby, Orin Grant, "Ramsay as a Plagiarist," *The American Historical Review* , Vol. 7, No. 4 (Jul., 1902), pp. 697-703 Ramsay, David, *The History of the American Revolution Vol. 1*, Foreword by Lester H. Cohen (Indianapolis: Liberty Fund 1990). Vol. 1., Jan. 2013

187. Greenberg, David ," Why Biden's Plagiarims Shouldn't be Forgotten," *Slate.com*, Aug. 25, 2008, Feb. 2013,

188. Lescaze, Lee and Saperstein, Saundra, "Bethesda Author Settles 'Roots' Suit for $500,000," *Washington Post*, p. A1, Dec 15, 1978, Feb 2013

189. Patry, William F., "Copyright Law and Practice," *Bloomberg News: The Bureau of National Affairs*, 1994, Feb. 2013, http://digital-law-online.info/patry/patry5.html

190. Ramsay, David, *History of South Carolina: From its First Settlement in 1670 to the Year 1808, Volumes 1 & 2*, W.J. Duffie, Newberry, S.C.: 1858 (1808), p. 226

191. Ibid, p. 201

192. Ibid, p. 215

193. Ibid, p. 219
194. Ibid, p. 220
195. Ibid, p. 226
196. Ibid, p. 227

EXHIBIT B.3 Regionalism: Diverging Histories of North and South

197. Boorstin, Daniel, *The Americans: The National Experience*, Vintage Books, New York: 1965, p. 368
198. Ibid.p.362
199. Ibid.p.363
200. Ibid.p.350
201. Hildreth, Richard, *The History of the United States of America from the Discovery of the Continent to the Organization of the Federal Constitution, Vol. 3*, Harper & Brothers, New York: 1863
202. Tucker, George, *The History of The United States From their Colonization to the End of the Twenty-Sixth Congress in 1841, Vol. 1*, Philadelphia, PA: 1856
203. Bancroft, George, *History of the United States from the Discovery of The Continent, Volume 10*, Little, Brown, and Company, Boston, MA: 1875, p. 207
204. Ibid, p. 209
205. Ibid, p. 328
206. Ibid, p. 340
207. Ibid, p. 466
208. Ibid, p. 479
209. Ibid, p. 481
210. Ibid, p. 482
211. Ibid, p. 524

EXHIBIT B.4 After the Civil War, Even Presidents Agree on King's Mountain

212. McCrady, Edward, *The History of South Carolina in The Revolution 1780-1783*, Macmillan company, New York: 1902, p. 536
213. Hall, Kermit L., Ely, James W. and Grossman, Joel B., *The Oxford Companion to the Supreme Court of the United States*, Oxford University Press, New York: 2005, p. 399
214. McCrady, Edward, *The History of South Carolina in The Revolution 1780-1783*, Macmillan company, New York: 1902 p. 53
215. Ibid, p. 719
216. Ibid, p. 737
217. Roosevelt, Theodore, *Winning the West, Volume 2*, G.P. Putnam's Sons, New York: 1889, p. 346
218. Gist, Margaret Adams, "Keepers of the Dead who Sleep on the Hill Top," *The Charlotte Observer*, 5 Oct. 1930: 3:5; Thomas, Nettie Allen, "President Hoover's North Carolina Progenitors," *The Charlotte Observer*, 5 Oct. 1930: 3:3

219. Gist, Margaret Adams, "Archibald Rutledge Chosen to Read An Original Poem At Kings Mountain Celebration," *The Charlotte Observer*, 5 Oct. 1930: 3:2; Watkins, Joseph, "All Roads Will Converge Towards Kings Mountain for Battleground's Birthday," *The Charlotte Observer*, 5 Oct. 1930: 3:5; Herbert Hoover: "Address on the 150th Anniversary of the Battle of Kings Mountain.", October 7, 1930. Online by Gerhard Peters and John T. Woolley, *The American Presidency Project*. http://www .presidency.ucsb.edu/ws/?pid=22379

EXHIBIT B.5 Counting Stolen Valor

220. Historical Section, U.S. Army War College per House Resolution HR 230, *The Battle of King's Mountain, South Carolina,* October 7, 1780 & *Battle of Cowpens, South Carolina,* January 17, 1781, U.S. Army War College, Carlisle, PA: 1928, p. 32

221. Ibid, p. 18

222. Ibid, p. 23

223. Ibid, p. 38

224. American Battlefield Protection Program, "Report to Congress on The Historic Preservation of The Revolutionary War and War of 1812 Sites in the United States," *National Park Service, U.S. Department of the Interior*, Sep. 2007, Dec. 2012; Heritage Preservation Services Division, "Scope and Methodology of Revolutionary War and War of 1812 Historic Preservation Study," *National Park Service, U.S. Department of the Interior*, Jun. 2000, Dec. 2012, http://tps.cr.nps.gov/gis/revwar/methodology .htm; Munn, David, "Battles and Skirmishes of the American Revolution in New Jersey," Bureau of Geology and Topography, New Jersey Geological Survey, 1976, Jan. 2013, http://slic.njstatelib.org/NJ_Information/ Digital_Collections/Revolution/BattlesandSkirmishes.php

225. Boatner, Mark Mayo, III, *Encyclopedia of the American Revolution,* Stackpole Books, Mechanicsburg, Pa.: 1994 (1966); Heitman, Francis, *Historical Register of Officers of the Continental Army During the War of American Revolution*, Rare Book Shop Printing Co. Washington DC: 1914

226. Ibid.

227. Ibid.

228. McCrady, Edward, *The History of South Carolina in The Revolution 1780-1783*, Macmillan company, New York: 1902, p. 735

229. O'Kelley, Patrick, *Nothing But Blood and Slaughter (Volumes 1, 2, 3 and 4)*, BookLocker.com, Inc., 2004, 2005

230. Vail, Henry H., *A History of the McGuffey Readers*, The Burrows Brothers, Cleveland, Oh.: 1911; Edited by Vail, Henry, *Eclectic Educational Series: McGuffey's Fifth Eclectic Reader*, American Book Company, New York: 1920 (1879); Edited by Vail, Henry, *Eclectic Educational Series: McGuffey's Sixth Eclectic Reader*, American Book Company, New York: 1921 (1879); *The New McGuffey Fourth Reader*, American Book Company, New York: 1901; Smith, Samuel J., "Mc-Guffey Readers," Encyclopedia of Educational Reform and Dissent

(2010), Mar 2013, http://digitalcommons.liberty.edu/cgi/viewcontent
.cgi?article=1118&context=educ_fac_pubs

231. *Journals of the Continental Congress, 1774-1789, (Vol. 18,19 & 21),*
Thirty Four Volumes Published by the Library of Congress, 1904-1937,
http://memory.loc.gov/ammem/amlaw/lwjclink.html

232. Ibid.

CLOSING ARGUMENT:
Crooks, Cronies, and Consequences of the War
on God, Guns, and Guts

Motives: "Long March" to Culture War

233. Hadro, Matt "CNN Analyst Suggests 'Right Wing Extremists' Could Be
Behind Boston Bombing," *Media Research Center: Newsbusters*, 15 Apr.
2013, Apr. 2013, http://newsbusters.org/blogs/matt-hadro/2013/04/15/
cnn-analyst-suggests-right-wing-extremists-could-be-behind-boston-
bombin; Sterman, David, "The Greater Danger: Military-Trained Right
Wing Extremists" *The Atlantic*, 24 Apr. 2013, Apr. 2013, http://www
.theatlantic.com/national/archive/2013/04/the-greater-danger-military-
trained-right-wing-extremists/275277/; Akram, Mohamed, "An Explan-
atory Memorandum on the General Strategic Goal for the Brotherhood
in North America," Shura Council of the Muslim Brotherhood, 19
May 1991, May 2013, http://www.investigativeproject.org/document/
id/20; Tett, Gillian, "The Physics of Terror," *The Financial Times*, 26
Apr 2013, May 2013, http://www.ft.com/intl/cms/s/2/b70eb990-ad40-
11e2-b27f-00144feabdc0.html#axzz2S8U5Xe1M; Clauset, Aaron,
and Woodward, Ryan, "Estimating the Historical and Future Probabil-
ities of Large Terrorist Events," *Cornell University "arxiv.org" Physics
Library,* 1 Sep. 2012, May 2013, http://www.paramuspost.com/article.
php/20091026152024744; "FBI's Most Wanted: Most Wanted Terrorists," *The Federal Bureau of Investigation*, 1 May 2013, May 2013,
http://www.fbi.gov/wanted/wanted_terrorists/@@wanted-group-listing;

234. Korte, Gregory, "IRS gave liberals a pass; Tea Party groups put on
hold," *USA Today*, 14 May 2013, May 2013, http://www.usatoday.
com/story/news/nation/2013/05/14/irs-gave-progressives-a-pass-tea-
party-groups-put-on-hold/2159983/; Korte, Gregory, "IRS Approved
Liberal Groups while Tea Party in Limbo," *USA Today*, 14 May 2013,
May 2013, http://www.usatoday.com/story/news/politics/2013/05/14/
irs-tea-party-progressive-groups/2158831/

235. Strassel, Kimberley, "The IRS Scandal Started at the Top," *The Wall
Street Journal, 19 May 2013, May 2013,* http://www.wsj.com/articles/SB1
0001424127887324767004578487332636180800

236. Trinko, Katrina, "Blame Palin," *The National Review*, 15 Jan.
2011, May 2013, http://www.nationalreview.com/article/257249/
blame-palin-katrina-trinko

237. "(U//FOUO) Rightwing Extremism: Current Economic and Political Climate Fueling Resurgence in Radicalization and Recruitment," *Prepared*

by the Extremism and Radicalization Branch, Homeland Environment Threat Analysis Division. Coordinated with the FBI, 07 Apr. 2009, Apr. 2013, http://www.fas.org/irp/eprint/rightwing.pdf; Benko, Ralph, "1.6 Billion Rounds Of Ammo For Homeland Security? It's Time For A National Conversation," *Forbes.com*, 11 Mar. 2013, Apr. 2013, http://www.forbes.com/sites/ralphbenko/2013/03/11/1-6-billion-rounds-of-ammo-for-homeland-security-its-time-for-a-national-conversation/; "Reps Challenge DHS Ammo Buys, Say Agency using 1,000 More Rounds Per Person than Army," *FoxNews.com*, 26 April 2013, Apr. 2013, http://www.foxnews.com/politics/2013/04/26/reps-challenge-dhs-ammo-buys-say-agency-using-1000-more-rounds-per-person-than/; Flock, Elizabeth, "DHS Denies Ammo Purchases Aimed at Civilians," *US News & World Report*, 25 Apr. 2013, Apr. 2013, http://www.usnews.com/news/blogs/washington-whispers/2013/04/25/dhs-denies-ammo-purchases-aimed-at-civilians; Dinan, Stephen, "Sequester, Tight Budgets Means DHS Buying Less Ammunition," *Washington Times*, 25 Apr. 2013, Apr. 2013, http://www.washingtontimes.com/news/2013/apr/25/sequester-tight-budgets-means-dhs-buying-less-ammu/print/; Flock, Elizabeth, "DHS Denies Massive Ammunition Purchase," *US News & World Report*, 22 Mar. 2013, May 2013, http://www.usnews.com/news/blogs/washington-whispers/2013/03/22/dhs-denies-massive-ammunition-purchase_print.html

238. Ibid.
239. Malkin, Michelle, "Confirmed: The Obama DHS Hit Job on Conservatives is Real," *MichelleMalkin.com*, 14 Apr. 2009, Apr. 2013, http://michellemalkin.com/2009/04/14/confirme-the-obama-dhs-hit-job-on-conservatives-is-real/
240. Ledeen, Michael A., *Tocqueville on American Character: Why Tocqueville's Brilliant Exploration of the American Spirit is as Vital and Important Today as it Was Nearly Two Hundred Years Ago*, St. Martin's Press, New York: 2000; Hunter, James Davison, *Before the Shooting Starts: Searching for Democracy in America's Culture War*, The Free Press, New York: 1994; Hunter, James Davison, *Culture Wars: The Struggle to Define America—Making Sense of the Battles Over the Family, Art, Education, Law, and Politics*, Basic Books, New York: 1991; Lipset, Seymour Martin, *American Exceptionalism: A Double-Edged Sword*, Norton & Company, New York: 1996
241. Cramer, Clayton, "James Davison Hunter, Culture Wars: The Struggle To Define America," *Claytoncramer.com*, May 2013, http://www.claytoncramer.com/bookreviews/culture.html; "Event Transcript: Is There A Culture War?," *The Pew Forum on Religious and Public Life*, 23 May. 2006, May 2013, http://www.pewforum.org/Politics-and-Elections/Is-There-A-Culture-War.aspx; Fonte, John, "Why there is a Culture War," *Policy Review #104, Hoover Institution, Stanford University*, 1 Dec. 2000, May 2013, http://www.hoover.org/publications/policy-review/article/7809; Congdon, Lee, "Virginia View Point: Culture War," Virginia Institute for Public Policy, Sep. 2005, May 2013, http://www.virginiainstitute.org/viewpoint/2005_09_5.html; Mouw, Ted and Sobel, Michael E., "Culture Wars and Opinion Polarization: The Case of

Abortion," American Journal of Sociology, AJS Volume 106 Number 4, Jan. 2001, May 2013, http://www.unc.edu/~tedmouw/papers/mouw%20 opinion%20polarization.pdf; Buchanan, Pat, *Republican National Convention "Culture War" Address delivered 17 August 1992*, http:// buchanan.org/blog/1992-republican-national-convention-speech-148; Carter, Stephen L., *The Culture of Disbelief: How American Law and Politics Trivialize Religious Devotion*, Anchor Books, New York: 1993

242. Ibid.

243. Ibid.

244. "A Decade Later, Iraq War Divides the Public" *The Pew Research Center*, 18 Mar. 2013, May 2013, http://www.people-press.org/files/ legacy-pdf/3-18-13%20Iraq%20Release.pdf; Bowen, Gordon, "Public Opinion and the Vietnam War," Mary Baldwin College, May 2013, http://www.mbc.edu/faculty/gbowen/PublicOpinionVietWar.htm; "Casualties, Public Opinion and Presidential Policy During the Vietnam War," *Rand: Project Air Force*, Mar. 1985, May 2013, http://www.rand .org/content/dam/rand/pubs/reports/2007/R3060.pdf; "Iraq Versus Vietnam: A Comparison of Public Opinion," *Gallup*, 24 Aug. 2005, May 2013, http://www.gallup.com/poll/18097/iraq-versus-vietnam-compar- ison-public-opinion.aspx?version=print; Fernia, Will, "'Hubris: Selling The Iraq War' to re-air March 22 at 9 p.m. ET," *MSNBC: The Maddow Blog*, 12 Mar. 2013, May 2013, http://maddowblog.msnbc .com/_news/2013/03/12/17287344-hubris-selling-the-iraq-war-to- re-air-march-22-at-9-pm-et?lite

245. Zoll, Rachel, "Report Says Protestants Lose Majority Status In U.S." *Associated Press*, 9 Oct. 2012, Dec. 2012, http://bigstory.ap.org/article/ report-us-protestants-lose-majority-status

246. Green, Joshua, "Why Republicans Won't Flip on Gay Marriage," *Bloomber Businessweek*, 29 Mar. 2013, May 2013, http://www.business- week.com/ articles/2013-03-29/why-republicans-wont-flip-on-gay-marriage; Murray, Mark, "NBC/WSJ poll: 53 Percent Support Gay Marriage," NBCNews.com, 12 Apr. 2013, Apr. 2013, http://firstread.nbcnews.com/_ news/2013/04/11/17708688-nbcwsj-poll-53-percent-support-gay- marriage?chromedomain=nbcpolitics&lite ; Miller, Dave, "Situation Ethics—Extended Version," *Apologetics Press*, 2004, Mar. 2013, http:// www.apologeticspress.org/APContent.aspx?category=7&article=645; Goodstein, Laurie, "Atheist Groups Promote a Holiday Message: Join Us," *The New York Times*, 9 Nov. 2010, Mar. 2013, http://www.nytimes .com/2010/11/10/us/10atheist.html?_r=3&scp=1&sq=atheist%20 groups%20promote%20a%20holiday%20message:%20join%20 us&st=cse&; Winston, Kimberly, "Study: Atheists Distrusted as Much as Rapists," *USA Today*, 10 Dec. 2011, Mar. 2013, http://usatoday30.usa- today.com/news/religion/story/2011-12-10/religion-atheism/51777612/1; Grewal, Daisy, "In Atheists We Distrust," *Scientific American*, 17 Jan. 2012, Mar. 2013, http://www.scientific\american.com/article.cfm?id=in- atheists-we-distrust; Gervais, Will, Et al. , "Do you believe in atheists? Distrust is central to anti-atheist prejudice," *Study conducted by Depart- ment of Psychology, University of British Columbia, Vancouver, BC*, 7

Nov. 2011, Mar. 2013, http://www.ncbi.nlm.nih.gov/pubmed/22059841; "APOSTLES OF ATHEISM: How the broadcast and print media helped spread the Gospel of Godlessness in 2007," *Culture and Media Institute at Media Research Center*, 2008, Mar. 2013, http://archive.mrc.org/cmi/uploads/pdf/CMI_Atheism_Report_nocover.pdf; "Global Index of Religiosity and Atheism – 2012," *Poll conducted by WIN-Gallup International*, 2012, Mar. 2013, http://redcresearch.ie/wp-content/uploads/2012/08/RED-C-press-release-Religion-and-Atheism-25-7-12 .pdf; Merritt, Jonathan, "Election 2012 Marks the End of Evangelical Dominance in Politics," *The Atlantic*, 13 Nov. 2012, May 2013, http://www.theatlantic.com/politics/archive/2012/11/election-2012-marks-the-end-of-evangelical-dominance-in-politics/265139/

247. Montanaro, Domenico, "No, Its Not Christians Fault Obama Won," *NBC News*, 16 Nov. 2012, Dec. 2012, http://firstread.nbcnews .com/_news/ 2012/11/16/15219396-no-its-not-christians-fault-obama-won?lite; Cillizza, Chris, and Cohen, "President Obama and the White Vote? No Problem.," *The Washington Post*, 08 Nov. 2012, May 2013, http://www.washingtonpost.com/blogs/the-fix/wp/2012/11/08/president-obama-and-the-white-vote-no-problem/; "Voter Analysis Shows Obama Would Have Lost in 2012 if Black Turnout had Mirrored 2008," *The Associated Press*, 28 Apr. 2013, May 2013, http://www.foxnews.com/politics/2013/04/28/in-first-black-voter-turnout-rate-passes-whites/; Trende, Sean, "The Case of the Missing White Voters," *RealClear Politics.com*, 8 Nov. 2012, May 2013, http://dyn.realclearpolitics.com/printpage/?url=http://www.realclearpolitics.com/articles/2012/11/08/the_case_of_the_missing_white_voters_116106-full.html; Cost, Jay, "After the Tumult and the Shouting," *The Weekly Standard*, 3 Dec 2012, May 2013, http://www.weeklystandard.com/articles/after-tumult-and-shouting_663841.html?nopager=1; "How the Faithful Voted: 2012 Preliminary Analysis," *The Pew Forum on Religion & Public Life*, 7 Nov. 2012, May 2013, http://www.pewforum.org/Politics-and-Elections/How-the-Faithful-Voted-2012-Preliminary-Exit-Poll-Analysis.aspx; Sullivan, Amy, "The Origins of the God Gap," *TIME*, 12 Jul. 2007, Mar. 2013, http://www.time.com/time/magazine/article/0,9171,1643038,00.html; "Barna Survey Examines Changes in Worldview Among Christians over the Past 13 Years," *The Barna Group*, 6 Mar. 2009, Nov. 2012, http://www.barna.org/barna-update/article/21-transformation/252-barna-survey-examines-changes-in-worldview-among-christians-over-the-past-13-years; "Election 2012 Priorities: How The Faith of Likely Voters Affects the Issues They Care About," *The Barna Group*, 18 Apr. 2012, Nov. 2012, http://www.barna.org/faith-spirituality/563-election-2012-priorities-how-the-faith-of-likely-voters-affects-the-issues-they-care-about; "Faith on the Hill: The Religious Composition of the 113th Congress and Appendix: Religious Affiliation of Each Member of Congress," *Pew Forum on Religion & Public Life*, 16 Nov. 2012, Nov. 2012, http://www.pewforum.org/Government/Faith-on-the-Hill--The-Religious-Composition-of-the-113th-Congress. aspx; "Athiests and Agnostics Take Aim at Christians," *The Barna Group*, 11 Jun. 2007, Nov. 2012, http://www.barna.org/barna-update/

article/12-faithspirituality/102-atheists-and-agnostics-take-aim-at-christians; "New Barna Report Examines Diversity of Faith in Various U.S. Cities," *The Barna Group*, 11 Oct. 2010, Nov. 2012, http://www.barna.org/faith-spirituality/435-diversity-of-faith-in-various-us-cities

248. Dickerson, John "Go for the Throat! Why if he wants to transform American politics, Obama must declare war on the Republican Party." *Slate.com*, 18 Jan. 2013, Feb. 2013, http://www.slate.com/articles/news_and_politics/politics/2013/01/barack_obama_s_second_inaugural_address_the_president_should_declare_war.single.html; Newton-Small, Jay, "White House Destruction Is Popular with Moviegoers; Why This is a Good and Bad Milestone," *TIME*, 1 Apr. 2013, May 2013, http://www.paramuspost.com/article.php/20091026152024744

249. Ryan, Danielle, "White House Receives Secession Pleas From All 50 States," *Los Angeles Times*, 14 Nov. 2012, Dec, 2012, http://articles.latimes.com/2012/nov/14/news/la-pn-white-house-secession-50-states-20121114; Carson, Jon, "Our States Remain United: Official White House Response to Nine Petitions for Peaceful Secession," *Office of Public Engagement, The White House*, 11 Jan. 2013, Jan. 2013, https://petitions.whitehouse.gov/response/our-states-remain-united; Richardson, Valerie, "White House Not Humoring Secession Pleas: Stresses Unity in Petition Response," The Washington Times, 13 Jan. 2013, Jan. 2013, http://www.washingtontimes.com/news/2013/jan/13/white-house-not-humoring-secession-pleas/

250. Buchanan, Pat, *Republican National Convention "Culture War" Address delivered 17 August 1992*, http://buchanan.org/blog/1992-republican-national-convention-speech-148; Irons, Peter, *God On Trial: Landmark Cases from America's Religious Battlefields*, Penguin Books, New York: 2007; Lexington, "How To Lose the Culture Wars, " *The Economist*, 1 Jun. 2006, http://www.economist.com/node/7008598; Buchanan, Patrick J. "The Culture War For The Soul of America," *Pat Buchanan's Official Blog*, 14 Sep. 1992, Nov. 2012, http://buchanan.org/blog/the-cultural-war-for-the-soul-of-america-149; Nagourney, Adam, "'Cultural War' of 1992 Moves In From The Fringe," *New York Times*, 29 Aug. 2012, Nov. 2012, http://www.nytimes.com/2012/08/30/us/politics/from-the-fringe-in-1992-patrick-j-buchanans-words-now-seem-mainstream.html?_r=0; Buchanan, Patrick J., *Suicide Of A Superpower: Will America Survive to 2025?*, St. Martin's Press, New York: 2011

251. Hunter, James Davison, *Before the Shooting Starts: Searching for Democracy in America's Culture War*, The Free Press, New York: 1994; Hunter, James Davison, *Culture Wars: The Struggle to Define America—Making Sense of the Battles Over the Family, Art, Education, Law, and Politics*, Basic Books, New York: 1991

252. Rei, Lisa, "Political Science Scholar Debunks Myth of America's Culture Divide in New Book," *Stanford Report*, 6 Oct. 2004, http://news.stanford.edu/news/2004/october6/onenation-106.html; Gates, Henry Louis Jr., "The Culture Wars Next Frontier: An excerpt from 'Tradition and The Black Atlantic,'" *The Daily Beast*, 17 Nov. 2012, Dec. 2012, http://www.thedailybeast.com/articles/2010/11/17/

henry-louis-gates-new-book-on-the-culture-wars.html; Lexington, "What's Eating Appalachia?" *Economist*, 7 Jul. 2012, Dec. 2012, http://www.economist.com/node/21558275; Cloud, John, "Gates Makes a Strong Defense of Multiculturalism and Afro-American Studies in Latest Collection of Essays," *The Harvard Crimson*, 1 May. 1992, May 2013, http://www.thecrimson.com/article/1992/5/1/gates-makes-a-strong-defense-of/;

253. Washington, George, *George Washington September 17, 1796, Farewell Address, George Washington Papers at the Library of Congress, 1741-1799 Series 2 Letterbooks, Letter Book 24*, Library of Congress, http://memory.loc.gov

254. Perliger, Arie, "Challengers from the Sidelines: Understanding America's Violent Far-Right", *Combating Terrorism Center, United States Military Academy*, 15 Jan. 2013, Jan. 2013, http://www.ctc.usma.edu/posts/challengers-from-the-sidelines-understanding-americas-violent-far-right; Scarborough, Rowan, "West Point Center Cites Dangers of 'Far Right' in U.S.,", *Washington Times*, 17 Jan. 2013, Jan. 2013, www.washington-times.com/news/2013/jan/17/west-point-center-cites-dangers-far-right-us/

255. Cassino, Dan, "Beliefs About Sandy Hook Cover-Up, Coming revolution Underlie Divide on Gun Control," *Fairleigh Dickenson University's PublicMind Poll*, 1 May 2013, May 2013, http://publicmind.fdu.edu/2013/guncontrol/; Knowles, David, "'Armed Revolution to Protect Liberties' May Soon be Necessary, 44% of Republicans Say," *The New York Daily News*, 1 May 2013, May 2013, http://www.nydailynews.com/news/national/armed-revolution-44-republicans-article-1.1332621; Michel, Casey, "Owning Guns Doesn't Preserve Freedom," *The Atlantic*, 25 Apr. 2013, May 2013, http://www.theatlantic.com/international/archive/2013/04/owning-guns-doesnt-preserve-freedom/275287/; Hutchinson, Bill, "Nutty New NRA President Jim Porter Still Fighting War Against 'Northern Aggression'," *The New York Daily News*, 2 May 2013, May 2013, http://www.nydailynews.com/news/national/nutty-new-nra-president-jim-porter-war-guns-article-1.1333864; Wing, Nick, "Open Carry March In Washington Seeks To Put 'Government On Notice' With Loaded Rifles," *The Huffington Post*, 6 May. 2013, May 2013, http://www.huffingtonpost.com/2013/05/06/open-carry-march-washington_n_3222511.html?view=print&comm_ref=false ; Seitz-Wald, Alex, "A March on Washington with Loaded rifles," *SALON.com*, 3 May 2013, May 2013, www.salon.com/2013/05/03/a_march_on_washington_with_loaded_rifles/

256. Ibid.

257. "Event Transcript: Is There A Culture War?," *The Pew Forum on Religious and Public Life*, 23 May. 2006, May 2013, http://www.pewforum.org/Politics-and-Elections/Is-There-A-Culture-War.aspx

258. Ibid.

Accomplices: Marxism Goes Mainstream

259. Edited by Graham, Hugh Davis and Gurr, Ted Robert, *The History of Violence in America: A Report to the National Commission on the Causes

and Prevention of Violence, Bantam Books, New York: 1969; Brown, Maxwell Richard, *Strain of Violence: Historical Studies of American Violence and Vigilantism,* Oxford University Press, New York: 1975; Brown, Maxwell Richard, *No Duty to Retreat: Violence and Values in American History and Society,* University of Oklahoma Press, Norman, OK: 1991

260. Carter, Jimmy, "Carter Raises Eyebrows With 'Superior' Comment (polarization quote)," *NBC Nightly News,* 20 Sep. 2010, May 2013, http:// www.nbcnews.com/video/nightly-news/39277980#39277980

261. Bibel, Sara, "Cable News Ratings for Monday, February 18, 2013," *TV by The Numbers,* 20 Feb. 2013, May 2013, http://tvbythe numbers.zap2it.com/2013/02/20/cable-news-ratings-for-monday-february-18-2013/170013/; Groseclose, Tim and Milyo, Jeffery, "A Measure of Media Bias," *UCLA Study,* Dec. 2004, Mar. 2013, http:// www.sscnet.ucla.edu/polisci/faculty/groseclose/Media.Bias.8.htm; Kurtz, Howard, "Suddenly Everyone's A Critic," *The Washington Post,* 3 Oct. 2005, Mar. 2013, http://www.washingtonpost.com/wp-dyn/ content/article/2005/10/02/AR2005100201296.html; Okrent, Dan, "THE PUBLIC EDITOR; Is The New York Times a Liberal Newspaper?" *The New York Times,* 25 Jul. 2004, Mar. 2013, http://www .nytimes.com/2004/07/25/opinion/the-public-editor-is-the-new-york-times-a-liberal-newspaper.html?pagewanted=all&src=pm; Bozell, Brent, "Bozell Column: Shameless Bias by Omission," *Media Research Center,* 22 May 2012, Feb. 2013, http://newsbusters.org/blogs/brent-bozell/2012/05/22/bozell-column-shameless-bias-omission; O'Reilly, Bill, *Culture Warrior,* Broadway Books, New York: 2006

262. "Media Bias Basics: Admissions of Liberal Media Bias," *Media Research Center,* Feb. 2013, http://archive.mrc.org/biasbasics/printer/ biasbasics2admissions.asp; Bozell, Brent, "Bozell Column: Shameless Bias by Omission," *Media Research Center,* 22 May 2012, Feb. 2013, http://newsbusters.org/blogs/brent-bozell/2012/05/22/ bozell-column-shameless-bias-omission

263. Lind, Michael, *Made In Texas: George W. Bush and the Southern Takeover of American Politics,* Basic Books, New York: 2003

264. Jenkins, Philip, "NEGOTIATIONS: Conflict Between North and South," *TIME,* 13 Jun. 1977, Mar. 2013, http://www.time.com/time/subscriber/ article/0,33009,919002,00.html; Grier, James F., "The Difference Between North and South Is Green," *Los Angeles Times,* 23 Nov. 2003, Mar. 2013, http://articles.latimes.com/2003/nov/23/opinion/oe-oc-grier23; Grossman, Andrew "Upstate Versus Downstate," *The Wall Street Journal,* 29 Sep. 2010, Mar. 2013, http://online.wsj.com/article/ SB10001424052748704791004575520432790728198.html; "Southie Rules' series set to premiere on A&E Network in January," *Boston Globe,* 18 Dec. 2012, Mar. 2013, http://www.boston.com/yourtown/ news/south_boston/2012/12/southie_rules_series_set_to_pr.html; Rimer, Sarah, "For Old South Boston, Despair Replaces Hope," *The New York Times,* 20 Aug. 2012, Mar. 2013, http://www.nytimes.com/1997/08/17/ us/for-old-south-boston-despair-replaces-hope.html?pagewant-ed=print&src=pm; Bariyo, Nicholas, and Gross, Jenny, "Sudans Sign

Deals to Resume Oil Exports," *The Wall Street Journal*, 27 Sep. 2012, Mar. 2013, http://online.wsj.com/article/SB10000872396390443916104578021823192692526.html; Kowsmann, Patricia, and Wall, Denise, "North-South Divide Marks Euro's Struggle," *Wall Street Journal*, 29 Jul. 2012, Mar. 2013, http://online.wsj.com/article/SB100008723963904448401045775492736130133702.html; Feher, Margit, and Emsden, Christopher, "Euro-Zone Data Point to North-South Divide," *Wall Street Journal*, 26 Jun. 2012, Mar. 2013, http://online.wsj.com/article/SB10001424052702304782404577489823734679622.html; Gale, Alister, "Provocations Escalate on Korean Peninsula," *The Wall Street Journal*, 8 Mar. 2013, Mar. 2013, http://online.wsj.com/article/SB10001424127887323362880457834756314131 2452.html; Dalton, Matthew, "Busting North-South Stereotypes," *The Wall Street Journal*, 14 Aug. 2011, Mar. 2013, http://www.realclearreligion.org/articles/2012/08/20/the_new_soviet_league_of_militant_godless.html; "Northern Ireland's Violent History Explained," *BBC*, 8 Jan. 2013, Mar. 2013, http://www.bbc.co.uk/newsbeat/20930976; Jung, Alexander, "An Economic Miracle in the Venetian Hinterlands," *Spiegel Online*, 8 Aug. 2012, Mar. 2013, http://www.spiegel.de/international/europe/booming-economy-in-northern-italy-could-be-a-model-for-the-country-a-848759-druck.html

265. Gould, Peter and White, Rodney, *Mental Maps (Second Edition)*, Routledge, New York, 1992; Christensen, Rob, *The Paradox of Tarheel Politics: The Personalities, Elections and Events that Shaped Modern North Carolina*, University of North Carolina Press, Chapel Hill, NC: 2008

266. Horwitz, Tony, *Confederates in the Attic: Dispatches From an Unfinished Civil War*, Vintage Books, New York: 1999

267. Twelve Southerners, *I'll Take My Stand: The South and the Agrarian Tradition*, Louisiana Sate University Press, Baton Rouge, LA: 1977 (1930)

268. Applebome, Peter, *Dixie Rising: How the South is Shaping American Values Politics and Culture*, Harcourt Brace & Company, Orlando, FL: 1997

269. Ibid.

270. Thompson, Chuck, *Better Off Without'em: A Northern Manifesto for Southern Succession*, Simon & Schuster, New York: 2012

271. Faircloth, Sean, *Attack of the Theocrats: How the Religious Right Harms Us All- And What We Can Do About It*, Pitchstone Publishing, Charlottesville, VA: 2012;

272. Frank, Thomas, *What's the Matter With Kansas? How Conservatives Won the Heart of America*, Picador, New York: 2004

273. Pearson, Michael, *Those Damned Rebels: The American Revolution as Seen Through British Eyes*, Da Capo Press, 1972 (2000), p. 352

274. Bass, Robert D., *The Green Dragoon: The Lives of Banastre Tarleton and Mary Robinson*, Sandlapper Publishing, Orangeburg, SC: 1973, p. 247

275. Cook, Don, *The Long Fuse: How England Lost the War of the American Colonies, 1760-1785*, Atlantic Monthly Press, New York: 1995, p. 348

276. Moynihan, Daniel Patrick, "Defining Deviancy Down," *American Scholar*, 1993, Apr. 2013, http://www2.sunysuffolk.edu/formans/DefiningDeviancy.htm; Moynihan, Daniel Patrick, "The Negro Family: The Case For National Action," *Office of Policy Planning and Research,*

United States Department of Labor, Mar. 1965, Apr. 2013, http://www
.dol.gov/oasam/programs/history/webid-meynihan.htm; Robinson,
Randall and Goodman, Amy, "The Debt: Randall Robinson Talks About
What America Owes to Blacks," Interview Transcript on *Democra-
cyNow.Org*, 17 Jan. 2000, Apr. 2013, http://www.democracynow
.org/2000/1/17/the_debt_randall_robinson_talks_about; Rector, Robert
"Testimony Before Committee on the Budget United States House of
Representatives: Examining the Means-ested Welfare State: 79 Programs
and $927 Billion in Annual Spending," *The Heritage Foundation*, 3 May
2012, Apr. 2013, http://www.heritage.org/research/testimony/2012/05/
examining-the-means-tested-welfare-state; Tanner, Michael, "CATO
Policy Analysis #694: The American Welfare State How We Spend Nearly
$1 Trillion a Year Fighting Poverty—and Fail," *The CATO Institute*, 11
Apr. 2012, Apr. 2013, http://www.cato.org/sites/cato.org/files/pubs/pdf/
PA694.pdf; Terrence, Jeffery, "Record 89,967,000 Not in LaboForce;
Another 663,000 Drop Out In March," *CNSNews.com*, 5 Apr. 2013,
May 2013, http://cnsnews.com/news/article/record-89967000-not-
labor-force-another-663000-drop-out-march; McKee, Guian, "Lyndon
B. Johnson and the War on Poverty: Introduction to the Digital Edition,"
*Presidential Recordings of Lyndon B. Johnson, University of Virginia
Press*, 2010, Apr. 2013, http://presidentialrecordings.rotunda.upress
.virginia.edu/essays?series=WarOnPoverty

Crooks & Cronies: Historical Malpractice Sells Books

277. *"Col. Gadsden presented to congress an elegant Standard, such as to be
used by the commander in Chief of the American navy, being a yellow
field, with a lively representation of a rattle-snake in the middle with the
attitude of going to strike, and these words underneath, "Don't tread on
me!" Ordered that said Standard be carefully preserved and suspended
in the Congress room." –Journal of the Provincial Congress of South
Carolina, February 1776*

278. Edited by Force, Peter, *Tracts and Other Papers Relating Principally to
the Origin, Settlement, and Progress of the Colonies in North America*,
Vol. 2, Peter Force, Washington: 1838 ("An Account of South Carolina Submitted by John Peter Purry, et al. in Charleston, 23 September,
1731")

279. Black, Earl & Black, Merle, *The Rise Of The Southern Republicans*,
Harvard University Press, Cambridge, MA:2002; Black, Earl & Black,
Merle, *Divided America: The Ferocious Power Struggle in American
Politics*, Simon & Schuster Paperbooks, New York: 2008; McKee, Seth
C., *Republican Ascendancy in Southern House Elections*, Westview Press,
Boulder, CO:2010; Kapeluck, Branwell DuBose (editor), *Paler Shade
of RED: The 2008 Presidential Election In The South*, University of
Arkansas Press, Fayetteville, AR: 2009

280. Gibson, Campbell and Jung, Kay, "Working Paper Series No. 56: Historical Census Statistics on Population Totals By Race, 1790 to 1990,
and By Hispanic Origin, 1970 to 1990, For The United States, Regions,
Divisions, and States," *U. S. Census Bureau*, Sep. 2002, Jan. 2013, http://

www.census.gov/population/www/documentation/twps0056/twps0056
.html; "Population Change for the United States, Regions, States, and
Puerto Rico: 1990 to 2000," *U. S. Census Bureau*, 2001, Jan. 2013,
http://www.census.gov/prod/2001pubs/c2kbr01-2.pdf; "Population
Change for the United States, Regions, States, and Puerto Rico: 2000 to
2010," *U. S. Census Bureau*, 2011, Jan. 2013, http://www.census.gov/
prod/cen2010/briefs/c2010br-01.pdf; Henninger, Daniel, "Romney's
Secret Voting Bloc," *Wall Street Journal*, 1 Nov. 2012, Dec. 2012, http://
online.wsj.com/article/SB10001424052970203707604578090962267200892.html; Milbank, Dana, "Confederacy of Takers," *Washington Post*,
13 Nov. 2012, Dec. 2012, http://www.washingtonpost.com/opinions/
dana-milbank-the-confederacy-of-takers/2012/11/13/d8adc7ee-2dd4-
11e2-beb2-4b4cf5087636_story.html; Burnett, Kristin, "2010 Census
Brief: Congressional Apportionment," U.S. Census Bureau, November
2011, http://www.census.gov/prod/cen2010/briefs/c2010br-08.pdf;
"Statistical Abstract of the United States 2012: State Population—Rank
, Percent Change, and Population Density: 1980 to 2010," *U.S. Census
Bureau*, http://www.census.gov/compendia/statab/2012/tables/12s0014.
pdf; Mackun, Paul, "2010 Census Brief: Population Distribution And
Change: 2000 to 2010," *U.S. Census Bureau*, Mar. 2011, http://www
.census.gov/prod/cen2010/briefs/c2010br-01.pdf
281. "STATISTICS OF THE CONGRESSIONAL ELECTION OF NO-
VEMBER 6, 2012," Clerk of the U.S. House of Representatives, Mar.
2013, http://history.house.gov/Institution/Election-Statistics/Election-
Statistics/; "STATISTICS OF THE CONGRESSIONAL ELECTION OF
NOVEMBER 5, 2002," Clerk of the U.S. House of Representatives, Mar.
2013, http://history.house.gov/Institution/Election-Statistics/Election-
Statistics/; "STATISTICS OF THE CONGRESSIONAL ELECTION OF
NOVEMBER 3, 1992," Clerk of the U.S. House of Representatives, Mar.
2013, http://history.house.gov/Institution/Election-Statistics/Election-
Statistics/; "Party Divisions of the House of Representatives 1789–
Present," Office of the Historian, U.S. House of Representatives, Mar.
2013, http://history.house.gov/Institution/Party-Divisions/Party-
Divisions/; "2009 Income, Expenditures, Poverty, & Wealth: Gross
Domestic Product (GDP)," *2012 Statistical Abstract, U.S. Census, U.S.
Department of Commerce*, 2012, Mar. 2013, http://www.census.gov/
compendia/statab/cats/income_expenditures_poverty_wealth/gross_
domestic_product_gdp.html; "World Bank Gross Domestic Product
Rankings, 2010," *World Development Indicators Database, World Bank*,
1 July 2011, Mar. 2013, http://siteresources.worldbank.org/
DATASTATISTICS/Resources/GDP.pdf
282. Black, Earl & Black, Merle, *The Rise Of The Southern Republicans*,
Harvard University Press, Cambridge, MA:2002; Black, Earl & Black,
Merle, *Divided America: The Ferocious Power Struggle in American
Politics*, Simon & Schuster Paperbooks, New York: 2008; McKee, Seth
C., *Republican Ascendancy in Southern House Elections*, Westview Press,
Boulder, CO: 2010; Kapeluck, Branwell DuBose (editor), *Paler Shade
of RED: The 2008 Presidential Election In The South*, University of Ar-
kansas Press, Fayetteville, AR: 2009; Blackmon, Douglas, "Republicans

Face Unexpected Challenges in Coastal South Amid Shrinking White Vote," *Washington Post*, 24 Nov. 2012, Dec. 2012, http://articles. washingtonpost.com/2012-11-24/politics/35511999_1_white-students-white-voters-black-votersWashington Post

283. Barone, Michael, and McCutcheon, Chuck, *The Almanac of American Politics 2012,* University Of Chicago Press, Chicago, IL: 2011

284. Klein, Joe "Blue Dogs Dumped," *TIME*, 4 Nov. 2010, May 2013, http:// swampland.time.com/2010/11/04/blue-dogs-dumped/

285. Black, Earl & Black, Merle, *The Rise Of The Southern Republicans*, Harvard University Press, Cambridge, Ma.:2002; Black, Earl & Black, Merle, *Divided America: The Ferocious Power Struggle in American Politics*, Simon & Schuster Paperbooks, New York: 2008;

286. King, Neil, "Deep in the Red of Texas, Republicans Fight the Blues," *The Wall Street Journal,* 04 Apr. 2013, Apr. 2013, http://online.wsj.com/ article/SB10001424127887324883604578397021579876246.html; Burns, Alexander, "Democrats Launch Plan to Turn Texas Blue," *Politico*, 24 Jan. 2013, Jan. 2013, http://www.politico.com/story/2013/01/democrats-launch-plan-to-turn-texas-blue-86651.html; Cox, Karen L., "A New Southern Strategy," *New York Times*, 17 Nov. 2012, Dec. 2012, http://www.nytimes .com/2012/11/18/opinion/sunday/a-new-southern-strategy.html

287. Lind, Michael, *Made In Texas: George W. Bush and the Southern Takeover of American Politics*, Basic Books, New York: 2003; Frank, Thomas, *What's the Matter With Kansas? How Conservatives Won the Heart of America*, Picador, New York: 2004; Henninger, Daniel, "The Racializing of American Politics," *Wall Street Journal*, 28 Nov. 2012, Dec. 2012, http://online.wsj.com/article/SB10001424127887324205404 578147360260072602.html

288. "A Decade Later, Iraq War Divides the Public" *The Pew Research Center*, 18 Mar. 2013, May 2013, http://www.people-press.org/files/ legacy-pdf/3-18-13%20Iraq%20Release.pdf , Bowen,Gordon, "Public Opinion and the Vietnam War," Mary Baldwin College, May 2013, http://www.mbc.edu/faculty/gbowen/PublicOpinionVietWar.htm; "Casualties, Public Opinion and Presidential Policy During the Vietnam War," *Rand: Project Air Force*, Mar. 1985, May 2013, http://www.rand.org/ content/dam/rand/pubs/reports/2007/R3060.pdf; "Iraq Versus Vietnam: A Comparison of Public Opinion," *Gallup*, 24 Aug. 2005, May 2013, http://www.gallup.com/poll/18097/iraq-versus-vietnam-comparison-public-opinion.aspx?version=print

289. Fonte, John, "Why there is a Culture War," *Policy Review #104, Hoover Institution, Stanford University*, 1 Dec. 2000, May 2013, http://www .hoover.org/publications/policy-review/article/7809; "Event Transcript: Is There A Culture War?," *The Pew Forum on Religious and Public Life*, 23 May. 2006, May 2013, http://www.pewforum.org/Politics-and-Elections/Is-There-A-Culture-War.aspx; Congdon, Lee, "Virginia View Point: Culture War," Virginia Institute for Public Policy, Sep. 2005, May 2013, http://www.virginiainstitute.org/viewpoint/2005_09_5.html

290. Ibid.

291. Cooke, Alistair, *Alistair Cooke's America*, Alfred A. Knopf, New York: 1973

292. Churchill, Winston S., *A History of the English Speaking Peoples, Volume 3: The Age of Revolution*, Dodd, Mead & Company, London:1957
293. Cooke, Alistair, *Alistair Cooke's America*, Alfred A. Knopf, New York: 1973
294. Maerz, Melissa, "Keith Olbermann taps Michael Moore, Ken Burns, Richard Lewis for 'Countdown'," *The Los Angeles Times*, 11 May 2011, Mar. 2013, http://latimesblogs.latimes.com/showtracker/2011/05/keith-olbermann-taps-michael-moore-ken-burns-richard-lewis-for-countdown.html
295. Gerstein, Josh; Parti, Tarini; Gold, Hadas; and Byers, Dylan, "Clinton Foundation donors include dozens of media organizations, individuals," *Politico.com*, 15 May, 2015, May 2015, http://www.politico.com/blogs/media/2015/05/clinton-foundation-donors-include-dozens-of-media-207228.html
296. Edited by Charles Francis Adams, *Familiar Letters of John Adams and His Wife Abigail Adams during the Revolution with a Memoir of Mrs. Adams*, Houghton Mifflin, New York: 1875, p. 397-8
297. Ibid, p. 403
298. Ibid, p. 395-399
299. Crader, Bo, "A Historian and Her Sources: Doris Kearns Goodwin's Borrowed Material," *The Weekly Standard*, 28 Jan. 2002, Feb 2013, http://www.weeklystandard.com/Content/Public/Articles/000/000/000/793ihurw.asp; Wiener, Jon, *Historians in Trouble: Plagiarism, Fraud and Politics in the Ivory Tower*, The New Press, New York: 2005, p. 182-200
300. Abel, David, "Prize-Winning Professor Suspended For Lying / Mount Holyoke Teacher Had Said He Served in Vietnam," *The Boston Globe*, 18 Aug. 2001, Mar. 2013, http://www.sfgate.com/education/article/Prize-winning-professor-suspended-for-lying-2887575.php; Tyrangiel, Josh, "A History of His Own Making," *TIME*, 24 Jun. 2001, Mar. 2013, http://www.time.com/time/nation/article/0,8599,165156,00.html; Smith, Lynn, and Rutten, Tim, Michael, "For Historian's Students, a Hard Lesson on Lying," *The Los Angeles Times*, 22 Jun. 2001, Mar. 2013, http://articles.latimes.com/2001/jun/22/news/mn-13419; Ferdinand, Pamela, "A Historian's Embellished Life: Joseph Ellis Took Meticulous Care With Facts — Except His Own Story," *The Washington Post*, 23 Jun. 2001, Mar. 2013, http://www.pamelaferdinand.com/a-historians-embellished-life-joseph-ellis-took-meticulous-care-with-facts-except-his-own-story/
301. Ellis, Joseph, "The Many Minded Man," *The New York Times*, 6 Jul. 2003, Mar. 2013, http://www.nytimes.com/2003/07/06/books/the-many-minded-man.html; Ellis, Joseph, "The Big Man: History vs. Alexander Hamilton," *The New Yorker*, 29 Oct. 2001, Mar. 2013, http://www.newyorker.com/archive/2001/10/29/011029crbo_books
302. Garrow, David J., "Ellis Broke Golden Rule of Teaching," *The Boston Globe*, p. A13, 20 Jun. 2001, Jan. 2013, http://www.davidgarrow-com.hb2hosting.net/File/DJG%202001%20BGlobeEllisOpEd20June.pdf
303. Editors, "The Lies of Joseph Ellis," *The New York Times*, 21 Aug. 2001, Mar. 2013, http://www.nytimes.com/2001/08/21/opinion/the-lies-of-joseph-ellis.html; Schulevitz, Judith, "THE CLOSE READER; The

Wound and the Historian," *The New York Times*, 15 Jul. 2001, Mar. 2013, http://www.nytimes.com/2001/07/15/books/the-close-reader-the-wound-and-the-historian.html

304. Ferdinand, Pamela, "A Historian's Embellished Life: Joseph Ellis Took Meticulous Care With Facts — Except His Own Story," *The Washington Post*, 23 Jun. 2001, Mar. 2013, http://www.pamelaferdinand.com/a-historians-embellished-life-joseph-ellis-took-meticulous-care-with-facts-except-his-own-story/

305. Ellis, Joseph "Jefferson: Post-DNA," *Frontline (reprinted from William & Mary Quarterly), Vol. LVII, No. 1*, Jan. 2000, Mar. 2013, http://www.pbs.org/wgbh/pages/frontline/shows/jefferson/enigma/ellis.html ; Turner, Robert, F., "The Myth of Thomas Jefferson and Sally Hemings," *The Richmond Times Dispatch*, 12 Aug. 2012, Mar. 2013, http://www.timesdispatch.com/news/the-myth-of-thomas-jefferson-and-sally-hemings/article_3c88372c-6b3e-5bbd-8756-36d29f13b58f.html?-mode=print; Turner, Robert, F., "The Truth about Jefferson," *Opinion Journal of the Wall Street Journal*, 4 Jul. 2001, Mar. 2013, http://www.tjheritage.org/newscomfiles/WSJArticle.pdf;

306. Ellis, Joseph, "Immaculate Misconception and the Supreme Court," *The Washington Post*, 7 May 2010, Mar. 2013, http://www.washingtonpost.com/wp-dyn/content/article/2010/05/02/AR2010050202446.html; "Bio for Anthony Lake, Executive Director of UNICEF," *The UNICEF Press Center*, 18 Aug. 2001, Mar. 2013 http://www.unicef.org/media/media_53427.html

307. Wiener, Jon, *Historians in Trouble: Plagiarism, Fraud and Politics in the Ivory Tower*, The New Press, New York: 2005, p. 168-181

308. Ellis, Joseph, J., *His Excellency: George Washington*, Random House, New York: 2004; Ellis, Joseph, J., *Founding Brothers: The Revolutionary Generation*, Knopf, New York: 2000

309. Robinson, Walter V., "Professor's Past in Doubt: Discrepancies Surface in Claim of Vietnam Duty," *The Boston Globe*, 18 Jun. 2001, p. A1;

310. Barton, David, *The Jefferson Lies: Exposing the Myths You've Always Believed About Thomas Jefferson*, Thomas Nelson, Nashville, TN: 2012

311. Brodie, Fawn M., *Thomas Jefferson: An Intimate History*, Bantam Books, New York: 1974; Bringhurst, Newell G., *Fawn McKay Brodie: A Biographer's Life*, University of Oklahoma Press, Norman, OK: 1999

312. Ibid.

313. Ibid.; Sowell, Thomas, *Black Rednecks and White Liberals*, Encounter Books, New York: 2005

314. Davis, Brion David, "Book Review: Thaddeus Stevens: Scourge of the South," Pennsylvania History vol. 27, no. 3, July 1960, Mar. 2013, http://ojs.libraries.psu.edu/index.php/phj/article/view/22755/22524

315. Edited by Duberman, Martin, *The Antislavery Vanguard: New Essays on the Abolitionists*, Princeton University Press, Princeton, NJ: 1965

Crooks & Cronies: The Ivory Tower is Really Red

316. Cunningham, David, *There's Something Happening Here: The New Left, The Klan, and FBI Counterintelligence*, University of California Press,

Berkley, Ca.:2004; Powers, Richard Gid, *BROKEN: The Troubled Past and Uncertain Future of the FBI*, Free Press, New York: 2004; Johnson, Paul, *Modern Times: The World From the Twenties to the Nineties*, Harper Collins, New York: 1992; Leebaert, Derek, *The Fifty-Year Wound: How America's Cold War Victory Shapes Our World*, Back Bay Books, New York: 2002; Horowitz, David and Glazov, Jamie, *Left Illusions: An Intellectual Odyssey*, Spence Publishing, Dallas, Tx: 2003; Horowitz, David and Johnson, Ben, *Party of Defeat: How Democrats and Radicals Undermined America's War on Terror Before and After 9/11*, Spence Publishing, Dallas, TX: 2008; Horowitz, David, *Destructive Generation: Second Thoughts About the Sixties*, Encounter Books, San Francisco, CA: 1989; Horowitz, David, *The Shadow Party: How George Soros, Hillary Clinton and Sixties Radicals Seized Control of the Democratic Party*, Nelson Current, Nashville, TN: 2006

317. Brinkley, Douglas, *The Boys of Pointe Du Hoc*, Harper Collins, New York: 2005, p.10; D'Souza, Dinesh, *Illiberal Education: the Politics of Race and Sex on Campus*, The Free Press, New York:1991

318. Gitlin, Todd, "Choosing our better history," *Social Science Research Council*, 1 Jun. 2009, Apr. 2013, http://blogs.ssrc.org/tif/2009/06/01/choosing-our-better-history/?disp=print

319. "Reviews for Marx in Soho, a Play by Howard Zinn," *MarxInSoho.com*, Mar. 2013, http://www.marxinsoho.com/reviews/reviews.html

320. 319 Herbert, Bob "A Radical Treasure," *The New York Times*, 29 Jan. 2010, May 2013, http://www.nytimes.com/2010/01/30/opinion/30 herbert.html?_r=0

321. "Federal Bureau of Investigation Files on Howard Zinn," The Vault: Federal Bureau of Investigation Files, Mar. 2013, http://vault.fbi.gov/Howard%20Zinn%20Zinn; Howard, *A People's History of The United States*, Harper Collins, New York: 2003

322. Easterling, Stuart, "Defending Howard Zinn," *SoicalistWorker.Org*, 11 Feb. 2010, Mar. 2013, http://socialistworker.org/2010/02/11/defending-howard-zinn; Kincaid, Cliff, "Leftist "Historian" Howard Zinn Lied About Red Ties," *Accuracy in Media*, 30 Jul. 2012, Mar. 2013, http://www.aim.org/aim-column/leftist-"historian"-howard-zinn-lied-about-red-ties/; "An Experts's History of Howard Zinn: Fellow Historians are Interviewed," *Los Angeles Times*, 1 Feb. 2010, Mar. 2013, http://articles.latimes.com/2010/feb/01/opinion/la-oe-miller1-2010feb01; Powell, Howard, "Howard Zinn, Historian, Dies at 87," *The New York Times*, 28 Jan. 2010, Mar. 2013, http://www.nytimes.com/2010/01/28/us/28zinn.html; Schuessler, Jennifer, "Giving Incredibility Its Due, Historically Speaking," *The New York Times*, 19 Jul. 2012, Mar. 2013, http://query.nytimes.com/gst/fullpage.html?res=9907E6D81F3F F93AA25754C0A9649D8B63&pagewanted=print

323. Glavin, Paul, and Morse, Chuck, "War is the Health of the State: An Interview with Howard Zinn," *Institute for Anarchist Studies, Perspectives on Anarchist Theory*, Vol.7 No. 1, Spring 2003, Mar. 2013, http://flag.blackened.net/ias/13zinn.htm; McCain, Robert Stacey, "The Case Against Howard Zinn," *The American Spectator*, 2 Aug. 2010, Mar. 2013, http://spectator.org/archives/2010/08/02/

the-case-against-howard-zinn; Prager, Dennis, "Dennis Prager Interview with Professor Howard Zinn," Dennis Prager radio Show Transcript, 30 Aug. 2006, Mar. 2013, http://www.dennisprager.com/transcripts. aspx?id=1071; "Reviews for Marx in Soho, a Play by Howard Zinn," *MarxInSoho.com*, Mar. 2013, http://www.marxinsoho.com/reviews/ reviews.html; Kazin, Michael, "Howard Zinn's History Lessons," *Dissent Magazine*, Spring 2004, Mar. 2013, http://www.dissentmagazine.org/ article/howard-zinns-history-lessons; Slessinger, David, "Howard Zinn Interview," *911Truth.Org*, 2 Feb. 2009, Mar. 2013, http://www.911truth .org/article.php?story=20090309141651530

324. Diggins, John Patrick, "Fate and Freedom in History," *The National Interest*, 1 Sep. 2002, Mar. 2013, http://nationalinterest.org/print/article/ fate-and-freedom-in-history-399

325. D'Souza, Dinesh, *What's So Great About Christianity?*, Tyndale House, Carol Stream, Il.:2008, D'Souza, Dinesh, *Illiberal Education: the Politics of Race and Sex on Campus*, The Free Press, New York:1991; Horowitz, David and Glazov, Jamie, *Left Illusions: An Intellectual Odyssey*, Spence Publishing, Dallas, TX: 2003; Horowitz, David and Johnson, Ben, *Party of Defeat: How Democrats and Radicals Undermined America's War on Terror Before and After 9/11*, Spence Publishing, Dallas, TX: 2008; Horowitz, David, *Destructive Generation: Second Thoughts About the Sixties*, Encounter Books, San Francisco, CA: 1989; Horowitz, David, *The Shadow Party: How George Soros, Hillary Clinton and Sixties Radicals Seized Control of the Democratic Party*, Nelson Current, Nashville, TN: 2006

326. Friedman, Milton, *Free to Choose*, University of Chicago Press, Chicago, Il.: 1990 (1980); Friedman, Milton, *Capitalism and Freedom*, University of Chicago Press, Chicago, IL: 2002 (1962)

327. Chambers, Whittaker, *Witness*, Regnery Publishing, Washington D.C.: 2001 (1952); Reinsch, Richard, *Whittaker Chambers: The Spirit of a Counterrevolutionary*, ISI Books, Wilmington, DE: 2010

328. Piven, Frances Fox and Cloward, Richard A., *Poor People's Movements: Why They Succeed, How They Fail*, Vintage Books, New York: 1979; Cloward, Richard and Piven, Frances Fox, "The Weight of the Poor: A Strategy to End Poverty," *The Nation*, 2 May. 1966, Apr. 2013, http:// www.commondreams.org/headline/2010/03/24-4; Piven, Frances Fox, "Mobilizing the Jobless," *The Nation*, 22 Dec. 2011, Apr. 2013, http:// www.thenation.com/article/157292/mobilizing-jobless#; Murray, Mark, "Review of "Poor People's Movements: Why They Succeed, How They Fail. By Frances Fox Piven and Richard A. Cloward. New York: Pantheon Books, 1977." *Western Sociological Review* , 1979, Apr. 2013, http://works.bepress.com/hkerbo/24

329. Rector, Robert "Testimony Before Committee on the Budget United States House of Representatives: Examining the Means-tested Welfare State: 79 Programs and $927 Billion in Annual Spending," *The Heritage Foundation*, 3 May 2012, Apr. 2013, http://www.heritage.org/research/ testimony/2012/05/examining-the-means-tested-welfare-state; Tanner, Michael, "CATO Policy Analysis #694: The American Welfare State How We Spend Nearly $1 Trillion a Year Fighting Poverty—and Fail," *The*

CATO Institute, 11 Apr. 2012, Apr. 2013, http://www.cato.org/sites/cato.org/files/pubs/pdf/PA694.pdf

330. Ibid.
331. Weiss, Phillip, "One, Two, Three, Four, Can a Columbia Movement Rise Once More? Amid echoes of 1968, a new kind of radicalism struggles to be born," *New York Magazine*, 24 Oct. 2007, Apr. 2013, http://nymag.com/news/features/30629/; Dawson, James, "Why liberals should recruit conservatives to Columbia," *The Columbia Daily Spectator*, 6 Sep. 2010, Apr. 2013, http://www.columbiaspectator.com/2010/09/06/why-liberals-should-recruit-conservatives-columbia; Kimball, Roger, "Columbia & the Poverty of Liberalism," *Real Clear Politcs.com*, 23 Sep. 2007, Apr. 2013, http://www.realclearpolitics.com/articles/2007/09/columbia_the_poverty_of_libera.html;
332. Kelly, James J., "Brink's Controversy Heats Up: Rockland PBA President Asks Columbia University President to Fire Kathy Boudin," *Rockland County Times*, 17 Apr. 2013, Apr. 2013, http://www.rocklandtimes.com/2013/04/07/brinks-controversy-heats-up-rockland-pba-president-asks-columbia-university-president-to-fire-kathy-boudin/; Delgado, AJ, "O'Reilly Blasts Columbia's Hiring Of Weather Underground 'Radical' And Left's 'Stranglehold' On Academia," *Mediaite.com*, 14 Apr. 2013, Apr. 2013, http://www.mediaite.com/tv/oreilly-blasts-columbias-hiring-of-weather-underground-radical-and-lefts-stranglehold-on-academia/;
333. Hofstadter, Richard, *Social Darwinism in American Thought*, Beacon Press, Boston, MA:1992 (1944)
334. Schraffenberger, Donny, "Karl Marx and the American Civil War Espionage," *International Socialist Review*, Nov-Dec. 2011, Mar. 2013, http://www.isreview.org/issues/80/feat-civilwar.shtml; Davenport, Tim, "Early American Marxist History: The Communist International (Comintern)," *MarxistHistory.Org*, Mar. 2013 http://www.marxisthistory.org/subject/usa/eam/index.html
335. Luraghi, Raimondo, *The Rise and Fall of the Plantation South*, New Viewpoints, New York: 1978; Genovese, Eugene D. *In Red and Black: Marxian Explorations in Southern and Afro-American History*, University of Tennessee Press, Knoxville, TN: 1968 (1984); Sowell, Thomas, *Black Rednecks and White Liberals*, Encounter Books, New York: 2005
336. Genovese, Eugene D., *The Southern Tradition: The Achievement and Limitations of an American Conservatism*, Harvard University Press, Cambridge, Ma.:1994; Davis, Brian David, "Southern Comfort: Review of Genovese's 'The Southern Tradition," *The New York Review of Books*, 5 Oct. 1995, Mar. 2013, http://www.nybooks.com/articles/archives/1995/oct/05/southern-comfort/?pagination=false&printpage=true; Douglas, Martin, "Eugene D. Genovese, Historian of South, Dies at 82," *The New York Times*, 30 Dec. 2002, Mar. 2013, http://www.nytimes.com/2012/09/30/us/eugene-d-genovese-historian-of-south-dies-at-82.html?_r=0
337. Genovese, Eugene D., *The Southern Tradition: The Achievement and Limitations of an American Conservatism*, Harvard University Press, Cambridge, MA: 1994, x-xii

338. Ibid.

339. Foner, Eric "Majority Report: Review of 'A People's History of the United States'," *The New York Times*, 2 Mar. 1980, Mar. 2013, *RealClearReligion.Com* http://query.nytimes.com/mem/archive/pdf?res=FA0817F63B5A12728DDDAB0894DB405B8084F1D3

340. Radosh, Ronald, "The Left's Lion: Eric Foner's History," *The National Review*, 1 Jul. 2002, Mar. 2013, http://old.nationalreview.com/comment/comment-radosh071002.asp

341. Froner, Eric "(Bush) He's The Worst Ever," *The Washington Post*, 3 Dec. 2006, Mar. 2013, http://www.washingtonpost.com/wp-dyn/content/article/2006/12/01/AR2006120101509_pf.html; Pipes, Daniel, "Profs Who Hate America," *The New York Post*, 12 Nov. 2002, Mar. 2013, http://www.danielpipes.org/923/profs-who-hate-america; McLemee, Scott, "Seeing Red," *The Chronicle of Higher Education*, 27 Jun. 2003, Mar. 2013, http://chronicle.com/free/v49/i42/42a01101.htm

342. Gottfried, Paul, "Guilt trip: Eric Foner Writes History to Suit the Politically Correct Left--and the Neocons.," *The American Conservative*, 9 Mar. 2013, Mar. 2013, http://www.thefreelibrary.com/_/print/PrintArticle.aspx?id=199069477

343. Radosh, Ronald, "The Left's Lion: Eric Foner's History," *The National Review*, 1 Jul. 2002, Mar. 2013, http://old.nationalreview.com/comment/comment-radosh071002.asp

344. Foner, Eric, *Reconstruction: America's Unfinished Revolution, 1863-1877*, Perennial Classics, New York: 2002 (1988); Tilley, John Shipley, *The Coming of the Glory*, Bill Coats, Nashville, TN: 1949 (1995); Pike, James Shepherd, *The Prostrate State: South Carolina Under Negro Government*, D.Appleton, New York: 1874; Andrews, E. Benjamin, *The United States in Our Own Time: A History from Reconstruction to Expansion*, Charles, Scribner & Sons, New York: 1895

345. Diggins, John Patrick, "Fate and Freedom in History," *The National Interest*, 1 Sep. 2002, Mar. 2013, http://nationalinterest.org/print/article/fate-and-freedom-in-history-399

346. Honan, William, "Jack D. Foner, 88, Historian And Pioneer in Black Studies," *The New York Times*, 16 Dec. 1999, Mar. 2013, http://www.nytimes.com/1999/12/16/arts/jack-d-foner-88-historian-and-pioneer-in-black-studies.html; Van Gelder, Lawrence, "Philip S. Foner, Labor Historian and Professor, 84," *The New York Times*, 15 Dec. 1994, Mar. 2013, http://www.nytimes.com/1994/12/15/obituaries/philip-s-foner-labor-historian-and-professor-84.html?pagewanted=print&src=pm

347. "Annual Report on the Committee on Un-American Activities for the Year 1949," *Committee on Un-American Activities U. S. House of Representatives*, 15 Mar. 1950, Mar. 2013, http://archive.org/stream/annualreportfory1949unit/annualreportfory1949unit_djvu.txt; Lincove, David, A. "Radical Publishing to 'Reach the Million Masses': Alexander L. Trachtenberg and International Publishers," *Left History*, 2004, Mar. 2013, https://pi.library.yorku.ca/ojs/index.php/lh/article/viewFile/5634/4827; Joffe, Alex, "Jews, Communism, and Espionage," *Jewish Ideas Daily*, 29 Jun. 2011, Mar. 2013, http://www.jewishideasdaily.com/913/features/jews-communism-and-espionage/?print; "Online Book

Catalog of International Publishers," *International Publishers*, Mar. 2013, http://www.intpubnyc.com/Authors.html;

348. Greenhouse, Steven, "Moe Foner, Labor Official and Movement's Unofficial Cultural Impresario, Dies at 86," *The New York Times*, 11 Jan. 2002, Mar. 2013, http://www.nytimes.com/2002/01/11/nyregion/moe-foner-labor-official-movement-s-unofficial-cultural-impresario-dies-86.html; "SEIU Moe Foner Scholarship Program," *Service Employees International Union (SEIU.org)*, Mar. 2013, http://www.seiu.org/a/members/seiu-moe-foner-scholarship-program.php;

349. Soyer, Daniel, "Henry Foner- ILGWU Heritage Project at Cornell University," 10 June 2009, May 2013, http://ilgwu.ilr.cornell.edu/archives/oralHistories/HenryFoner.html

350. 349 Edited by Trachtenberg, A.L., *A Political Guide for Workers: Socialist Party Campaign Book 1920*, Socialist Party of the United States, Chicago, Il.: 1920; Lincove, David, A. "Radical Publishing to 'Reach the Million Masses': Alexander L. Trachtenberg and International Publishers," *Left History*, 2004, Mar. 2013, https://pi.library.yorku.ca/ojs/index.php/lh/article/viewFile/5634/4827;

351. Chambers, Whittaker, *Witness*, Regnery Publishing, Washington D.C.: 2001 (1952) p. 264; Davenport, Tim, "Early American Marxist History: The Communist International (Comintern)," *MarxistHistory.Org*, Mar. 2013 http://www.marxisthistory.org/subject/usa/eam/index.html ; Lincove, David, A. "Radical Publishing to 'Reach the Million Masses': Alexander L. Trachtenberg and International Publishers," *Left History*, 2004, Mar. 2013, https://pi.library.yorku.ca/ojs/index.php/lh/article/viewFile/5634/4827; Edited by Trachtenberg, A.L., *A Political Guide for Workers: Socialist Party Campaign Book 1920*, Socialist Party of the United States, Chicago, Il.: 1920; McLemee, Scott, "Seeing Red," *The Chronicle of Higher Education*, 27 Jun. 2003, Mar. 2013, http://chronicle.com/free/v49/i42/42a01101.htm, "Annual Report on the Committee on Un-American Activities for the Year 1949," *Committee on Un-American Activities U. S. House of Representatives*, 15 Mar. 1950, Mar. 2013, http://archive.org/stream/annualreportfory1949unit/annualreportfory1949unit_djvu.txt ; Lincove, David, A. "Radical Publishing to 'Reach the Million Masses': Alexander L. Trachtenberg and International Publishers," *Left History*, 2004, Mar. 2013, https://pi.library.yorku.ca/ojs/index.php/lh/article/viewFile/5634/4827; Joffe, Alex, "Jews, Communism, and Espionage," *Jewish Ideas Daily*, 29 Jun. 2011, Mar. 2013, http://www.jewishideasdaily.com/913/features/jews-communism-and-espionage/?print; Haynes, John Earl and Klehr, Harvey, *Venona: Decoding Soviet Espionage in America*, Yale University Press, New Haven, CT: 2000; Haynes, John Earl and Klehr, Harvey and Vasiliev, Alexander, *Spies: The Rise and Fall of the KGB in America*, Yale University Press, New Haven, CT: 2009; *Marxists.Org*, Apr. 2015 https://www.marxists.org/archive/marx/works/1843/critique-hpr/intro.htm

352. Ibid.

353. Ibid.

354. Ibid.

355. Marx, Karl, "A Contribution to the *Critique of Hegel's Philosophy of Right*," *Marxists.Org*, Apr. 2015 https://ww.marxists.org/archive/marx/works/1843/critique-hpr/intro.htm

356. Lamson, Peggy, *Roger Baldwin: Founder of the American Civil Liberties Union*, Houghton, Mifflin, Boston, Ma.:1976; American Civil Liberties Union (ACLU), *aclu.org History*, 24 Jul. 2009, http://www.aclu.org/aclu-history; Rossomando, John, "The ACLU's Untold Stalinist Heritage," The Daily Caller, 1 Apr. 2011, http://dailycaller.com/2011/01/04/the-aclu's-untold-stalinist-heritage/; Baldwin, Roger, "Freedom in the USA and the USSR," *Soviet Russia Today*, Sept 1934, May 2013, http://www2.law.ucla.edu/volokh/blog/baldwin.pdf

357. Ibid.

358. Barton, David, *Original Intent: The Courts, the Constitution, and Religion*, Wallbuilder Press, Aledo, TX: 1996 (2008)

359. Ibid, p. 15

Crooks & Cronies: ACLU, from Tennessee to Hollywood

360. Buchanan, Patrick J., *Suicide Of A Superpower: Will America Survive to 2025?*, St. Martin's Press, New York: 2011

361. Parker-Pope, Tara, "Suicide Rates Rise Sharply in U.S.," *The New York Times*, 2 May 2013, May 2013, http://www.nytimes.com/2013/05/03/health/suicide-rate-rises-sharply-in-us.html?_r=0; "Percentage* of U.S. High School Students Reporting Considering, Planning, or Attempting Suicide in the Past 12 Months, by Sex, United States, 2009," *Centers for Disease Control and Prevention*, 2 Apr. 2013, May 2013, http://www.cdc.gov/violenceprevention/suicide/statistics/youth_risk.html; "Suicide Among Adults Aged 35–64 Years—United States, 1999–2010," Morbidity and Mortality Weekly Report (MMWR) - Centers for Disease Control and Prevention, 3 May 2013, May 2013, http://www.cdc.gov/mmwr/preview/mmwrhtml/mm6217a1.htm?s_cid=mm6217a1_w; "Regional Variations in Suicide Rates- United States 1990-1994" Center for Disease Control, Morbidity and Mortality Weekly Report, 29 Aug. 97, Nov. 2012, http://www.cdc.gov/mmwr/preview/mmwrhtml/00049117.htm;

362. Irons, Peter, *God On Trial: Landmark Cases from America's Religious Battlefields*, Penguin Books, New York: 2007; Taranto, James, "Those Courageous Racists: Left wing Bigots Pat Themselves on the Back," *The Wall Street Journal*, 2 Apr. 2013, Apr. 2013, http://online.wsj.com/article/SB10001424127887323296504578398731336938160.html?mod=us_most_pop_newsreel; Sullivan, Amy, "The Origins of the God Gap," *TIME*, 12 Jul. 2007, Mar. 2013, http://www.time.com/time/magazine/article/0,9171,1643038,00.html; Butler, Jon, *Awash in the Sea of Faith: Christianizing the American People*, Harvard University Press, Cambridge, MA: 1992 "Atheists and Agnostics Take Aim at Christians," *The Barna Group*, 11 Jun. 2007, Nov. 2012, http://www.barna.org/barna-update/article/12-faithspirituality/102-atheists-and-agnostics-take-aim-at-christians; "New Barna Report Examines Diversity of Faith in Various U.S. Cities," *The Barna Group*, 11 Oct. 2010, Nov. 2012, http://www.barna.org/faith-spirituality/435-diversity-of-faith-in-various-us-cities

363. American Civil Liberties Union (ACLU), *aclu.org History*, 24 Jul. 2009, http://www.aclu.org/aclu-history ; Rossomando, John, "The ACLU's Untold Stalinist Heritage," The Daily Caller, 1 Apr. 2011, http://dailycaller.com/2011/01/04/the-aclu's-untold-stalinist-heritage/

364. Moran, Jeffrey P., *The Scopes Trial: A Brief History with Documents*, Bedford/St.Martin's, Boston Ma.: 2002; Dershowitz, Alan M., *Trials of the Century: Courtroom Battles that Changed the Nation, 1913-Today*, Recorded Books - Barnes & Noble Publishing, New York: 2006; Kazin, Michael, *A Godly Hero: The Life of William Jennings Bryan*, Anchor Books, New York: 2006; Bryan, William Jennings and Bryan, Mary Baird, *The Memoirs of William Jennings Bryan*, Universal Book and Bible House, Philadelphia, PA: 1925; Edited by the Rhea County Historical Society, *The World's Most Famous Court Trial: A Word-for-Word Report of the Famous Court Test of the Tennessee Anti-Evolution Act, at Dayton, July 10 to 21, 1925, Including Speeches and Arguments of Attorneys, Testimony of Noted Scientists and Bryan's Last Speech*, The Rhea County Historical Society, Dayton, TN: 1978 (1928); Levine, Lawrence, *Defender of The Faith: William Jennings Bryan-The Last Decade 1915-1925*, Harvard University Press, Cambridge, MA.: 1987

365. Ibid.

366. Ibid.

367. Radosh, Ronald, "Case Closed: the Rosenbergs Were Soviet Spies," *The Los Angeles Times*, 17 Sep. 2008, Mar. 2013, http://www.latimes.com/news/opinion/commentary/la-oe-radosh17-2008sep17,0,864776.story; Haynes, John Earl and Klehr, Harvey, *Venona: Decoding Soviet Espionage in America*, Yale University Press, New Haven, CT: 2000; Haynes, John Earl and Klehr, Harvey and Vasiliev, Alexander, *Spies: The Rise and Fall of the KGB in America*, Yale University Press, New Haven, CT: 2009

368. Menton, David, "Inherit The Wind: An Historical Analysis," *Creation*, 1 Dec. 1996, Cloud, John, " Inherit The Wind," *TIME*, 12 Apr. 2011; Blankenship, Bill, "Inherit The Controversy," *The Topeka Capital Journal*, 2 Mar. 2001; Benen, Steve, " Inherit the Myth?" *Church & State*, Jul 2000 Vol. 53 No. 7; Benen, Steve, "Its Not A Christian Nation," *Blog, Washington Monthly*,7 Apr. 2009; Americans United for Separation of Church and State, Website Mission & History, Nov. 2012, https://www.au.org/about/our-mission, https://www.au.org/about/our-history; Center for Responsive Politics, OpenSecrets.org Lobbying & Expenditure Report on Americans United For Separation of Church and State for 2009, 2010, 2011, 2012, Nov. 2012, http://www.opensecrets.org/lobby/firmbills.php?id=D0000477098&year=2009

369. Hoffman, David, "St. Marks Players unveil new 'Inherit The Wind' Production," *Washington Blade*, 13 Jan. 2011, http://www.washingtonblade.com/2011/01/13/arts-news-in-brief-5/; "Auntie Mame coauthor Jerome Lawrence dead at 88," Advocate.com, Nov. 2012, http://www.advocate.com/arts-entertainment/entertainment-news/2004/03/03/ltigtauntie-mameltigt-coauthor-jerome-lawrence-dead

370. Mencken, H.L., "Homo Neanderthalensis," *The Baltimore Evening Sun*, 29 Jun. 1925, Mar. 2013, http://www.positiveatheism.org/hist/menck01

.htm#SCOPES1; Mencken, H.L., "Mencken Finds Daytonians Full of Sickening Doubts About Value of Publicity," *The Baltimore Evening Sun*, 9 Jul. 1925, Mar. 2013, http://www.positiveatheism.org/hist/menck01 .htm#SCOPES1; Mencken, H.L., "Impossibility of Obtaining Fair Jury Insures Scopes' Conviction, Says Mencken," *The Baltimore Evening Sun*, 10 Jul. 1925, Mar. 2013, http://www.positiveatheism.org/hist/ menck01.htm#SCOPES1 ; Klinkenborg, Verlyn, "Editorial Observer; Remembering the Permanent Opposition of H. L. Mencken," *The New York Times*, 30 Dec. 2002, Mar. 2013, http://www.nytimes .com/2002/12/30/opinion/editorial-observer-remembering-the-permanent-opposition-of-h-l-mencken.html?ref=henrylouismencken

371. Cash, W.J., *The Mind of the South*, Random House, New York, 1991 (originally Knopf 1941), Woodward, C. Vann "W.J. Cash Reconsidered," *The New York Review of Books*, 4 Dec. 1969, Mar. 2013, http://www .nybooks.com/articles/archives/1969/dec/04/wj-cash-reconsidered/? pagination=false; Cash, W.J., "The Mind of the South," *The American Mercury*, Oct. 1929, Mar. 2013, http://www.wjcash.org/WJCash1/WJCash/ WJCash/mindofthesouth.htm; Cash, W.J., "Genesis of the Southern Cracker," *The American Mercury*, May. 1935, Mar. 2013, http://www .wjcash.org/WJCash1/WJCash/WJCash/genesisofthesoutherncracker.htm

372. Faulkner, William, *William Faulkner, Novels 1936-1940: Absalom, Absalom!, The Unvanquished, If I Forget Thee Jerusalem, The Hamlet*, Literary Classics of the U.S., New York: 1990 (Absalom! Absalom! Copyright 1936), Keener, Joseph B., *Shakespeare And Masculinity in Southern Fiction: Faulkner, Simms, Page, and Dixon*, Palgrave Macmillan, New York: 2008; Blotner, Joseph, *Faulkner: A Biography*, University Press of Mississippi, Jackson, Ms.: 1974 (2005); Cantwell, Robert, "BOOKS: When the Dam Breaks (William Faulkner cover story)," *TIME Magazine*, 23 Jan. 1939, Mar. 2013, http://www.time .com/time/subscriber/article/0,33009,760655,00.html; Lehmann-Haupt, Christopher, "Love Songs of a Crocodile: Review of Tennessee Williams' 'Memoirs'," *The New York Times*, 7 Nov. 1975, Mar. 2013, http://www .nytimes.com/books/00/12/31/specials/williams-memoirs.html; Woodward, C. Vann, *Thinking Back: The Perils of Writing History*, Louisiana State University Press, Baton Rouge, La.: 1986; Woodward, C. Vann, "The Siege: A review No Ivory Tower: McCarthy and the Universities," *New York Review of Books*, 25 Sep. 1986, Apr. 2013, http://www .nybooks.com/articles/archives/1986/sep/25/the-siege/?pagination=false

373. Higginbotham, Don, *The War Of American Independence*, Northeastern University Press, Lebanon, N.H.: 1983; Edited by Stapleton, John, "U.S. Military Academy: Officer's Professional Reading Guide," U.S. Military Academy, West Point, N.Y., Jan. 2013, http://www .westpoint.edu/history/sitepages/american%20revolution.aspx; Severo, Richard, "C. Vann Woodward, Historian Who Wrote Extensively About the South, Dies at 91," *The New York Times*, 19 Dec. 1999, Mar. 2013, http://www.nytimes.com/1999/12/19/us/c-vann-woodward-historian-who-wrote-extensively-about-the-south-dies-at-91.html? pagewanted=all&src=pm; Wyatt-Brown, Bertram, "C. Vann Woodward, 1908-1999" *Perspectives, The Magazine of the American*

Historical Association, Mar. 2000, Mar. 2013, http://www.historians
.org/perspectives/issues/2000/0003/0003mem8.cfm

374. Shales, Tom, "'The People Speak': A Revisionist History of These
     United States," *The Washington Post*, 12 Dec. 2009, Mar. 2013,
     http://www.washingtonpost.com/wp-dyn/content/article/2009/12/11/
     AR2009121103855_pf.html; O'Connell, Libby, "The People
     Speak-Democracy is Not a Spectator Sport," *HISTORY Channel*,
     Mar. 2013, http://www.history.com/shows/the-people-speak/articles/
     the-people-speak-story

375. McIntyre, Gina, "'Abraham Lincoln: Vampire Hunter': Fake
     history, but an honest Abe," Los Angeles Times, 16 Apr. 2012, Dec. 2012,
     http://herocomplex.latimes.com/2012/04/16/abraham-
     lincoln-vampire-hunter-fake-history-but-an-honest-abe/print/#/0

376. Wells, William, *The Life And Public Services of Samuel Adams, being a
     narrative of His Acts and Opinions and of his Agency in Producing and
     Forwarding the American Revolution with Extracts of his Correspon-
     dence, State Papers, and Political Essays*, Little Brown, And Company,
     Boston, Ma,: 1866; Benen, Steve, " Inherit the Myth?" *Church & State*,
     Jul 2000 Vol. 53 No. 7; Benen, Steve, "Its Not A Christian Nation,"
     Blog, Washington Monthly,7 Apr. 2009; Americans United for Sep-
     aration of Church and State, Website Mission & History, Nov. 2012;
     https://www.au.org/about/our-mission>, <https://www.au.org/about/
     our-history; Center for Responsive Politics, OpenSecrets.org Lobbying
     & Expenditure Report on Americans United For Separation of Church
     and State for 2009, 2010, 2011, 2012, Nov.; 2012http://www
     .opensecrets.org/lobby/firmbills.php?id=D0000477098&year=2009;
     Wattenberg, Daniel, "Sacred Mystery: Blockbuster Ratings for 'The
     Bible' Confound Hollywood," *The Washington Times*, 14 Mar. 2013,
     Mar. 2013, http://www.washingtontimes.com/news/2013/mar/14/
     sacred-mystery-blockbuster-ratings-bible-confound-/

377. Meacham, Jon, *American Gospel: God, The Founding Fathers and
     the Making of a Nation*, Random House, New York: 2006; Hagey,
     Keach "Newsweek Quits Print," *Wall Street Journal*, 19 Oct. 2012,
     Dec. 2012, http://online.wsj.com/article/SB100008723963904447348
     04578064300216922258.html; Kirk, Russell, "Civilization Without
     Religion?," *The Heritage Lectures Series, The Heritage Foundation*,
     24 Jul. 1992, Mar. 2013, http://www.heritage.org/research/lecture/
     civilization-without-religion

378. Federer, William, J., *The Original 13: A Documentary History of Reli-
     gion in America's First Thirteen States*, Amerisearch, St Louis, Mo: 2008;
     Edited by Francis Newton Thorpe, *The Federal And State Constitutions
     Colonial Charters and Other Organic Laws of the States, Territories,
     and Colonies Nor or Heretofore Forming The United States of America*,
     Government Printing Office, Washington DC: 1909; Kraminick, Isaac
     and Moore, Laurence R., *The Godless Constitution: A Moral Defense of
     the Secular State*, W.W. Norton, New York: 1997 (2005)

379. Ibid.

380. Barton, David, *Original Intent: The Courts, the Constitution, and Reli-
     gion*, Wallbuilder Press, Aledo, TX.: 1996 (2008)

Epilogue: Cling to Your Guns and Your Religion

381. Kumar, Anita, "Obama Proposes Assault Weapons Ban, Other Controls on Guns," *McClatchy News Papers*, 16 Jan. 2013, Jan. 2013, http://www .mcclatchydc.com/2013/01/16/180042/obama-proposes-ban-on-assault. html; Ohman, Jack, "Cartoon: The United States of Paranoia," *Sacramento Bee*, 16 Jan. 2013, Jan. 2013, http://www.mcclatchydc .com/2013/01/14/179809/mcclatchy-cartoons-for-the-week.html; "States With the Most Legal Guns in 2012," *The Daily Beast*, 29 Jan. 2013, Jan. 2013, http://www.thedailybeast.com/articles/2012/12/15/states-with-the-most-legal-guns-in-2012.html; "Gun Ownership by State," *Washington Post*, May. 2006, Jan. 2013, http://www.washingtonpost.com/wp-srv/ health/interactives/guns/ownership.html; Frosch, Dan, "Some Sheriffs Object to Call for Tougher Gun Laws," *The New York Times*, 31 Jan. 2013, Mar. 2013, http://www.nytimes.com/2013/02/01/us/some-sheriffs-object-to-call-for-tougher-gun-laws.html ; "NSA Position Statement on Gun Control," *National Sheriff's Association*, 1 Feb. 2013, Mar. 2013, http://www.sheriffs.org/content/nsa-position-statement-gun-control; Tavernise, Sabrina, and Gebeloff, Robert, "Share of Homes With Guns Shows 4-Decade Decline," *The New York Times*, 9 Mar. 2013, Mar. 2013, http://www.nytimes.com/2013/03/10/us/rate-of-gun-ownership-is-down-survey-shows.html?pagewanted=all; Deluca, Matthew, and Briggs, Bill, "Gun Stores Running Low on Weapons as Sales Surge, Owners Say," *NBC News* 18 Jan. 2013, Mar. 2013, http://usnews.nbcnews.com/_ news/2013/01/18/16570552-gun-stores-running-low-on-weapons-as-sales-surge-owners-say?lite

382. Buchanan, Patrick J. "The Dead Soul of Adam Lanza," *Pat Buchanan's Official Blog*, 18 Dec. 2012, http://buchanan.org/blog/ the-dead-soul-of-adam-lanza-5428

383. Kleinfield, N.R et al., "Newtown Killer's Obsessions, in Chilling Detail," *The New York Times*, 28 Mar. 2013, May 2013, http://www.nytimes. com/2013/03/29/nyregion/search-warrants-reveal-items-seized-at-adam-lanzas-home.html?pagewanted=all&_r=0; Childress, Charlotte and Childress, Harriet, "White men have much to discuss about mass shootings," *The Washington Post*, 29 Mar. 2013, Apr. 2013, http://www.washington-post.com/opinions/white-men-have-much-to-discuss-about-mass-shootings/2013/03/29/7b001d02-97f3-11e2-814b-063623d80a60_story .html

384. Lt Colonel Grossman, Dave, *On Combat: The Psychology and Physiology of Deadly Conflict in War and Peace*, PPCT Research Publications, 2004

385. "The Massacre has been certified five times platinum by the RIAA and has sold 11 million copies worldwide." 50 Cent (artist) Website: Biography, Mar. 2013, http://www.50cent.com/Bio/; Edwards, Terrence, "The Public Must Reject 2 Live Crew's Message; Clearly Obscene," *Letter to the New York Times*, 3 Jul. 1990, May 2013, http://www.nytimes. com/1990/07/03/opinion/l-the-public-must-reject-2-live-crew-s-message-clearly-obscene-872890.html?pagewanted=print&src=pm; Rimer, Sarah, "Obscenity or Art? Trial on Rap Lyrics Opens," *The New*

York Times, 17 Oct. 1990, May 2013, http://www.nytimes.
com/1990/10/17/us/obscenity-or-art-trial-on-rap-lyrics-opens.html?
pagewanted=all&src=pm; Gates, Henry Louis, "The Case of 2 Live
Crew Tells Much About the American Psyche," *Letter to the New York
Times*, 15 Jul. 1990, May 2013, http://www.nytimes.com/1990/07/15/
opinion/l-the-case-of-2-live-crew-tells-much-about-the-american-
psyche-574190.html?ref=henrylouisjrgates&pagewanted=print

386. Greenberg, Zack, "50 Cent's Next Beverage Bonanza," *Forbes*,
27 Mar. 2013, May 2013, http://www.forbes.com/sites/
zackomalleygreenburg/2013/03/27/50-cents-next-beverage-bonanza/

387. Wiener, Jon, *Historians in Trouble: Plagiarism, Fraud and Politics in the
Ivory Tower*, The New Press, New York: 2005, pg 74-93

388. Cramer, Clayton E., *Armed America: The Story of How and Why Guns
Became as American as Apple Pie*, Nelson Current, Nashville, Tn.: 2006

389. Ibid.

390. "Population Change for the United States, Regions, States, and Puerto
Rico: 2000 to 2010," *U. S. Census Bureau*, 2011, Jan. 2013, http://www
.census.gov/prod/cen2010/briefs/c2010br-01.pdf; "Population Representation in the Military Services Fiscal Year 2000," Office of the Under
Secretary of Defense, Personnel and Readiness, *Department of Defense*,
2000, Jan. 2013, http://prhome.defense.gov/RFM/MPP/ACCESSION%20
POLICY/PopRep2000/assets/pdf/chapters2000.pdf; "Population Representation in the Military Services Fiscal Year 2005," Office of the Under
Secretary of Defense, Personnel and Readiness, *Department of Defense*,
2005, Jan. 2013, http://prhome.defense.gov/rfm/MPP/ACCESSION%20
POLICY/PopRep2005/download/download.html; "Population Repre-
sentation in the Military Services Fiscal Year 2010," Office of the Under
Secretary of Defense, Personnel and Readiness, *Department of Defense*,
2010, Jan. 2013, http://prhome.defense.gov/RFM/MPP/ACCESSION%20
POLICY/PopRep2010/index.html; "Military Recruitment 2010," *National
Priorities Project (NPP)*, June 30, 2011, Jan. 2013, http://nationalpriorities.
org/analysis/2011/military-recruitment-2010/; Operation Iraqi Freedom,
US Casualties," *iCasualty.org*, Jan. 2013, http://icasualties.org/Iraq/
USCasualtiesByState.aspx; Operation Enduring Freedom, US Casualties,"
iCasualty.org, Jan. 2013, http://icasualties.org/OEF/USCasualtiesByState.
aspx; Schudel, Matt, "Bertram Wyatt-Brown, Historian Who Illuminated
'Southern Honor,' Dies at 80," *The Washington Post*, 15 Nov. 2012, Mar.
2013, http://articles.washingtonpost.com/2012-11-15/local/35503308_1_
bertram-wyatt-brown-southern-honor-b; Boot, Max, "After the Sands of
Iwo Jima," *The Wall Street Journal*, 18 Dec. 2012, Jan. 2013, http://online
.wsj.com/article/SB10001424127887324407504578185230593926380.
html ; Boot, Max, "The Guerilla Myth," *The Wall Street Journal*, 18 Jan.
2013, Jan. 2013, http://online.wsj.com/article/SB10001424127887323596
20457824370240419338.html?mod=googlenews_wsj

391. Schmitt, Gary and Miller, Cheryl, "The Military Should Mirror the
Nation" *Wall Street Journal*, 26 Aug. 2010, Jan. 2013, http://topics.wsj
.com/article/SB20001424052748703632304575451531529098478.
html; Herbig, Katherine L., "Technical Report 08-10: Allegiance in a
Time of Globalization," *Defense Personnel Security Research Center*,

Dec. 2008, Jan. 2013, http://www.dhra.mil/perserec/reports/tr08-10
.pdf; Smith, Tom, "Public Attitudes Towards Security and Counter-
Espionage Matters in 1994 and 1996," *Defense Personnel Security
Research Center*, Nov. 1996, Jan. 2013, http://www.fas.org/sgp/othergov/
perssur2.html; Segal, David, and Segal, Mady, "America's Military Population," *Population Bulletin, Volume 59, No. 4*, Dec. 2004, Jan. 2013,
http://www.prb.org/source/acf1396.pdf; Michael C. Desch, "Explaining
the Gap: Vietnam, the Republicanization of the South, and the End of
the Mass Army," in Feaver and Kohn, *Soldiers and Civilians: The Civ-
il-Military Gap and American National Security* (2001), Pgs. 289–324;
Szayna, Thomas, et al., "The Civil-Military Gap in the United States:
Does It Exist, Why, and Does It Matter?," *RAND Corporation Mono-
graph 379*, 2007, Jan. 2013, http://www.rand.org/pubs/monographs/
MG379.html ; Druckman Daniel, "Nationalism, Patriotism, and Group
Loyalty: A Social Psychological Perspective," *Mershon International
Studies Review*, Vol. 38, No. 1 (Apr., 1994), pp. 43-68 , Published by:
Blackwell Publishing on behalf of The International Studies Association,
Jan. 2013, http://bev.berkeley.edu/Ethnic%20Religious%20Conflict/
Ethnic%20and%20Religious%20Conflict/2%20National%20Identity/
Druckman%20nationalism.pdf; Morales, Lymari, "One in Three Ameri-
cans 'Extremely Patriotic' Republicans, Conservatives, and Seniors Most
Likely to Say So," *Gallup Politics* (Results for this USA Today/Gallup
poll are based on telephone interviews conducted June 11-13, 2010, with
a random sample of 1,014 adults, aged 18 and older, living in the continental U.S., selected using random-digit-dial sampling.), 2 Jul. 2010,
Jan. 2013, http://www.gallup.com/poll/141110/one-three-americans-
extremely-patriotic.aspx

392. Luttrell, Marcus, *Lone Survivor: The Eyewitness Account of Operation
Redwing and the Lost Heroes of SEAL Team 10*, Little, Brown And Co.,
New York: 2007

393. Dedman, Bill, "Reading Hillary Rodham's hidden thesis: Clinton White
House asked Wellesley College to close off access," *NBCNews.com*, 9
May. 2007, Apr. 2013, http://www.nbcnews.com/id/17388372/#
.UWghHY5S2TM

394. Alinsky, Saul D., *Rules for Radicals: A Practical Primer for Realistic
Radicals*, Random House, Inc. Vintage Books edition, New York: 1989
(1971)

395. Henninger, Daniel "Henninger: Clinging to Guns—and Abortion" *The
Wall Street Journal*, 17 Apr. 2013, Apr. 2013, http://online.wsj
.com/article/SB10001424127887323330960457842890086762001 8
.html?mod=opinion_newsreel; Smith, Ben, "Obama on small-town Pa.:
Clinging to religion, guns, xenophobia," *Politico.com*, 11 Apr. 2008, Apr.
2013, http://www.politico.com/blogs/bensmith/0408/Obama_on_
smalltown_PA_Clinging_religion_guns_xenophobia.html

PARTIAL LISTING OF
ADDITIONAL WORKS CONSULTED

Buchanan, John, *The Road to Guilford Courthouse: The American Revolution in the Carolinas*, John Wiley &Sons, New York: 1997

Gordon, William, *The History of the Rise, Progress, and Establishment of the Independence of the United States Of America, Volumes 1, 3 & 4*, Charles Dilly, London, England: 1788

Martin, Joseph Plum, *Private Yankee Doodle*, Edited by George Scheer, Eastern National, (Originally Published in 1830 Maine as *A Narrative of Some of The Adventures, Dangers and Sufferings of a Revolutionary Soldier, Interspersed with Anecdotes of Incidents That Occurred Within His Own Observations*)

Edited by Robert Bray and Paul Bushell, *Diary of a Common Soldier of the American Revolution 1775-1783: An Annotated Journal of Jeremiah Greenman*, Northern Illinois University Press, Dekalb, IL: 1978

Draper, Lyman C., *Kings Mountain and its Heroes and The Events Which Led to it*, Heritage Books Facimile Reprint (1881), Westminster, MD 2008

Fischer, David Hackett, *Albion's Seed: Four British Folkways in America*, Oxford University Press, New York: 1989

Muhlenberg, Henry A., *The Life of Major General Peter Muhlenberg of the Revolutionary Army*, Carey and Hart, Philadelphia, PA: 1849

Olmsted, Frederick Law, *A Journey in the Back Country*, Mason Brothers, New York: 1860

Beller, James R., *America in Crimson Red: The Baptist History of America*, Prairie Fire Press, Arnold, MI: 2004

Beale, Robert Baylor Semple, *The History of the Rise and Progress of the Baptists in Virginia*, Pitt & Dickinson, Richmond, VA: 1894 (originally published in 1810)

Colonel Creecy, James R., *Scenes of The South and Other Miscellaneous Pieces*, Thomas McGill, Washington, DC: 1860

Kercheval, Samuel, *A History of the Valley of Virginia*, Samuel Davis, Winchester, VA: 1833

Landers, H.L. Lt Col., *Battle of Camden South Carolina: Historical Statements*, Kershaw Historical Society Facimile reprint (1929), Camden, SC: 1997

Alden, John Richard, *The South in the Revolution 1763-1789*, Louisiana State University Press, Baton Rouge, LA: 1957

Durant, Will and Ariel, *Rousseau and Revolution: A History of Civilization in France, England, and Germany from 1756 and in the remainder of Europe from 1715 to 1789*, Simon & Schuster, New York: 1967

Edited by Ford, Worthington Chauncey, *The Writings of George Washington, Volume 8, 1779-1780*, G.P. Putnam's Sons, New York: 1890

Edited by Ford, Worthington Chauncey, *The Writings of George Washington, Volume 9, 1780-1782*, G.P. Putnam's Sons, New York: 1891

Simms, William Gilmore, *The Partisan: Romance of the Revolution*, Belford, Clarke & Co. New York: 1886 (1986)

Bennett, William J., *America, The Last Best Hope: Volume 1:From the Age of Discovery to the World at War*, Thomas Nelson, Nashville, TN: 2006

Edgar, Walter, *Partisans & Redcoats: The Southern Conflict That Turned the Tide of the American Revolution*, Harper Collins, New York: 2001

Taylor, Alan, *The Civil War of 1812: American Citizens, British Subjects, Irish Rebels, Indian Allies*, Vintage Books, New York: 2010

Ferling, John, *Almost A Miracle: The American Victory in the War of Independence*, Oxford University Press, New York: 2007

Marston, Daniel, *The American Revolution 1774-1783*, Osprey Publishing, New York: 2002

Rankin, Hugh F., *The Moores Creek Bridge Campaign, 1776*, Eastern National, Currie, NC: 1986

Gordon, John W., *South Carolina And The American Revolution: A Battlefield History*, University of South Carolina Press, Columbia, SC: 2003

Swisher, James K., *The Revolutionary War in the Southern Back Country*, Pelican Publishing, Gretna, LA: 2008

Davis, Burke, *The Cowpens-Guilford Courthouse Campaign*, University Pennsylvania Press, Philadelphia, PA: 2003

Wood, Gordon S., *The Empire of Liberty: A History of the Early Republic, 1789-1815,*Oxford University Press, New York: 2009

Bass, Robert D., *The Green Dragoon: The Lives of Banastre Tarleton and Mary Robinson,* Sandlapper Publishing, Orangeburg, SC: 1973

Swager, Christine R., *The Heroes of Kettle Creek 1779-1782,* Infinity Publishing, West Conshohocken, PA: 2008

Tierney, John J. Jr., *Chasing Ghosts: Unconventional Warfare in American History,* Potomac Books, Dulles, VA: 2007

Babits, Lawrence E. & Howard, Joshua B., *Long Obstinate, and Bloody: The Battle of Guilford Courthouse,* University of North Carolina Press, Chapel Hill, NC: 2009

Rankin, Hugh F., *The North Carolina Continentals,* University of North Carolina Press, Chapel Hill, NC: 2005

Jones, Randall, *Before They Were Heroes at King's Mountain,* Daniel Boone Footsteps, Winston-Salem, NC: 2011

Southern, Ed (editor), *Voices Of The American Revolution In The Carolinas,* John F. Blair, Winston-Salem, NC: 2009

Russell, David Lee, *Victory On Sullivan's Island: The British Cape Fear/ Charles Town Expedition of 1776,* Infinity Publishing, Haverford, PA:2002

Berleth, Richard, *Bloody Mohawk: The French And Indian War & American Revolution on New York's Frontier,* Black Dome Press, Hendersonville, NY: 2010

Middlekauff, Robert, *The Glorious Cause: The American Revolution, 1763-1789,* Oxford University Press, New York, 2005

Spring, Matthew H., *With Zeal And Bayonets Only: The British Army On Campaign in North America, 1775-1783,* University of Oklahoma Press, Norman, OK: 2008

Jasanoff, Maya, *Liberty's Exiles: American Loyalists In the Revolutionary World,* Knopf, New York: 2011

Brumewell, Stephen, *White Devil: A True Story Of War, Savagery, And Vengeance In Colonial America,* Da Capo Press, Cambridge, MA: 2004

Allen, Thomas B., *Tories: Fighting For The King In America's First Civil War,* Harper Collins, New York: 2010

Babits, Lawrence E., *A Devil Of A Whipping: The Battle of Cowpens,* University of North Carolina Press, Chapel Hill, NC: 1998

Sparrow, W. Keats (editor), *"The First Of Patriots And Best Of Men": Richard Caswell In Public Life,* Lenoir County Historical Commission, Kinston, NC: 2007

Todish, Timothy J., *The Annotated And Illustrated Journals Of Major Robert Rogers*, Purple Mountain Press, Fleischmanns, NY: 2002

Moss, Bobby Gilmer, *Uzal Johnson, Loyalist Surgeon: A Revolutionary War Diary*, Scotia Hibernia Press, Blacksburg, SC: 2000

Scheer, George F. & Rankin, Hugh F., *Rebels & Redcoats: The American Revolution Through The Eyes Of Those Who Fought It And Lived It*, Da Capo Press, Cambridge, MA: 1957

Bailey, De Witt, Ph.D., *Pattern Dates For British Ordnance Small Arms 1718-1783*, Thomas Publications, Gettysburg Publications, PA: 1997

Darling, Anthony D., *Red Coat And Brown Bess*, Museum Restoration Service, Alexandria Bay, NY: 1971

McCrory, R.H., *Lock Stock And Barrel: Antique Gun Repair*, Pioneer Press, Union City, TN: 1966

Dykeman, Wylma, *With Fire And Sword: The Battle of Kings Mountain 1780*, National Park Service, Washington DC: 1991

National Park Service, *The American Revolution: Official National Park Service Handbook*, National Park Service, Washington DC: 1991

Minetor, Randi S., *Passport To Your National Parks Companion Guide: Southeast Region*, Falcon Guides, Guilford, CT: 2008

Barefoot, Daniel W., *Touring North Carolina's Revolutionary War Sites*, John F. Blair, Winston-Salem, NC: 1998

Barefoot, Daniel W., *Touring South Carolina's Revolutionary War Sites*, John F. Blair, Winston-Salem, NC.: 1999

Gragg, Rod, *Forged In Faith: How Faith Shaped The Birth Of The Nation 1607-1776*, Howard Books, New York: 2010

Goldwater, Barry, *The Conscience Of A Conservative*, Princeton University Press, Princeton, NJ: 1960,2007

Dunkerly, Robert M. ed., *The Battle of Kings Mountain: Eyewitness Accounts*, The History Press, Charelston, SC: 2007

Reverend Lathan, Robert, *Historical Sketches of the Revolutionary War in the Upcountry of South Carolina*, Yorkville Enquirer, Yorkville, SC: 1877 (Transcribed by West, Robert Jerald, Broad River Basin Historical Society, 1998)

Gallup, Andrew, *A Sketch of The Virginia Soldier in the Revolution*, Heritage Books, Westminster, MD: 2008

Lossing, Benson J., *Pictorial Field-Book of the Revolution Vol. 2*, Harper & Brothers , New York: 1855

Lossing, Benson J., *Pictorial Field-Book of the Revolution Vol. 3*, Pelican Publishing, Gretna, LA: 2008 (1850)

Reverend Caruthers, Eli W. D.D., *Revolutionary Incidents and Sketches of Character Chiefly in "The Old North State" in 1776, Vol. 1 &*

2, Hayes & Zell, Philadelphia, Pa.:1854, 1856 (Transcribed by Thompson Ruth, Guilford County Genealogical Society, 1985)

Parker, John C. Jr, *Parker's Guide to the Revolutionary War in South Carolina*, Hem Branch Publishing, Patrick, SC: 2009

Graham, James, *The Life of Daniel Morgan of the Virginia Line of the United States Army*, 1859 (Reprinted by Applewood Books, Bedford, MA)

Weems, Mason Locke & Peter, Horry, *The life of General Francis Marion, a Celebrated Partisan Officer, in the Revolutionary War, Against the British and Tories in South Carolina and Georgia*, 1884 (Reprinted form the Library of Congress)

Lumpkin, Henry, *From Savannah to Yorktown*, iUniverse.com, Lincoln, NE: 1987

Brooks, David, *BoBos in Paradise: The New Upper Class and How They Got There*, Simon & Schuster, New York: 2000

Wyatt-Brown, Bertram, *The Shaping of Southern Culture: Honor, Grace, and War 1760s-1880s*, University of North Carolina Chapel Hill, Chapel Hill, NC: 2001

Mapp, Alf, J., *The Faiths of Our Fathers: What America's Founders Really Believed*, Fall River Press, New York: 2006

Haberski, Raymond, Jr., *God and War: American Civil Religion Since 1945*, Rutgers University Press, Rutgers, NJ: 2012

Beckwith, Francis, J., *Politics for Christians: Statecraft as Soulcraft*, InterVarsity Press, Downers Grove, IL: 2010

Remini, Robert V., *The Battle of New Orleans: Andrew Jackson and America's First Military Victory*, Penguin Books, New York: 1999

Tilley, John Shipley, *Lincoln Takes Command: How Lincoln Got the War he Wanted*, Bill Coats, Nashville, TN: 1941 (1991)

Bain, Robert, *The Clans and Tartans of Scotland*, William Collins Sons & Co. Ltd, London: 1938 (1970)

Ross, Anne, *The Folklore of the Scottish Highlands*, Barnes & Noble Books, 1976

Laing, Lloyd and Jenny, *The Picts and the Scots*, Sutton Publishing Ltd, 1993

Butler, Jon, *Awash in the Sea of Faith: Christianizing the American People*, Harvard University Press, Cambridge, MA.: 1992

Edited by Charles Francis Adams, *Letters of John Adams, Addressed to his Wife, Vol. 1*, Little And Brown, Boston, MA: 1841

Ricks, Thomas, *Making the Corps*, Scribner, New York, 1997

Gold, Philip, *The Coming Draft: The Crisis in our military and Why Selective Service is Wrong for America*, Ballantine Books, New York: 2006

Edited by Tracy, James, *The Military Draft Handbook: A Brief History & Practical Advice for the curious and Concerned*, Manic D Press, San Francisco, CA: 2006

Flynn, George, *The Draft 1940-1973*, University Press , Wichita, KS 1993

Roth-Douqet, Kathy and Schaeffer, Frank, *AWOL: The Unexcused Absence of America's Upper Class from Military Service- And How it Hurts our Country*, Harper Collins, New York: 2006

Goad, Jim, *The Redneck Manifesto: How Hillbillies, Hicks, And White Trash Became America's Scapegoats*, Simon & Schuster, New York: 1997

Edited by Stiles, T.J., *Warriors and Pioneers: In Their Own Words*, Perigree Books, New York: 1996

Chaves, Mark, *American Religion: Contemporary Trends*, Princeton University Press, Princeton, NJ: 2011

Edited by Lawson, Lewis A. and Kramer, Victor A., *Conversations with Walker Percy*, University Press of Mississippi, Jackson, MS: 1961 (1985)

Edited by Hooker, Richard, J., *The Carolina Backcountry on the Edge of the Revolution: The Journal and other writings of Charles Woodmason, Anglican Itinerant*, University of North Carolina Press, Chapel Hill, NC: 1953

McWhiney, Grady, *Cracker Culture: Celtic Ways in the Old South*, University of Alabama, Tuscaloosa, AL: 1988

Boatner, Mark Mayo, III, *Encyclopedia of the American Revolution*, Stackpole Books, Mechanicsburg, PA: 1994 (1966)

McMaster, John Bach, *A History of the People of the United States: From the Revolution to the Civil War- Volume 1*, originally published by D. Appleton Company in 1883, Cosimo Books, New York: 2005 (1883)

National Emergency Council, *Report on the Economic Conditions of the South prepared for the President of the United States*, 1938, http://www.archive.org

Edited by Matthews, Mitford, *Dictionary of Americanisms, Volumes 1 & 2*, The University of Chicago Press, Chicago, IL: 1951

Edited by Graham, Hugh Davis and Gurr, Ted Robert, *The History of Violence in America: A Report to the National Commission on the Causes and Prevention of Violence*, Bantam Books, New York: 1969

Brown, Maxwell Richard, *Strain of Violence: Historical Studies of American Violence and Vigilantism*, Oxford University Press, New York: 1975

Brown, Maxwell Richard, *No Duty to Retreat: Violence and Values in American History and Society*, University of Oklahoma Press, Norman, OK: 1991

Nisbett, Richard E. and Cohen, Dov, *Culture of Honor: The Psychology of Violence in the South*, Westview Press, Boulder, CC: 1996

Putnam, Robert and Campbell, David E., *American Grace: How Religion Divides and Unites Us*, Simon & Schuster, New York: 2010

Thomas, Emory M., *The Confederacy as a Revolutionary Experience*, University of South Carolina Press, Columbia, SC: 1991 (1971)

Mathews, Donald G., *Religion in the Old South*, The University of Chicago Press, Chicago, IL: 1977

Foxworthy, Jeff, *Complete Redneck Dictionary*, Villard Books, New York: 2005

Collected by Muehlhausen, Jaimie, *Redneck Words of Wisdom: Real-life Expressions, Advice, Commentary and Observations From Some of the Smartest People Around . . . Rednecks*, Raincoast Books, Vancouver, BC: 2006

Ruark, Howard, *The Old Man and the Boy*, Holt, Rinehart, and Winston, New York: 1957

Leuba, James H., *The Belief in God and Immorality: A Psychological, Anthropological and Statistical Study*, Sherman, French & Company, Boston, MA: 1916

Cox, Karen L., *Dreaming of Dixie: How the South Was Created in American Popular Culture*, University of North Carolina Press, Chapel Hill, NC, 2011

Smith, Adam, *The Wealth of Nations*, Random House, New York: 2003 (1776)

Bryan, William Jennings and Bryan, Mary Baird, *The Memoirs of William Jennings Bryan*, Universal Book and Bible House, Philadelphia, PA: 1925

Warren, Robert Penn, *All The King's Men*, Harcourt, Orlando, FL: 2001 (1946)

Warren, Robert Penn, *The Legacy of the Civil War: Meditations on the Centennial*, University of Nebraska Press, NE: 1998 (1961)

Edited by Watkins, Floyd and Hiers, John T., *Robert Penn Warren Talking: Interviews: 1950-1978*, Random House, New York: 1980

LaPierre, Wayne, *Guns, Crime, and Freedom*, Regnery Publishing, Washington DC: 1994

Edited by Ashton, John F., *In Six Days: Why Fifty Scientists Choose To Believe in Creation*, Master Books, Green Forest, AR: 2002

Lt General Boykin, William, *Never Surrender: A Soldier's Journey to the Crossroads of Faith and Freedom*, FaithWords, New York: 2008

Greene, Francis Vinton, *Great Commanders: General Greene*, D. Appleton and Company, New York: 1893 (2006)

Edited by Conrad, Dennis M., Nathanael, *The Papers of General Nathanael Greene: Vol. 6, June 1780- December 1780*, University of North Carolina Press, Chapel Hill, NC: 1994

Edited by Conrad, Dennis M., Nathanael, *The Papers of General Nathanael Greene: Vol. 7, December 1780- March 1781*, University of North Carolina Press, Chapel Hill, NC: 1994

Edited by Conrad, Dennis M., Nathanael, *The Papers of General Nathanael Greene: Vol. 10, 3 December 1781 – 6 April 1782*, University of North Carolina Press, Chapel Hill, NC: 1994

Edited by Conrad, Dennis M., Nathanael, *The Papers of General Nathanael Greene: Vol. 13, 22 May 1783- 13 June 1786*, University of North Carolina Press, Chapel Hill, NC: 1994

Edited By Ian Saberton, *The Cornwallis (Marquis Charles Cornwallis) Papers: The Campaigns of 1780 and 1781*, Vol. 4, Naval & Military Press, East Sussex, England: 2010

Edited by Lieber, Francis, *Encyclopedia Americana: A Popular Dictionary of Arts, Sciences, Literature, history, Politics, and Biography*, Vol. 7, Desilver, Thomas, & Co., Philadelphia, PA: 1836

Washington, George, *George Washington September 17, 1796, Farewell Address, George Washington Papers at the Library of Congress, 1741-1799 Series 2 Letterbooks, Letter Book 24*, Library of Congress, http://memory.loc.gov

Warren, Mercy, *History of the Rise, Progress and Termination of the American Revolution Interspersed with Biographical, Political and Moral Observations Vols.1 & 3*, Manning and Loring, Boston, MA: 1805

Hardin, Robert V., *Overmountain Victory Trail: Then And Now*, Self-Published in NC: 2005

Crawford, Earle W., *Samuel Doak*, The Overmountain Press, Johnson City, TN: 1980

Howard, Robert A. and Gerhardt, Alvin E., *Mary Patton: Powder Maker of the Revolution*, Rocky Mount Historical Association, Piney Flats, TN: 1980

Dixon, Max, *The Wataugans: First Free and Independent Community of the Continent*, The Overmountain Press, Johnson City, TN: 1976

Brown, Stephen and Hirschman, Elizabeth, and Maclaran, Pauline, *Two Continents One Culture: The Scotch-Irish in Southern Appalachia*, The Overmountain Press, Johnson City, TN: 2006

Turner, Francis Marion, *Life of General John Sevier*, The Overmountain Press, Johnson City, TN: 1910

Barone, Michael, and McCutcheon, Chuck, *The Almanac of American Politics 2012*, University Of Chicago Press, Chicago, IL: 2011

Dameron, J. David, *King's Mountain: The Defeat of the Loyalists October 7, 1780*, Da Capo Press, Cambridge, MA: 2003

White, Katherine Keogh, *The King's Mountain Me: The Story of the Battle with Sketches of the American Soldiers Who Took Part*, Genealogical Publishing Co. Baltimore, MD: 1924 (1977)

Greene, Evarts and Harrington, Virginia, *American Population Before The Federal Census of 1790*, Columbia University Press and Genealogical Publishing Co., Baltimore, MD: 1993 (1932)

Edited by Smith, Sam B. and Owsley, Harriet, *The Papers of Andrew Jackson, Volume 1, 1770-1803*, University of Tennessee Press, Knoxville, TN: 1980

Dobson, David, *The Original Scots Colonists of Early America: 1612-1783*, Genealogical Publishing Co. Inc., Baltimore, MD: 1989

Kephart, Horace, *Our Southern Highlanders*, The Macmillan Company, New York: 1921

Wilson, Howard McKnight, *The Tinkling Spring Headwater of Freedom: A Study of a Church and Her People 1732-1952*, The Tinkling Spring and Hermitage Presbyterian Churches, Fishersville, VA: 1954

Compiled By Bockstruck, Lloyd DeWitt, *Revolutionary War Bounty Land Grants Awarded by State Governments*, Genealogical Publishing Company, Baltimore, MD: 1996

Calendar of the Tennessee and King's Mountain Papers of the Draper Collection of Manuscripts, Compiled and Published by the State Historical Society of Madsion, WI: 1929

Hurt, Frances Hallam, *An Intimate History of the American Revolution in Pittsylvania County, Virginia*, The Womack Press, Danville, VA: 1976

Brumbaugh, Gaius Marcus, *Revolutionary War Records, Volume 1, Virginia, Virginia Army and Navy Forces with Bounty Land Warrants For Virginia Military District of Ohio and Virginia Military Scrip; from Federal and State Archives*, Lancaster Press, Lancaster PA: 1936

Clement, Maud Carter, *The History of Pittsylvania County Virginia*, Pittsylvania Historical Society, Chatham, VA: 1988 (1929)

Pat Alderman, *The Overmountain Men: Early Tennessee History*, The Overmountain Press, Johnson City, TN: 1970

Cox, William E., *Battle of Kings Mountain Participants, October 7, 1780*, Eastern National Park & Monument Association, reprinted by permission, to Historical Society of Washington County, VA: 1972

General Sherman, W.T., *Sherman: Memoirs of General W.T. Sherman*, Literary Classics, New York: 1990 (1885)

Hayek, F.A., *The Road to Serfdom: Text and Documents* (Edited by Bruce Caldwell), University of Chicago Press, Chicago, IL: 2007 (1944)

Lillback, Peter A., *George Washington's Sacred Fire*, Providence Forum Press, Pennsylvania, PA: 2006

Feaver, Peter D. and Kohn, Richard H. editors, *Soldiers and Civilians: The Civil-Military Gap and American National Security*, The MIT Press, Cambridge, MA: 2001

Nash, Gary, *The Unknown American Revolution⊠: The Unruly Birth of Democracy and the Struggle to Create America⊠*, Penguin, New York: 2006

Ericson, David, *The Debate Over Slavery: Antislavery and Proslavery Liberalism in Antebellum America*, New York University Press, New York: 2000

Tucker, George, *The History of The United States From their Colonization to the End of the Twenty-Sixth Congress in 1841, Vol. 1*, Philadelphia, PA: 1856

Hildreth, Richard, *The History of the United States of America from the Discovery of the Continent to the Organization of the Federal Constitution, Vol. 3*, Harper & Brothers, New York: 1863

Stanhope, Philip Henry (Lord Mahon), *History of England From the Peace of Utrecht to the Peace of Versailles 1713-1783*, Little Brown and Company 1854

Edited by Force, Peter, *Tracts and Other Papers Relating Principally to the Origin, Settlement, and Progress of the Colonies in North America, Vol. 2*, Peter Force, Washington: 1838 ("An Account of South Carolina Submitted by John Peter Purry, et al. in Charleston, 23 September, 1731")

Barton, David, *The Second Amendment: Preserving the Inalienable Right of Individual Self Protection*, Wall Builders, Aledo, TX: 2000

Lott, John R., *More Guns Less Crime: Understanding Crime and Gun Control Laws, 3rd Edition*, University of Chicago Press, Chicago, IL: 2010